AND K

SPEAKING TO EACH OTHER

VOLUME TWO

By the Same Author

AUDEN
An Introductory Essay

THE USES OF LITERACY

Speaking To Each Other

Essays by

RICHARD HOGGART

VOLUME II

About Literature

1970

Chatto & Windus

LONDON

PUBLISHED BY
CHATTO & WINDUS LTD.
40 WILLIAM IV STREET
LONDON W.C.2

*

CLARKE, IRWIN & CO. LTD.
TORONTO

SBN 7011 1514 9

© Richard Hoggart 1970

PRINTED IN GREAT BRITAIN BY
NORTHUMBERLAND PRESS LIMITED
GATESHEAD

CONTENTS

For
Simon, Nicola and Paul

ACKNOWLEDGEMENTS

The essays in this volume have, with one or two exceptions, all been published previously in a somewhat different form, Acknowledgement is made to the following sources of original publication:

WHY I VALUE LITERATURE: *Times Educational Supplement*, 1963; subsequently included in the collection of essays, *The Critical Moment*, Faber & Faber, 1964.

LITERATURE AND SOCIETY: *A Guide to the Social Sciences*, ed. Norman Mackenzie, Weidenfeld & Nicolson and The New American Library. Reprinted by permission.

THE FORCE OF CARICATURE: *Essays in Criticism*, Vol. 3-4, October 1953.

THE LONG WALK: THE POETRY OF W. H. AUDEN: British Council Series *Writers and their Work*, Longmans 1957-66, and University of Nebraska Press.

A MATTER OF RHETORIC: *The Nation*, April 27th, 1957.

ART AND SEX: THE RHETORIC OF HENRY MILLER: *The Guardian*, April 5th, 1963.

LAWRENCE'S VOICES: *The Listener*, October 29th, 1964.

WALKING THE TIGHTROPE: ANIMAL FARM: A talk given on BBC External Services.

GEORGE ORWELL AND THE ROAD TO WIGAN PIER: Introduction to *The Road to Wigan Pier*, Heinemann Educational Books.

THE DANCE OF THE LONG-LEGGED FLY: *Encounter* 27-2, August 1966.

SAMUEL BUTLER AND THE WAY OF ALL FLESH: Introduction to *The Way of All Flesh*, Penguin Books.

THE NEED FOR LOVE: KILVERT'S DIARY: *New Statesman*, June 18th, 1960 under the title THE CHARISMATIC CURATE.

SPEAKING TO EACH OTHER

A QUESTION OF TONE: The Tredegar Memorial Lecture of the Royal Society of Literature. Reprinted in *Essays by Divers Hands*, Vol. 33, Oxford University Press.

TEACHING WITH STYLE: *Of Books and Humankind*, ed. J. Butt, Routledge & Kegan Paul, 1964.

TEACHING LITERATURE: 'English Studies in Extramural Education' first appeared in *Universities Quarterly*, 5-3, May 1951. 'Poetry and Adult Classes', originally a talk to the Annual Conference of the Society of Teachers of English, April 1952, first appeared in *Adult Education*, 25-3, Winter 1952. 'Notes on Extramural Teaching' was first issued by the Department of Adult Education, University of Hull, 1959. All three were reprinted in *Teaching Literature*, published by the National Institute of Adult Education and Department of Adult Education, University of Hull, 1963.

SCHOOLS OF ENGLISH AND CONTEMPORARY SOCIETY: Inaugural Lecture, University of Birmingham, 1963.

THE LITERARY IMAGINATION AND THE SOCIOLOGICAL IMAGINATION: Given as a talk to the Sociology Section of the British Association at its 1967 Annual Conference. Subsequently distributed as a pamphlet.

Thanks are due to the following for permission to reprint copyright material quoted or referred to in this volume:

W. H. Auden, Faber & Faber Ltd. and Random House Inc; Saul Bellow, Weidenfeld & Nicolson Ltd. and The Viking Press Inc; the Trustees of the Joseph Conrad Estate and J. M. Dent & Sons Ltd; E. M. Forster and Edward Arnold Ltd; Graham Greene, William Heinemann Ltd. and Monica McCall Inc; the Trustees of the Hardy Estate and Macmillan & Co. Ltd; Tom Harrisson and Victor Gollancz Ltd; James Kirkup and Curtis Brown Ltd; the Estate of the late Mrs. Frieda Lawrence, Laurence Pollinger Ltd. and The Viking Press Inc; Laurie Lee, The Hogarth Press Ltd. and William Morrow & Co. Inc.; William Plomer and Jonathan Cape Ltd; The Society of Authors as agent for the Bernard Shaw Estate; and Tom Wolfe, Jonathan Cape Ltd. and Farrar, Straus & Giroux Inc.

PREFACE

A<small>LL</small> but three or four of these essays were written during
the last ten years; they represent just over a third of
my published writing in that period. Looking at their dates,
I notice that two in three of the essays about culture were
written between 1965 and 1967, and half of those about
literature between 1963 and 1966. So 1965 and 1966 seem
to have been fuller years than usual. During 1968 almost all
the essays were greatly amended, for publication, chiefly by
pruning; and some have been given new titles.

Most were prompted by particular occasions: a request for
a long essay or special lecture, or for a book review. I virtually
never accept such an invitation unless it gives the chance
to work somewhere near my main interests. I am a slow
writer and can hardly ever afford to 'knock something out'
in a spirit of only casual interest.

I can see, now that these essays have been put side by
side, that I tend to work at the same group of themes again
and again, though from different angles. At least, this is what
I have done in the past decade. So there is a good deal of
interweaving and movement of cross-currents in and between
these two volumes.

The main social themes seem to circle around how one
understands, interprets and evaluates cultural change—as
seen in attitudes to class and education, the debate about
'brows', mass communication, 'public voices' (who speaks to
whom, about what, and in what tones of voice?), and in questions about intellectual freedom and responsibility in a
commercial democracy.

Where the literary essays are about particular authors,
their special interest for someone with my kind of outlook
is self-evident. The others seem as often as not to settle on such
subjects as the peculiar nature of the 'subjective' literary
imagination and its contribution to understanding society;

9

or—and this I really do want to take much further if I can
—they are about questions of tone and how very much a
reading of tone can reveal.

I have noticed some changes—some quite marked changes
—in my own attitudes over the decade, and some changes of
style. I've noted also some recurrent patterns in my ways of
thinking, of approaching problems; and so some recurrent
habits of style. But I'm not yet sure what these contrasting
characteristics mean.

I owe a great deal to a great many people, but most of all
to the following nine, whom I want to thank as strongly as
ever I can: Catharine Carver, Stuart Hall, Eleanor Insch,
G. E. T. Mayfield, Felicity Reeve, Roy Shaw, Mary Weate,
my daughter Nicola and my wife Mary.

October 1969   Richard Hoggart

WHY I VALUE LITERATURE

I VALUE literature because of the way—the peculiar way—
in which it explores, re-creates and seeks for the meanings
in human experience; because it explores the diversity, complexity and strangeness of that experience (of individual men
or of men in groups or of men in relation to the natural
world); because it re-creates the texture of that experience;
and because it pursues its explorations with a disinterested
passion (not wooing nor apologizing nor bullying). I value
literature because in it men look at life with all the vulner-
ability, honesty, and penetration they can command . . . and
dramatize their insights by means of a unique relationship
with language and form.

'Exploring human experience' is a useful phrase, but not
quite sufficient. It is too active. 'Contemplating' or 'cele-
brating' human experience might be better for a beginning,
to indicate the preoccupied passivity before life in which
the imagination often starts its work. And 'exploring' can
sound too much like wandering for its own sake, as though
literature simply opens up successive territories of human
response. 'Searching' or even 'ordering' would be better, so
long as we didn't imply by either of them an 'irritable reaching after fact and reason'. Every writer—not necessarily in
an obvious sense nor necessarily consciously, and whether in
a tragic or comic or in any other manner—means what he
says. Sometimes he will deny that there is a meaning. "I only
wanted to write an interesting tale," he will say, ignoring
that the interest of a story almost always comes from seeing
the human will in action—against chaos or against order.
Sometimes the meaning he intends will not be the work's
achieved meaning. The ebb and flow of imaginative power
within the work may reveal attitudes hidden from the
writer himself. But there will be a meaning, a kind of order—

11

expressed or implied. Whether he knows it or not, the writer will be testing the validity of certain ways of seeing life; he will be offering, no matter how provisionally, a way of ordering the flux of experience. By his choice and arrangement of materials, by the temper of his treatment of them, a writer is implicitly saying: this is one way in which we can face experience or succumb to it or seek to alter it or try to ignore it.

The attention good literature pays to life is both loving and detached. It frames experience and, in a sense, distances it. But it always assumes the importance, the worthwhileness, of human experience even when—as in tragedy—it finds much in that experience evil. So, if a writer is imaginatively gifted, his work helps to define and assert that importance, to bring experience up fresh before us. This is not a way of saying that a good writer makes an evil experience good. But his exploration is good, since it defines more clearly the nature of the evil we suffer and perform. It helps to make us believe more in the freely willing nature of man; and it helps us to feel more sharply the difficulties and limits of that freedom. Good literature insists on 'the mass and majesty' of the world—on its concreteness and sensuous reality, and on its meanings beyond 'thisness'. It insists on the importance of the inner, the distinctive and individual, life of man, while much else in our activities and in our make-up—fear, ambition, fatigue, laziness—tries to make that life generalized and typecast.

Not all writing acts in this way. Roughly, we can say there are two kinds of literature: conventional literature and live literature. Conventional literature usually (though it may sometimes do better than its author knows) reinforces existing assumptions, accepted ways of looking at the world. Properly read, live literature—even the quietest or most light-hearted —may be disturbing, may subvert our view of life.

'Properly read' is the key-phrase in that last sentence. I said at the beginning that literature explores, re-creates and orders human experience in a *unique* way. Other activities of the human mind explore human experience, and some re-create it, and some seek to order it. One can think of philosophers or theologians or of composers or painters. I am not concerned to set literature against any of those. Literature can be discursive in the way that some philosophy is; it has, like painting and music but unlike most philosophy, an imaginative architecture. Its peculiarity is its special relationship with, its special form of engagement with, language . . . a relationship which is intellectual and emotional at the same time and is almost always a relationship by values. Ruskin said, "Tell me what you like and I'll tell you what you are." We could just as easily say, "Tell me what language you use and I will tell you what you are." Language is not simply a range of conventional signs, increasing and altering so as to express the complexity of experience; the business of grappling with the complexity of experience, with the life by time and the life by values, is itself partly carried on through and within language.

Literature can never be aesthetically pure or abstractly contemplative. There can be no such thing as 'abstract literature' as there is abstract painting. By its nature—because its medium, language, is used by almost everybody in all sorts of everyday situations; and because it tries both to say and to be—literature is an art which invites impurities.

It is the most creaturely of the arts. No other art makes us feel so much that the experience must have been just like that, that desire and will and thought would all have been caught up with those gestures, those smells, those sounds. It's not reality; it's a mirroring; but it mirrors more nearly than any other imaginative activity the *whole* sense of an experience.

Literature is both in time and outside time. It is in time because it works best when it creates a sense of a certain time and place and of particular persons, when it works through and re-creates identifiable life and manners . . . Tom Jones hiding in a particular copse with Molly Seagrim, Marvell lying in a certain garden, Dimitri Karamazov in *that* prison cell, Will and Anna Brangwen in *that* cottage bedroom.

It is outside time in two ways. First, in a sense we are all used to: that, if it is rooted in time and place and is imaginatively penetrating, it will go beyond particular time and place and speak about our common humanity, will become —as we used to say more readily—universal.

Literature goes beyond time in a more subtle sense. To describe discursively, fully to paraphrase, all that an imaginatively successful scene in fiction or drama or a poem says, means and is—to do this would take an impossibly long time and would be futile. It is of the essence of the scene's or the poem's meaning that all its elements simultaneously co-exist, do their work at the same time . . . so that we feel them all at once as we would in heightened moments of life, if we were sufficiently sensitive. The resources of language and form then work together to produce the peculiarly literary achievement, full of simultaneous meanings . . . Yeats writing 'the salmon-falls, the mackerel-crowded seas', Cordelia replying 'No cause, no cause', Margaret Wilcox crying, 'Not any more of this! You shall see the connection if it kills you, Henry!', Sophia looking down on Gerald Scales' body after all those years of desertion. One could not, even at six-volume length, 'write out the meaning' of any one of these; in separating the elements by space and time we would destroy the meaning.

To respond to these meanings is not necessarily easy. It is not sensible to expect a work of any depth to yield all its meanings on a first reading by almost anyone in almost any mood. Literature is 'for delight', it is true—delight in recognition, in exploration and in ordering, in the sense of increased apprehension, of new and unsuspected relationships, and in aesthetic achievement. But beyond a fairly simple level (for example, rhythmic incantation) we have to work more and attend better if we want the best rewards, here as in any other activity.

It follows that wide hospitality is good. Nor need it be the enemy of good judgment. The fact that some people use their claim to being hospitable as an excuse for refusing to make distinctions is another matter; catholicity is not promiscuity. Almost every writer with imaginative ability (that is, with some capacity, no matter how intermittent or partial, to explore aspects of experience through language), almost every such writer will have some insights to give if we read him disinterestedly, with a 'willing suspension of disbelief'.

Such a man may in general, or in particular things, be immature or irresponsible; we may think his statements or assumptions about human life untrue or perverse. If we do feel any of these things we should say so, as exactly and strongly as we think necessary. But we ought to be clear what we are attacking. Otherwise we may dismiss a man with some imaginative ability, but whose outlook we find antipathetic, and will claim we are judging his literary powers; or we may come to believe that we find imaginative insight in a writer whose views fit our own but who is without creative ability. If we do not 'entertain as a possibility' the outlook of a writer while we are reading him we shall not know what his outlook is, and will attack or praise a caricature of it.

'To entertain as a possibility' is not the best form of words but it is hard to find a better. It does not mean 'to accept', because the process is more subtle than that. It means to exercise intellectual and emotional openness and charity. It means to be able to see for a while how someone can have such an outlook and to know what it feels like to have it, what the world looks like from that angle. To do this is not to 'surrender'. All the time, though not necessarily consciously, we are testing that outlook against life as we think we know it ourselves. With certain writers we will be all the time in a sharp double state . . . of entertaining and rejecting at once; but even then there are likely to be moments when light is thrown on a part of human experience, and some attitude which we had pushed out of the field of our consciousness will prove to have more power than we had wanted to think.

In my experience, this is likely to be true of all but two kinds of literary effort. It is not true of work which, though

full of 'right instincts' and intelligent technicalities, shows
no effective literary imagination. Think, for example, of many
of the thematic novels about moral conflict published during
the past twenty years. Worse, is the bodilessly aesthetic production which tries to treat words and forms as ends in
themselves. I believe that literature is certainly in one sense
'play'—grave and absorbed play. But these are pointless
arabesques. They do not explore, and their patterns neither
mean nor mirror.

I do not think a trivial outlook will produce great literature. It may produce odd incidental insights; but, overall, a
shallow view of life will produce a shallow penetration into
experience. But I agree also with R. P. Blackmur who noted
that we could learn something from second- and third-rate
work, so long as we supplied our own irony towards it. You
salt it yourself.

The *effects* of literature cannot be simply described—the
moral effects, that is. I do not think these effects are direct,
or our experience would be a simpler matter than it is. Good
readers might then be good people, and good writers better
human beings even than their good readers. In speaking about
the moral impact of art we are not talking about a more complicated form of those ethically improving tales for children,
most of which are irrelevant to the way imaginative literature
actually works. Obviously, we can learn morally even if evil
appears to triumph. 'Moral impact' does not mean a direct
ethical prompting but the effect literature may have on the
temper with which we face experience.

But first, and as we have seen, literature does seek to articulate something of the 'mass and majesty' of experience.
Most of us (and most of our societies) are constantly tending
to narrow our focus, to ignore embarrassing qualifications
and complexities, to make much of the rest of the world and
all experience with which we are not comfortable—to make
all this into merely a backcloth to the stage on which our egos
do act comfortably. Literature can help to bring us up short,
to stop the moulds from setting firm. It habitually seeks to

break the two-dimensional frame of fixed 'being' which we just as habitually try to put round others, to make us see them again as three-dimensional people in a constant state of 'becoming'. Literature can have only a formal use for utterly damned souls—or for saints.

It is all the time implicitly inviting us to remain responsive and alert and to extend our humanity; we do not talk quite so easily about 'all farm labourers' or even about 'all Russians' after we have read Hardy or Turgenev. It is implicitly inviting us to widen and deepen our knowledge of ourselves and of our relations with others, to realize that life is more this—and more that—than we had been willing to think (Emma at Box Hill, Queequeg looking down into the whale-nursery).

All this, we have to remember, may be achieved—may sometimes only be achieved—in a mythic and parabolic way. When we speak of the 'moral intelligence of art' we are not speaking only of the will in action but also of a world outside the will, of the unconscious psychic life of men. It is almost impossible not to sound pretentious here; but literature—along with the other arts, which have their own ways of informing the imagination—can help us to rediscover awe.

What is true of individuals is true also of societies. A society without a literature has that much less chance of embodying within its temper and so within its organizations something of the fullness of human experience. We only know certain things by articulating them or bodying them out. This does not mean that we have to 'argue them out'. We may know some things only by approaching them metaphorically, as dramatic 'play'.

So literature can make us sense more adequately the fullness, the weight, the inter-relations and the demands of human experience—and the possibilities for order. It can make us feel all this, but not necessarily act on it. We can see and do otherwise, always. But we are not then acting quite so much out of blindness or inarticulateness; we are selfishly or fearfully or wilfully trying to short-circuit what we know underneath to be more nearly the true state of things. Works of literature, properly read, give us the opportunity to extend our imaginative grasp of human experience; if we *will* to act well thereafter we may be able to do so with greater flexibility and insight. In this special sense literature can be morally educative. It can guide the moral will in so far as its illuminations depreciate certain modes of conduct and, conversely, reinforce others. But it cannot direct the moral will. In so far as it embodies moral intelligence and psychic insight it may *inform* the moral will, be 'the soul of all (our) moral being'.

The relation of literature to 'the moral will' is not simple. Literature is 'a criticism of life' which must itself be judged. But we can only understand that criticism and make our own judgment on it if we first—in a sense—suspend the will, if we attend to the literature as itself, as if it were an autonomous object, and let it work in its own way. It may then be in an active relationship with our sense of ourselves, with our sense of life in time and life by values. Like the other arts, literature is involved with ends beyond itself. Things can never be quite the same again after we have read—really read —a good book.

1963

LITERATURE AND SOCIETY

MANY students of society—historians, social scientists, political scientists, philosophers—find the study of works of literature useful and readily say so. They do not feel threatened by a different kind of discipline or tempted to over-stress their own subject's special mysteries. The high degree of imagination necessary for distinguished work in the humanities or social sciences ensures that men with these powers do not mistake the technical boundaries between academic disciplines for divisions within human experience.

Yet it is not easy to define exactly in what ways literature illuminates society. One is pointing to something more than the use of literature as documentary illustration, a source of raw material from whatever period one is studying, a quarry to be raided for 'background'. One is not simply talking about a mass of evidence that interestingly shows the life of an age but acts only as illustration of the judgments one then makes about a society *from outside literature,* as a historian or philosopher or social scientist. One is arguing that literature provides in its own right a form of distinctive knowledge about society.

It would be foolish to underestimate the documentary use of literature. Literature can serve such a purpose very well. Imagine a long line of books, all of them normally studied in courses on literature. At one end might be books felt by historians or political scientists or philosophers to belong to their fields as much as to the literary student's—memoirs, works of philosophy, diaries, letters, essays (and writers such as Defoe, Bunyan, Swift, Pepys, Burke, Newman). Towards the middle are mixed kinds of writing such as philosophical poetry (for example, *An Essay on Man*) and those novels that most evidently illustrate elements in their ages (there is a huge range within a range here, from Sterne through Samuel Butler's *The Way of All Flesh* to much of Charles

Dickens). Right at the other end of the line are works that seem more 'purely literary', in the sense that their value to students of society is not at first obvious (T. S. Eliot's *Four Quartets* would be a recent example).

Not all these works will have to anything like the same degree that 'something more' than illustrative value we have hinted at. How much they have depends on two things: on their intrinsic power, their power as works of literature; and on our ability to read them as works of literature, rather than to use them as quarries for extraneous buildings. Read in and for themselves, with an openness to the author's imagination and art, works of literature give an insight into the life of an age, a kind and intensity of insight, which no other source can give. They are not a substitute for these other sources; to think so would be foolish. It is just as foolish to think that these other sources can be sufficient in themselves. Without the literary witness the student of society will be blind to the fullness of a society's life.

What are these 'intrinsic', these peculiar, qualities of literature to which a good reader attends? Good literature re-creates the experiential wholeness of life—the life of the emotions, the life of the mind, the individual life and the social life, the object-laden world. It creates these things all together and interpenetrating, as they do in the lives we live ourselves. Tolstoy knew that a whole range of dissatisfactions felt by an upper-middle-class Russian woman in the nineteenth century would suddenly find their focus and demand action when she saw, as for the first time, the hair sprouting from her distinguished husband's ears. Conrad never ceased to wonder (even more than other novelists) at the way a little gesture, something about a man's clothing or a woman's voice, could focus a whole personal and social situation. Experience is much more complicatedly, much more fluidly, inter-involved than we like to remember; literature makes it harder for us to forget.

Good literature re-creates the immediacy of life—that life was and is all these things, all these different orders of things, *all at once.* It embodies the sense of human life developing in a historical and moral context. It re-creates the pressure of value-laden life so that—to the extent of the writer's gifts and art—we know better what it must have meant to live and make decisions in that time and place, to have smelled roast beef, been troubled by falling hair and wondered what we were making of our lives.

Most important of all, literature seeks a new kind of wholeness—to trace the pattern or movement that can lie behind the apparently inchoate details of life. Henry James's novels, to take an obvious instance, often work out polarities between innocence and experience in the life of individuals and between societies (innocent America and experienced Europe), polarities not 'objectively' evident but nevertheless—he believed—at work deep within individual and national psyches.

Through literature 'we know better what it must have meant . . .', I said. Perhaps I should have said 'we feel we know better'. For is our response to literature really a form of knowledge? Some people say it is not. Novels are all very interesting, they may say, but one shouldn't confuse them with knowledge. Novels are inventions, fabrications, imaginings. They don't tell us 'what it must have meant' or, if they are about contemporary life, 'what it really means'; they tell us what someone imagines it must have meant or mean. They tell us something about him—the writer, in there; not about them—other people, out there. They have no representative significance or meaningful outer reference. They do not therefore belong to the pursuit of knowledge, which is the effort after and the considered interpretation of objectively verifiable material, independent of the personality of the inquirer.

As a deliberately adopted professional position (a technical stance) this can, in certain circumstances, be admirable; as a general statement about human life it is one-eyed. In some disciplines one must act as though all knowledge were scientifically verifiable (and in some subjects it is). In the study of society it cannot be. Sociological and social-psychological techniques are already sophisticated and rightly grow more sophisticated every day; they are still crude by comparison with the complexity of what an unskilled labourer feels on his pulses every day of the week.

Cyberneticians say that even the most advanced computers have only a minute proportion of the operational efficiency of the brain of a not very well-endowed or well-trained human being. You have to go further than that if you want to describe adequately the intellectual or, harder, the emotional life of human beings. Yet it is plain that social scientists as social *scientists* must act as if all knowledge about the life of human beings can be caught within their procedures. Experimental social scientists are therefore likely to suspect those in their number who mix knowledge and opinion, objectivity and intuition. Like the early natural scientists, they fear a relapse into alchemy.

But as an overall view about human experience the idea that there is only one gate to knowledge, one kind of gate, is a form of mental colour blindness; and the second kind of knowledge is as difficult to describe to some people as colour to a colour-blind person:

> Thus they fall to denying what they cannot comprehend . . .
> they like to discern the object which engages their attention
> with extreme clearness . . . their disposition of mind soon
> leads them to condemn forms, which they regard as useless
> and inconvenient veils placed between them and the truth.

Somewhat earlier than Tocqueville, who wrote that passage, Blake put it more tartly:

> May God us keep
> From single vision and Newton's sleep.*

The heart of the case is that poetic, metaphoric, intuitive understanding is a form of knowledge although it cannot be

---

* A more recent advocacy of the double (and unified) vision is to be found in Herbert Marcuse's *One-Dimensional Man*.

objectively measured; that its validity depends on the imaginative power of the author ('imagination' includes penetration, complexity, honesty) and on our capacity as readers to test it against our own sense of experience. We will 'go along with' an author so long as he keeps our confidence on all these counts. Such knowledge is not as finally provable as 'objective' knowledge. It is not a whit less difficult to arrive at:

> Poetry is as exact a science as geometry. Induction is as good as deduction. . . . No doubt my poor Bovary is suffering and weeping in twenty different French villages at this very moment.

A hundred years later Auden made the same point as Flaubert, less colourfully but with more argumentative weight. He was writing about Henry James's *The American Scene* (James, of course, thought persistently and with an absorbed sense of craft about those 'facts' which, seen from the exactly right angle, throw a revealing light on a whole life or class):

> In grasping the character of a society, as in judging the character of an individual, no documents, statistics, 'objective' measurements can ever compete with the single intuitive glance. Intuition may err, for though its judgment is, as Pascal said, only a question of good eyesight, it must be good, for the principles are subtle and numerous, and the omission of one principle leads to error; but documentation, which is useless unless it is complete, must err in a field where completeness is impossible.*

Poetry is 'as exact a science as geometry'; the principles of intuition are 'subtle and numerous'. There is nothing easy here, no vague sense that because 'X', the writer, 'feels it down there' and feels he feels it deeply then it must be true, interesting and important.

---

* W. H. Auden, 'The American Scene', *The Dyer's Hand* (1963).

A good writer can give us a sense of the formative but largely submerged currents in an age's life. From his books, quite apart from their considerable value as social documents, one of the rewards is this sense of the way life was lived 'in the bone' at the time—that behind people's actions and reactions lay *this* particular sense of a nation's destiny, *these* assumptions about the relations between the sexes, about class and money and duty.

Occasionally a single moment, placed at just the right point, brings together and contains within itself a world of individual and social meanings, becomes a comprehensive unstated statement about those people and that sense of values (and in so doing transcends its time and place). Tolstoy and Dostoevsky especially have this power. My own favourite among the great Russian novels is the scene in Turgenev's *Fathers and Sons* when the brilliant young Bazarov dies. The reaction of his parents, loving but conservative and uncomprehending, brings together a whole range of insights about the gaps between and the love between generations, about youthful idealism, about Russian political and intellectual life, about the tragic absurdity that the universe can seem to be. (It is a moment not unlike that in which Lear refuses to believe that Cordelia is dead; to do so would be to admit that a meaningless cruelty pervades the world.)

As night approached he sank into a state of coma, and, on the following day, expired. Father Alexis performed over him the last rites of religion, and at the moment when Extreme Unction was being administered, and the holy oil touched his breast, one of the dying man's eyelids raised itself, and over the face there seemed to flit something like an expression of distaste at the sight of the priest in his vestments, the smoking censer, and the candles before the *ikon*.

Finally, when Bazarov's last breath had been drawn, and there had arisen in the house the sound of 'the general lamentation', something akin to frenzy came upon Vasili Ivanitch [the father].

"I declare that I protest!" he cried with his face blazing and quivering with fury, and his fist beating the air as in menace of some one. "I declare that I protest, that I protest, that I protest!"

Upon that old Arina Vlasievna, suffused in tears, laid her arms around his neck, and the two sank forward upon the floor. Said Anfisushka later, when relating the story in the servants' quarters: "There they knelt together—side by side, their heads drooping like those of two sheep at midday."*

Among English novelists Hardy had similar powers (it is part of what we mean by calling him a 'poetic' novelist). Think of the scene in *Tess of the D'Urbervilles* in which Tess realizes that her illegitimate baby is about to die and decides to baptise it herself. In that ceremony Hardy brings together an intricate network of observations about the terms of life for such a girl in such a society (and about much else in human nature at any time). But it is crucial to realize that what makes the scene effective is not that Hardy overtly makes it 'representative', but that he keeps his eye on the particulars. Tess's face, far from being some generalized symbol for outraged womanhood or the plight of peasant maidens, is seen and described as a rough-skinned country girl's face but now, because of the softening weak light of the candle, transformed:

> Tess then stood erect with the infant on her arm beside the basin, the next sister held the Prayer Book open before her, as the clerk at church held it before the parson; and thus the girl set about baptizing her child.
> Her figure looked singularly tall and imposing as she stood in her long white nightgown, a thick cable of twisted dark hair hanging straight down her back to her waist. The kindly dimness of the weak candle abstracted from her form and features the little blemishes which sunlight might have revealed—the stubble scratches upon her wrists and the weariness of her eyes—her high enthusiasm having a transfiguring effect upon the face which had been her undoing, showing it as a thing of immaculate beauty, with a touch of dignity which was almost regal. The little ones kneeling round, their sleepy eyes blinking and red, awaited her prepara-

* Ivan Turgenev, *Fathers and Sons*, trans. C. J. Hogarth (1921).

tions full of a suspended wonder which their physical heaviness at that hour would not allow to become active.

This is the way art releases its meanings, by looking honestly at the object until the meaning emerges as if of its own volition, not by rigging the scene as symptomatic documentation.

What the novel can supremely give is a sense of the texture of life as it is lived; and of the way in which that texture is all the time shot through with moral choices. 'Moral' in this context does not mean 'moralizing', enunciating ethical precepts. It means exploring the ways in which we are day after day involved in value judgments, whether by commission or omission; it means recognizing that our lives are irradiated with qualitative commitments, and recognizing too the almost incredible complexity of these relationships. I sometimes wonder whether the irritation of some social scientists at the irruption, into the discussion of society, of evaluative opinion comes less from professional strictness than from an awful sense of the difficulty of measuring and assessing these qualitative elements.

In some respects it is easier to talk about the social relevance of novels than about that of plays or—even more—poetry. The poet speaks, more often than the novelist, in his own person. His witness is more direct and contemporary. He is less likely to explore and re-create how people a century or so ago lived and moved and had their being; he is more likely to be saying, in effect, "This is how *I* feel" or "This is what a hawk looks like to me from the middle of a city street in 1966."

Moreover, the poet's relation to language is more sensitive than the novelist's. It is even more difficult to paraphrase him. Language is for him, even more than for the novelist, organically a part of what he is saying, not only a vehicle for thought or feeling but a fulfilling of, a bodying out of the pressure of that thought and feeling. Fourteenth-century England, the early seventeenth century, the Commonwealth and Restoration: we shall only discover what Chaucer, Donne and Milton illuminate in these periods if we read their poetry as poetry, not as evidence. Then it may become evidence. Their language expresses the temper of their minds, and their tempers exemplify crucial elements in their ages.

And the poet is likely to be more concerned about technique than the novelist. But again the form, like the texture of the language, is part of what is being said; the structure chosen and the other technical devices are not an escape from experience but a way of holding experience under pressure.

Wordsworth is a good example of the different ways a poet can speak for his age. Involved in that important movement from eighteenth-century to nineteenth-century ways of thought, he responded to the change at the deepest psychic levels, as a challenge to define one's humanity and one's relations to the world outside man. At times he wrote directly and discursively; for instance, in the Preface to *Lyrical Ballads* with Coleridge (after these two the line of direct social criticism by poets runs up through Matthew Arnold to T. S. Eliot). But his greatest explorations of the pressure of his age are in his poetry itself. It is not surprising that John Stuart Mill should have stressed in his *Autobiography* the value of Wordsworth's poetry to him:

> What made Wordsworth's poems a medicine for my state of mind was that they expressed, not mere outward beauty, but states of feeling, and of thought coloured by feeling, under the excitement of beauty. They seemed to be the very culture of the feelings, which I was in quest of.

'The very culture of the feelings.' Some of the great Victorians still had a sense of the unity of being. Darwin in his own *Autobiography* could say with impressive humility that when, late in life, he found himself no longer able to read poetry he knew that—whatever the achievements of his long service to science—something had withered in him:

> My mind seems to have become a kind of machine for grinding general laws out of large collections of facts, but

why this should have caused the atrophy of that part of the brain alone, on which the higher tastes depend, I cannot conceive. . . . If I had to live my life again, I would have made a rule to read some poetry and listen to some music at least once every week. . . . The loss of these tastes is a loss of happiness, and may possibly be injurious to the intellect, and more probably to the moral character, by enfeebling the emotional part of our nature.

In Wordsworth's poetry the outstanding text in this connection is *The Prelude*. But the hundred and fifty lines of 'Tintern Abbey' provide a marvellous introduction to a crucial moment for Wordsworth and his age, in their questioning of the interrelations between the natural and human orders:

> *I have owed to them,*
> *In hours of weariness, sensations sweet,*
> *Felt in the blood, and felt along the heart;*
> *And passing even into my purer mind,*
> *With tranquil restoration:—feelings too*
> *Of unremembered pleasure: such, perhaps,*
> *As have no slight or trivial influence*
> *On that best portion of a good man's life,*
> *His little, nameless, unremembered, acts*
> *Of kindness and of love. Nor less, I trust,*
> *To them I may have owed another gift,*
> *Of aspect more sublime; that blessed mood,*
> *In which the burthen of the mystery,*
> *In which the heavy and the weary weight*
> *Of all this unintelligible world,*
> *Is lightened . . .*

There is an interesting comparison with Tennyson's 'In Memoriam' which, on the face of it, might seem more likely to illuminate its age than much of Wordsworth. Certainly that poem is an essential document in the development of the argument about belief during the mid-nineteenth century. Yet, no matter how much one admires 'In Memoriam', one has to say that it reveals less about its age than some of Wordsworth's poetry, even when Wordsworth's poetry is not directly about its age.

Finally, a modern instance. The poetry of W. B. Yeats provides unusually good evidence of the different ways in which poetry may speak for its time. I am thinking of the movement from Yeats's early poetry of the Celtic Twilight to his directly political poetry and finally to the apparently unpolitical but more deeply representative late poems.

If one special strength of fiction is the fullness of its re-creation of an age's life, and of poetry a particular attention to language and form as means of inquiry, then a peculiar strength of drama is its capacity to reveal truths about an age by indirection, mythically, by an oblique 'showing': "Tell all the truth but tell it slant/Success in circuit lies." Some of the more difficult truths about the soul of an age best reveal themselves when told 'slant'. Look, today, at the work of Beckett and Pinter, work unmistakably about the quality of men's lives in the mid-twentieth century but work that scarcely ever makes a direct statement about those lives.

To read a book is harder than we realize, a difficult effort in giving dispassionate and full attention to language and form. A book of any worth cannot be gutted or winnowed; it is a complex organism. It is also difficult to state analytically, once a book has been read, what its representativeness really consists in. T. S. Eliot could make particularly fascinating and seminal correlations, but has rightly been criticized for a kind of cavalier quality in some of them:

> The difference is not a simple difference of degree between poets. It is something which had happened to the mind of England between the time of Donne or Lord Herbert of Cherbury and the time of Tennyson and Browning; it is

the difference between the intellectual poet and the reflective poet. Tennyson and Browning are poets, and they think; but they do not feel their thought as immediately as the odour of a rose. A thought to Donne was an experience; it modified his sensibility.

The assumptions that passage from 'The Metaphysical Poets' (1921) makes are staggering. They may be true; yet neither Eliot nor those who have since used the passage have thoroughly examined its extra-literary implications. Eliot acknowledged this need, with particular reference to the essay on 'The Metaphysical Poets', in his British Academy lecture on Milton, in 1947. In this sort of analysis we do need to work at the frontiers shared with other students of society; and we have to recognize that it is difficult work.

It is as hard to describe the imaginative whole that is a great work of literature as to describe a symphony or a great painting. At his best a good literary critic shows respect for the author's creation in itself, an openness before the author's way of looking at experience, a recognition of his own biases and a refusal to cut corners on their behalf in discussing the texts. A literary work of any consequence is not a collection of impressions, of 'pure emotion' (whatever that may mean), or the product of some nonsignificant formal or aesthetic game. A work of literature, and so the skill (criticism) that analyses it, differs from non-artistic explorations of experience (for example, philosophy) because it does not abstract-out the elements of experience; it starts and finishes with experience as a whole, 'blood, imagination, intellect running together'. To recognize this wholeness, this intellectual/emotional/mythopoeic immediacy, and to learn how to respond to it in literature, is a necessary part of knowledge, without which we shall not see far in other humane disciplines (or in our own lives, since they will even less bear the abstractions of the single vision).

The use of literary criticism in understanding popular art,

mass art and some other forms of mass communication has been developed to a limited extent by a small number of British literary critics for the past few decades. In America more has been done.* In Britain, the close, practical analysis of this material has usually been supported by a number of generally accepted ideas about contemporary cultural conditions (about the relations between folk, mass and popular art; about minorities or élites; about high, middle and low brows). Some of its foundation documents are the Preface to *Lyrical Ballads*, Matthew Arnold's *Culture and Anarchy* (1869) and, in this century, Ortega y Gasset's *The Revolt of the Masses* and T. S. Eliot's *Notes Towards the Definition of Culture*.

In general the cultural picture assumed by most British teachers of literature who have worked in this field is too limited. They are insufficiently responsive to the complications of contemporary cultural conditions and so to the meanings of much contemporary art at all levels. Popular and mass art is more varied than they recognize (and what professes to be 'high art' sometimes no more than a profession), and the continuity and change within working-class attitudes more complex than they allow.†

In close analysis the main aim is to see better the thing as it is, its texture and inner nature. There are two main lines of approach: detailed analysis of rhetoric, and the study of larger meanings (myth, archetype, pattern, theme). In both, the assumption must be that the productions have *in some ways* the kind of relation to language and to their audiences that 'high art' has, and are therefore open to similar analytic

---

* A useful first guide, for some of its essays and for its bibliography, is *Mass Culture*, a Free Press/Macmillan paperback (New York, 1967). Although most of the essays it reprints are by social scientists, it includes some literary critics' work, names others and gives an idea of the close relations between parts of the two disciplines. In Britain the more important earlier contributors include Dr. and Mrs. Leavis and Denys Thompson; and, from a different angle, George Orwell.

† Among recent books Raymond Williams' *Culture and Society* and *The Long Revolution* and Edward Thompson's *The Making of the English Working Class* valuably extend our understanding here.

approaches. (That these relations are often simpler, more 'stereotyped' in 'mass art' than in 'high art' does not disprove the assumption; and part of the purpose of the inquiry is to test these terms themselves.) This needs stressing to those literary critics who think that only recognized works of literary art can be critically analysed, and that the rest—'lowbrow art', to use a favoured portmanteau expression which conflates a number of different forms—is as simple as bubble gum. This is a crude error in the face of an interesting set of relationships.

A related view—more common among social scientists—is that mass art can be explained simply in commercial and economic terms; that it is wholly and deliberately a devised product, for an audience whose tastes are pretty exactly known. The commercial and economic connections of mass art certainly need to be understood better. But views like these, whether they are held by social scientists or by 'highbrow' critics, simplify the relationship between the producers and their audiences, the producers and their material, the audiences and the material, and the interactions between different forms and levels of taste.

Suppose we assume that the products of the mass media can sometimes be analysed in the same way as traditional works of art. A few social scientists will nevertheless still see no point in such analysis; no point for the social scientist, that is. They will argue that there can be no such thing as 'the work in itself', that the formulation is a way of claiming absoluteness for what is itself a socially conditioned matter; that what is meant by 'the work of art in itself' is what particular authors, with their kind of background, thought they were creating, thought they were effecting in their readers; or it is simply what a group of critics, at a particular time or in a particular 'literary tradition', agree to call 'the work of art in itself'. So, although social scientific analysis of these assumptions themselves might be useful, since it would tell you something about these authors and critics, it would tell you little about what any individual reader or viewer made of or took away from any work. With the mass arts this is a crucial consideration, since audiences and would-be literary critics of the mass media certainly do not 'share a tradition'. Therefore, such a social scientist would continue, to study the effects of mass communications it is best to confine oneself to effects-analysis drawn directly from audience studies. We know from existing effects-analysis that what is taken from the same production varies from person to person, that we are all highly selective in our responses.

We can agree that certain kinds of effects-analysis (particularly psychological analysis) must keep themselves clinically to themselves. Outside that, it is important on several grounds for the student of mass communications within the social sciences to have a good sense of the contribution literature and literary criticism can make to his studies. They can help to bring to the light better, like a brass-rubbing, the face and body of mass communications, and so inform consideration of their impact below the 'objective' level. They can help the social scientist to avoid setting up questionnaires or other tests that contain assumptions which a closer sense of the 'things in themselves' could have corrected. The social scientist who began an essay on the significance of television with the assumption that television is essentially 'entertainment' might have been saved if he had thought more carefully in the first place about the nature of social structures, and so of the degree to which what a medium is is pre-decided by the structure within which a society makes it operate. The same result could have been achieved if he had thought more about the material itself. Another social scientist who, in assessing the effects of television on 'serious' cultural pursuits, constructed a scale of ascending seriousness running from comic books through the *Reader's Digest* to the Book-of-the-Month could only have been saved from such unreality by a closer analytic understanding of the nature of 'things in themselves'.

Social scientific content analysis is much more sophisticated than it was a few years ago, but is still insufficiently alert to

33

the inner character—and so, to the likely effect—of many forms of mass communication (for example, most sociological analyses of crime-and-violence series on television leave you wondering whether their authors have ever felt the appeal of one of them). Literary critical practice can help make content analysis more subtle. And, in co-operation with other relevant disciplines, it can help to set the phenomena of mass communications in a fuller social and historical context than any of us, working alone, have so far managed. It is not a substitute for social scientific analysis but a useful—an essential—adjunct.

In the analysis of rhetoric—using 'rhetoric' as a comprehensive term for qualities of style, particularly those that assist persuasion or assent, that carry the relations between writer and reader—special attention needs to be paid to tone and manner. Compare, for instance, the opening paragraphs of Forster's *A Passage to India* and Lawrence's *Sons and Lovers*.* The contrast is striking. The passages have very different emotional keyboards—partly because the authors are different individuals, partly because the passages serve different artistic purposes, partly for socio-cultural reasons. By close attention to individual words and images, to syntax, to stress, to the movement of each passage, the literary critic can just begin to make some assumptions about each author's sense of his audience and his society, about the assumed relations between literature and social class and about other assumptions shared and unshared.

A comparison across a stretch of time shows such differences even more clearly. Here are two moments of vocational-revelation in fiction, separated by three-quarters of a century. George Eliot describes the moment at which Lydgate in *Middlemarch* becomes destined to be a doctor:

> The page of the Cyclopaedia he chanced to open was under the head of Anatomy, and the first passage that drew his eyes was on the valves of the heart. He was not much acquainted with valves of any sort, but he knew that valva were

* The paragraphs are quoted in full in 'A Question of Tone', pp. 194 & 198.

folding-doors, and through this crevice came a sudden light startling him, with his first vivid notion of finely-adjusted mechanism in the human frame. A liberal education had of course left him free to read the indecent passages in the school classics, but beyond a general sense of secrecy and obscenity in connection with his internal structure, had left his imagination quite unbiased, so that for anything he knew his brain lay in small bags at his temples, and he had no more thought of representing to himself how his blood circulated than how paper served instead of gold. But the moment of vocation had come, and before he got down from his chair, the world was made new to him by a presentiment of endless processes filling the vast spaces planked out of his sight by that wordy ignorance which he had supposed to be knowledge. From that hour Lydgate felt the growth of an intellectual passion.

Tench, the broken-down expatriate dentist in Graham Greene's *The Power and the Glory** has a similar moment of revelation:

> "Oh, it will be hours yet," Mr. Tench assured him again.
> "Hours? Are you certain? It's very hot in the sun."
> "You'd better come home."
> Home: it was a phrase one used to mean four walls behind which one slept. There had never been a home. They moved across the little burnt plaza where the dead general grew green in the damp and the gaseosa stalls stood under the palms. Home lay like a picture postcard on a pile of other postcards: shuffle the pack and you had Nottingham, a Metroland birthplace, an interlude in Southend. Mr. Tench's father had been a dentist too—his first memory was finding a discarded cast in a waste-paper basket—the rough toothless gaping mouth of clay, like something dug up in Dorset—Neanderthal or Pithecanthropus. It had been his favourite toy: they tried to tempt him with Meccano, but fate had struck. There is always one moment in childhood when the door opens and lets the future in. The hot wet river-port and the vultures lay in the waste-paper basket, and he picked them out. We should be thankful we cannot see the horrors

---

* London: Heinemann, 1940; New York: The Viking Press, 1946. All quotations are by permission of the publishers.

and degradations lying around our childhood, in cupboards and bookshelves, everywhere.

Even within the context of a whole book, it is difficult to define social and cultural changes accurately—to distinguish between elements peculiar to the author, those that are part of his artistic strategy, and those that are representative, that hint at changes in society, in assumptions, in the sense of available audiences. But insofar as it does succeed, this kind of analysis can uniquely assist understanding of the society within which a book has been written.

Less intensively, the same kind of approach can be applied to any piece of persuasive prose—to advertisements, speeches, public statements. There are a fair number of books that describe and give practice in this sort of work. This recent advertisement could be the starting point for an essay on the Sixties, on one society's image of itself:

> Cliff Adams is like that. He faces a situation, makes a decision and sticks to it. Commercial TV started and he started with it. Writing and arranging music for commercials. One of his first for Fry's Turkish Delight is still around. And he still likes it.
> This is the new type of Englishman. The professional. There's nothing of the dilettante about Cliff. Nothing of the frustrated musician who apologises for commercial work saying he'd really like to write a symphony. Cliff Adams works to order. He works for money. And what he does, he does very well indeed. He says this attitude is what the English revolution is all about. He talks about how people have changed. How they face things squarely. Want life to be straightforward, not full of unwritten rules. He says it shows in everything they do. The way they dress, talk, write, think, even drink. He talks about what people drink nowadays. He says it's vodka. Cossack Vodka because it's a clean drink. Cossack Vodka because it's straightforward and makes no pretence.*

Or consider the mild persuasive sophistication of this defence of commercial television:

* With acknowledgments to the Distillers Co. and S. H. Benson Ltd.

If you decide to have a system of people's television, then people's television you must expect it to be. It will reflect their likes and dislikes, their tastes and aversions, what they can comprehend and what is beyond them. Every person of common sense knows that people of superior mental constitution are bound to find much of television intellectually beneath them. If such innately fortunate people cannot realize this gently and considerately and with good manners, if in their hearts they despise popular pleasures and interests, then of course they will be angrily dissatisfied with television. But it is not really television with which they are dissatisfied. It is with people.

More difficult and interesting is a comparison of the literature of violence at different 'levels'; we soon find that many of our assumptions about the differences between good and bad literature do not serve well under pressure, and that the social implications of the comparisons are not easily grasped or, when grasped, always palatable. In all such exercises it is important to work outward from close analysis of style, to have each general judgment rooted in that kind of illustration. This is the essential guide to knowing just what any passage really says. One gets closer to its character by watching the words, listening for changes of stress, noting what it doesn't say as well as what it does.

In the second approach, through examining myth, symbol, thematic patterns—larger elements in a work than 'rhetorical' analysis implies—one of the most interesting discoveries is that social scientists and literary critics can be very close to each other. They can not only reach similar conclusions but are likely to use similar illustrations and emphases en route.*

But, to end near where I started, for a student of society great works of literature are more important than popular

---

* See, for instance, an essay in *Mass Culture* by two sociologists—'How to Read "Li'l Abner" Intelligently' by Arthur J. Broadbeck and David M. White—which could be compared with essays on similar subjects by literary critics. So might several essays by the American sociologist David Riesman. Kingsley Amis' book on Ian Fleming is, so far as I know, a unique instance of a thoroughly ambivalent work in the field—part critically perceptive, part evasive of its own implications.

literature. One way of defining great art is as that art which transcends the conditions that gave it birth and so penetrates further into human experience, sees more, than those conditions promised.

The better the art, the better the witness; and this is a judgment of quality, not quantity. Zola is not as great an artist as Stendhal, although he went to much greater pains to get his social detail correct and full to overflowing.

The quality of the perception brought to bear is the crux of the matter: a capacity to see not only individual instances but long-term movements below the surface detail; an ability to unite dissimilars, to reveal a pattern out of a mass and mess, like a magnet placed into iron filings. This quality is presumably the basis of any significant hypothesis in any discipline; in no discipline is it a matter of simple aggregation.

Behind the writing and reading of all good literature lie a number of extraordinary assumptions. The literary student takes them for granted, but should remind himself of their extraordinariness. The student of society can benefit by looking at them. Why *should* men try to 're-create' their personal and social worlds? Why should they—as well as analysing them, probing them, generalizing about them, taking them to pieces, finding their component parts—have felt moved to 'make them again'?

One reason seems to be that men do so not to effect anything but, so to speak, for its own sake; because they feel wonder and awe about the nature of their lives; and because they feel amusement, irony and pride at their—at man's—attempts to cope.

Another reason seems to be the wish to be in touch with others. Literature implies an audience: perhaps not a very large audience, perhaps an audience that is 'fit though few'—but always an audience. It assumes the possibility and the worthwhileness of communication with other human beings. Without having to say so explicitly, it says at the back of its mind: we are not alone. Though we may be 'poor, bare, forked animals', we can try and hope to get in touch. And this, though it may not at first glance seem to have much to tell the student of society, has a significance for him that he would be wrong to neglect.

1966

THE FORCE OF CARICATURE

*Aspects of the art of Graham Greene, with particular
reference to* The Power and the Glory

ADMIRERS of Graham Greene usually reserve a special place
for *The Power and the Glory*,* the story of a priest's flight
through a land which has forsaken the Faith. I have in mind
not so much specialists and critics as the large number of
people who normally read few novels and yet are devoted
readers of Graham Greene. Why should this novel be so highly
regarded? Does it possess some typical qualities in stronger
measure than Greene's other books? Are the theme, the
manner or the setting particularly attractive, and if so why?

Setting is always important and constitutive in Graham
Greene, but in *The Power and the Glory* even more than
elsewhere. The theme is indivisibly priest-and-land, his
journey through a country against whose condition, simply
by being what he is, he makes a charge. The land is given
over to a 'huge abandonment'; it rolls through time 'like a
burning and abandoned ship'. Variations on these phrases
echo throughout the book. So far as this country likes to
think itself modern, it has chosen the sterile progressivism
of the police lieutenant; so far as it is what it always was,
though now without acknowledging its condition, it is 'a
landscape of terror and lust'. Here the echoes are even more
insistent: this is a world 'of treachery, violence and lust', of
'violence everywhere . . . was there no end to violence'; this
is the land of the corrupt and cowardly Jefe, of the fang-
toothed Judas ('they [the priest and the Judas] might have
been the only survivors of a world which was dying out'), of
a whole people who 'carried the visible marks of the dying
about with them'.

* London: Heinemann, 1940; New York: The Viking Press, 1946. All
quotations are by permission of the publishers.

40

But the darkness is occasionally illuminated by evidence of grace, by the courage of the girl Coral, by the unwillingness of his fellow-prisoners to betray the priest after he has made himself and the price on his head known, by the lieutenant's gift of money to help the unrecognized priest on his way. The priest is a whisky-priest, a coward, the father of a child born of his loneliness and weakness, a once arrogant man who quickly recovers his old attitudes when he reaches safety. Yet, 'after all . . . he carries on', says a minor character; he carries on, continually touched by conscience, and finally goes back from safety to administer the last sacrament to a dying murderer, knowing the call to be a trap. After his execution a new priest follows in the abandoned land.

One could scarcely miss the allegory. I say allegory rather than symbolism to indicate a manipulation of the material in accordance with a view of the world which the writer has from outside that material, so to speak. I reserve symbolism for a more inward embodiment of the writer's attitude to experience, in which the attitude does not so much precede the creation of the fiction as find itself in the fiction. I would therefore apply the adjective 'symbolic' to Kafka's novels but not to *The Power and the Glory*.

This society is clearly our society, allegorically heightened: "This place [the prison] was very like the world: overcrowded with lust and crime and unhappy love; it stank to Heaven. . . ." This is our world, as it presents itself to Graham Greene: corrupt but denying sin; man-centred but still in the presence of God. The primary characteristics of Greene's view of the world are unhappiness and sin; it is 'stinking to heaven', the priest repeats, and later, 'the world's unhappy whether you're rich or poor'. One believes in God and original sin, to begin with, because not to believe would be to find the whole situation meaninglessly cruel. The long and frequently quoted passage from Cardinal Newman which forms the motto to *The Lawless Roads* (the quarry for *The Power and the Glory*) makes the general point most clearly, ending:

What shall be said to this heart-piercing, reason-bewildering fact [of evil in the world]? I can only answer, that either there is no Creator, or this living society of men is in a true sense discarded from His presence . . . *if* there be a God, *since* there is a God, the human race is implicated in some terrible aboriginal calamity.

Greene gives the personal application on the third page of *The Lawless Roads*:

And so faith came to one—shapelessly, without dogma, a presence above a croquet lawn, something associated with violence, cruelty, evil across the way. One began to believe in heaven because one believed in hell, but for a long while it was only hell one could picture with a certain intimacy.

Seedy settings attract because there one sees life as it really is, with none of the thin platforms over the abyss which normal social life constructs. Speaking in *The Lost Childhood* of the blitzed cities, Greene says: "That, I think, is why one feels at home in London or in Liverpool or Bristol . . . because life there is what it ought to be." One cannot fail to see there the vast struggle which is for ever being played out in human existence. Greene's vision of the world is intensely dramatic—it alternates between the rubbish tip at the far end of the town and the outer stars, between Father José the apostate priest, standing in his nightshirt in his miserable compound, laughed at by the boys and called for by his gross wife, and the galaxies towards which his hands ineffectually gesture.

Hell is certainly pictured with a certain intimacy, with more intimacy than heaven, than the instances of goodness and love. They are included, are recognized intellectually, but do not seem to be felt anywhere near as strongly as the wickedness. Indeed, Greene sometimes finds only sinfulness where many of us would find something less reprehensible. Ida, the fat Guinness-and-oysters barmaid of *Brighton Rock*, who has clearly all kinds of virtues, even though she may not recognize sin and will go on talking about right-and-wrong, is several times directly and violently disparaged by Greene. I think particularly of the way he vilifies her as she prepares to spend the night in an hotel with Phil Corkery. Or of his comment on the workers who come in thousands for a day at Brighton, people very like Ida: "Her amusements were their amusements, her superstitions their superstitions . . . she had no more love for anyone than they had."

It is the last clause which grates, which is—one's own experience of life insists, and without being simply a jolly humanist—just not the whole truth. Greene has misunderstood; his obsession has blinded him to an important part of the truth. So it is also as the priest in *The Power and the Glory* sits at the side of the dying murderer. The murderer knows, and thinks the priest does not, that the call to the deathbed is a trap, and spends his last few minutes trying to persuade the priest to take his revolver and escape, cursing 'the bastards' who have laid the trap. Immediately after the death of the gunman the priest prays, " 'O merciful God, after all he was thinking of me, it was for my sake . . .' but he prayed without conviction. At the best, it was only one criminal trying to aid the escape of another—whichever way you looked there wasn't much merit in either of them." The priest presumably prays 'without much conviction' because, in terms of doctrine, confession for the gunman is the only relevant action at this moment, and his refusal to confess a final refusal of grace. But both the interpretations of the attitude which is preventing the gunman from making the act of confession are unconvincing. He was not likely to be prompted simply by unselfish thought for the priest or simply by the wish of one criminal 'to aid the escape of another'. His response was probably lower than the former, but certainly higher than the latter. 'The bastards' is partly an angry moral assertion against the lowness of the trick, and not therefore to be dismissed so flatly.

What Greene does seem to feel very strongly for others is not so much love as pity. The history of Scobie, in *The Heart of the Matter*, is the history of a man drawn to his death by

43

overweening pity. For Greene knows—it accounts for much of the ambiguity in his relation to his characters—that 'pity can corrupt', as Auden said of his work. Yet Greene can never still the promptings of pity. It is surely this which causes him, whenever his characters are particularly reduced, to slip into the imagery of lost children . . . Loo and Anthony at the end of their short-lived relationship in *England Made Me*, or Mr. and Mrs. Fellows at the beginning of *The Power and the Glory*: "There was no meaning anywhere outside their hearts; they were carried like children in a coach through the huge spaces without any knowledge of their destination." And later in the bedroom of the capital's only hotel, after the death of Coral: "They gave an odd effect of being children, lost in a strange town, without adult care."

This world of Greene's is presented in such vivid allegory, is so obviously intensely felt, that for a time we find it absorbing. At the back of our minds, becoming more insistent as we re-read, questions about it thrust themselves upon us. But perhaps our doubts about the nature of Greene's world and our interest in the sources of his novels' appeal are really aspects of the same question. If so, we should be able, by a detailed textual examination, to discover something not only about the technical bases of their attraction, but also about the connection between Greene's way of writing and his outlook on experience.

Greene's style is nervous, vivid, astringent, the vehicle of a restless and pungent imagination: it picks out the shopkeeper in the Lehrs' village with his 'three commercial chins'; the 'hooded and cramped pleasure' of the act of sex in prison; the mean-spirited, self-righteous sisters leaving jail in the early morning, "they were both tied up in black shawls like things bought in the market, things hard and dry and secondhand"; and the director of Private Tutorials Ltd., 'Henry Beckley, B.A.'—the name presents him at once . . . a third in English at Oxford; behind the shiny rimless glasses a bright

'let me be your father' smile; an incipient predatory harden-
ing of the mouth which would like to be charming. Or one
recalls the effect of the word 'bastard' on the priest, catching
at his heart like the name of someone you love heard in a
strange company; or the creation of the atmosphere of collapse in heat and disillusion in the very first paragraph as
Mr. Tench, the ruined dentist, goes out hopelessly for the
ether cylinder he's bound to miss getting.

These are in themselves important qualities, and need only
to be recalled. Yet their effect over any length is of something over-generalized and rhetorical. On looking more
closely one finds that the epithets, for instance, are often
either unusually arresting or just cliché—'patience' is likely
to be either 'monstrous patience' or simply 'stony patience'.
The emotions are being pulled out of shape, put into over-
bold relief: Mr. Tench had been seized by the desire to be
a dentist after finding a discarded cast in a wastepaper basket,
"Fate had struck. . . . We should be thankful we cannot see
the horrors and degradations lying around our childhood, in
cupboards and bookshelves, everywhere": Coral feels the
first pains of menstruation, "The child stood in her woman's
pain and looked at them: a horrible novelty enclosed her
whole morning: it was as if today everything was memorable"
(and why should it be only 'horrible'?—Greene seems almost
to hate the physical aspects of sex): the mother of the priest's
child speaks about her, "She said 'She's bad through and
through'. He was aware of faith dying out between the bed
and the door." Or one remembers the water-pipes which
gurgle through Greene's novels. Like the Wurlitzer organ—
'the world's wet mouth lamenting over life'—they are among
the telltale voices of modern civilization, this time of the
individual's loneliness behind all the mechanics. Anthony,
the wastrel ex-public-schoolboy in *England Made Me*, tries
to make yet another anonymous hotel bedroom look friendly:
"He stood in the middle of the room wondering what to do
next to make the room look like home, listening to the hot-
water pipes wailing behind the wall." In *The Power and the*

Glory, the water-pipes play a sad background music to the scene, again in an hotel bedroom, in which the priest's communion wine is drunk for him, "somewhere in the distance a pipe gurgled and the beetles detonated against a bare globe".

Greene uses the selectively typical catalogue as much as Auden, partly because they naturally tend to handle their material similarly, partly because they both began to write in the Thirties when reportage made the catalogue very popular. More importantly, it seems to me, Greene's use of the catalogue follows from his way of looking at life. If life is seen as a vast pattern then all the details of life can easily become parts of the pattern; they can be 'placed' with a certain sureness and inevitability. At its best the manner is illuminating; at its worst it can suggest a kind of contempt, as though the author is saying, "One knows that people such as these will always dress like this, have this kind of house, this kind of furniture." On the reader the effect may be quietly flattering, though, of course, the author may not intend this. The reader may appear to be invited to collaborate by the suggestion that he, like the author, has seen this kind of thing before; nothing is unexpected to the wide eye of the intelligentsia. This is the detail you will expect to find, it seems to say, if you are one of the cognoscenti; the items are typical of a whole genre.* For instance, the cheap bookie's house in *Brighton Rock*:

> He looked with contempt down the narrow hall—the shell-case converted into an umbrella stand, the moth-eaten stag's head bearing on one horn a bowler hat, a steel helmet used for ferns. . . . He lit the gas fire, turned on a stand lamp in a red silk shade with a bobble fringe. The light glowed on a silver-plated biscuit box, a framed wedding-group.

The garage of the gimcrack villa where Pinky hides:

> A spade, a rusty lawn-mower, and all the junk the owner had

* Sir G. Rostrevor Hamilton has discussed the use of this kind of catalogue in *The Tell-Tale Article: A Critical Approach to Modern Poetry* (1949).

46

no room for in the tiny house: an old rocking horse, a pram which had been converted into a wheelbarrow, a pile of ancient records: 'Alexander's Rag Time Band', 'Pack up your Troubles', 'If you were the only Girl'; they lay with the trowels, with what was left of the crazy paving, a doll with one glass eye and a dress soiled with mould.

Anthony undressing in *England Made Me*:

> . . . the rather torn photograph of Annette which he had stripped from its frame (he leant it against his tooth mug), the ties which he had crammed into his pocket at the lodgings, his new pants, his new vests, his new socks, *The Four Just Men* in a Tauchnitz edition, his dark blue pyjamas, a copy of *Film Fun*. He turned out his pockets: a pencil, a half-crown fountain pen, an empty card-case, a packet of De Reszke cigarettes.

Or the empty Fellows' bungalow in *The Power and the Glory*:

> He looked in through the window—perhaps this was the child's room. Everything had been removed from it except the useless or the broken. There was a cardboard box full of torn paper and a small chair which had lost a leg. There was a large nail in the white-washed wall where a mirror perhaps had been hung—or a picture. There was a broken shoe-horn. . . . The priest opened the door on the left—perhaps it had been the bedroom. In a corner lay a pile of old medicine bottles: small fingers of crudely coloured liquid lay in some of them. There were medicines for headaches, stomach-aches, medicines to be taken after meals and before meals. Somebody must have been very ill to need so many? There was a hairbrush, broken, a ball of hair-combings— very fair hair turning dusty white.

The detail is acutely observed, but is all too typical—we are in the world of *New Statesman* competitions.

Greene's similes are almost always short and sharply juxtapose the concrete, actual or temporal with the abstract, subjective or eternal. They can therefore have a genuine and important function in an allegory. But some of them seem to have been written by rote, and there are so many that the cumulative effect is dulling. These are some from *The Power and the Glory* only:

Evil ran like malaria in his veins.
The memory was like a hand, pulling away the past, exposing him.
Heat stood in the room like an enemy.
She carried her responsibilities carefully like crockery across the hot yard [of Coral].
The old life peeled away like a label.
He could feel his prayers weigh him down like undigested food.
Pride wavered in his voice, like a plant with shallow roots.

Sometimes the abstract/concrete relationship is reversed:

It was like hate on a death-bed [of a dog's snarl].
He drank the brandy down like damnation.

The repeated three-steps-down ending gives the effect of a flat 'not with a bang but a whimper', hopeless, corner-of-the-mouth tailing-off.

This was what he was used to: the words not striking home, the hurried close, the expectation of pain coming between him and his faith.

You cannot control what you love—you watch it driving recklessly towards the broken bridge, the torn-up track, the horror of seventy years ahead.

Their little shameless voices filled the patio, and he smiled humbly and sketched small gestures for silence, and there was no respect anywhere left for him in his home, in the town, in the whole abandoned star.

The effect of all these stylistic qualities is of repeated jabs from a hypodermic syringe, of overforcing, of distortion, of a boldly caricaturish manner.

The narrative of *The Power and the Glory* derives its

undoubted force from three main structural features: (i) the extreme simplicity of the overall pattern, and the skill and complexity with which the themes are interwoven through its three parts; (ii) the striking visual quality of the scenes; (iii) the speed of transition between those scenes. Henry James said that he composed his novels dramatically; one could say that Greene composes his cinematically. The construction here could hardly be simpler; the parts deal respectively with the setting and the arrival of the priest; the pursuit to its apparent end in safety; and the return, the execution and the arrival of the new priest. Indeed, the pattern is too neat; the new priest comes too pat on his cue, becomes a mechanical metaphor for the assertion that the Faith goes on and the horror is always repeated.

Throughout, the eye shifts constantly, without explanatory links. In the first paragraph the solitary figure of Mr. Tench is picked up crossing the hot deserted square; a few vultures look down at him; he tosses something off the road at them and one rises; with it goes the camera and introduces us to the town, the river, the sea. As the paragraph closes we drop to Mr. Tench again, now at the far side of the plaza, and now in his setting. Thereafter the camera moves from the dentist to the police-chief, to the pious woman reading, to the Fellows. The process is repeated with variations in the last chapter; the execution is presented as it *affects* the minor characters, and only seen, not through the narrator, but through the eyes of Mr. Tench as he looks from the window of his dingy surgery, whilst the Jefe moans with fright in the chair. Greene can assume an audience familiar with unusual camera angles and quick fadings in and out, and uses both with great skill.

The power of the individual scenes comes primarily from Greene's ability to see them in the most striking way, to know how to place them and where to let the light fall—as when the priest and a mangy dog circle a rotten bone, or when the priest turns back. At that point a mule is ready to take him forward to full safety; Miss Lehr stands ready to give

49

a good missionary's 'godspeed'; the half-caste has arrived with his story which the priest recognizes as a lie but cannot refute. There is a moment in which he stands between the two, between safety and death; only he knows all that is happening. The moment is held, and then—the mule is wheeled about and the priest sets off back.

The predilection for striking juxtaposition which informs Greene's similes is given extended exercise in the composition of scenes. The pious mother reads the silly literary life of a martyr as the hunt starts for one she rejects as a bad priest but who will be martyred; at the close the same situation is picked up again—she is reading yet another literary martyrdom as the real one takes place not far away. The priest, dirty and exhausted in the South American heat, shelters from the savage pursuit in the Fellows' deserted bungalow, and reads with difficulty Coral's English literature test paper:

I come from haunts of coot and hern . . .

This rapid alternation of stripped narrative and highly-charged scene is, I think, the second main cause of Greene's attraction. He presents everything visually heightened, and with immense deftness. But his manner of composition promotes over-excitement, is not sufficiently complex and qualified. He never bores; he rarely even taxes. This is structure as caricature.

Greene's characters have a kind of intense nervous life which at first almost convinces but is soon seen to be breathed into them by Greene's breath, and always by his breath. They surprise us, as the scenic juxtaposition surprises us, but they surprise so regularly and neatly that they eventually fail to surprise. They are flat characters given a series of twists; they are revolved rapidly or stood on their heads at intervals; but when one has mastered the direction of the twist and the timing of its recurrence the pattern is exposed and there is no more surprise. We do not take it any longer for more than set movements with a wooden figure. So the priest, in spite of the great skill that has gone to make him, is no more than an intensely felt idea presented through a puppet. He seems to come to odd life at intervals, but we soon cease to regard it as anything other than one of the puppet's regular reactions. In tight corners he almost invariably gives a surprised giggle—'a little gulp of astonished laughter'—at some inconsequential memory. The lieutenant's appearance of life comes from the tension between the cold progressive on top and the wish to love underneath, which reveals itself occasionally in unexpected actions, like the giving of a coin to the priest as he dismisses him from prison. But again, the over-management kills, as in the lieutenant's inexpressible emotion and his gesture with the hands in these extracts; one accepts the first, but the second resembles it so closely that we are irritated into feeling that not only the characters but we, too, are being manipulated. With the boys of the town the lieutenant finds himself moved by feelings he does not understand: "He wanted to begin the world again with them in a desert . . . [He] put out his hand in a gesture of affection—a touch, he didn't know what to do with it." To the villagers he is interrogating soon afterwards he says:

"In my eyes—can't you understand—you are worth far more than he is. I want to give you"—he made a gesture with his hands which was valueless, because no one saw him— "everything."

Mr. Fellows is beefy, stupid, muddled; his wife a bourgeoise driven neurotic by the strain of exile:

He was powerless and furious; he said, "You see what a hole you've put us in." He stumped back into the house and into his bedroom, roaming aimlessly among the boot-trees. Mrs. Fellows slept uneasily, dreaming of weddings. Once she said aloud, "My train. Be careful of my train."

A passage like this is surely cartoon-art; 'dreaming of weddings' belongs to the same stylized regions as the huge

51

mothers-in-law of the picture postcards, and 'roaming among the boot-trees' is near-Thurberesque fantasy (how many boot-trees were there? were they larger than life? was there a seal behind each of them?).

The characters are being constantly pushed around, put into positions which are more effective for the pattern than probable; for example, the half-caste finally betraying the priest to the soldiers, simply saying 'Father' from the clearing as the priest reaches the door of the hut—it is too obviously the Judas kiss. Or the priest's child sniggering evilly at him from among the refuse-heaps—the cracked vessel of the Truth facing the evidence of original sin; or the prison-companions who do not betray; or the boy who has admired the lieutenant and sensibly rejected the sickly tales of martyr-dom, changing without warning when the priest has been executed, spitting at the lieutenant and opening the door for the new priest. Or the frequent, too appropriate, dreams. The priest sleeps, with guilt on his soul at the thought of his child:

> His eyes closed and immediately he began to dream. He was being pursued: he stood outside a door banging on it, begging for admission, but nobody answered—there was a word, a password, which would save him, but he had forgotten it. He tried desperately at random—cheese and child, California, excellency, milk, Vera Cruz. His feet had gone to sleep and he knelt outside the door. Then he knew why he wanted to get in: he wasn't being pursued at all: that was a mistake. His child lay beside him bleeding to death and this was a doctor's house. He banged on the door and shouted, "Even if I can't think of the right word, haven't you a heart?" The child was dying and looked up at him with middle-aged complacent wisdom. She said, "You animal," and he woke again crying.

The lieutenant should be happy now that he has finally caught the enemy of the new perfectionism, but is only lost and miserable:

> He went into the office: the pictures of the priest and the

gunman were still pinned up on the wall: he tore them down—they would never be wanted again. Then he sat at his desk and put his head upon his hands and fell asleep with utter weariness. He couldn't remember afterwards anything of his dreams except laughter, laughter all the time, and a long passage in which he could find no door.

The dialogue is occasionally made to fit in the same way, as in the scene—brilliant as what it aims at being—in which the priest's illicit wine and brandy are drunk by the corrupt official and his hangers-on. The dialogue is trimmed to give a despondent, dribbling effect, e.g. the repeated 'salud' as the precious drink disappears:

"Is this the only bottle?" The man in drill watched him with frigid anxiety.

"I'm afraid the only bottle."

"Salud!"

"And what," the Governor's cousin said, "were we talking about?"

"About the first thing you could remember," the beggar said.

"The first thing I can remember," the Jefe began with deliberation, "but this gentleman is not drinking."

"I will have a little brandy."

"Salud!"

"Salud!"

"The first thing I can remember with any distinctness is my first communion. Ah, the thrill of the soul, my parents round me. . . ."

"How many parents then have you got?"

"Two, of course."

"They could not have been around you—you would have needed at least four—ha, ha."

"Salud!"

"Salud!"

And so on till all the drink has gone, and the priest is in tears. The scene lives in its dialogue, which has been formalized to the ends of the dramatic situation.

One's uneasiness increases as these kinds of detail pile up.

It all finally confirms the impression of management from outside, of a lack of submission from within to the difficult and subtle matter of characterization.

'Immense readability', the reviewers say, and they are right; considerable immediate power from skilled overforcing of style, structure and character, and from a refusal to allow half-tones, uncertainties, complexities. I do not mean to imply that Greene deliberately aims at being 'readable' in the popular sense, that he aims at commercial success. It seems more likely that both the distortion and the excessive control are results of Greene's view of life. This view is so insistent that it leads him consistently to falsify his fictional life. It has prevented him from producing, up to the present (though in *The End of the Affair* he was clearly disciplining both his structural and stylistic habits), a novel whose life we can 'entertain as a possibility' whilst we are reading. But we continue to find his novels interesting simply because of the power of the view of life behind them, that very power which is causing the over-manipulation. We do not find experience convincingly recreated; we know all the time that we are in the presence of an unusually controlled allegory, a 'show', to use Gerontion's word. The characters, I suggested, have a kind of life, but that life is always breathed into them by Greene's breath. The novels as a whole have a kind of life, but not the life of, say, *The Possessed*, in which we forget Dostoevsky and explore the revolutionary mentality. In Greene's novels we do not 'explore experience'; we meet Graham Greene. We enter continual reservations about what is being done to experience, but we find the novels up to a point arresting because they are forceful, melodramatic presentations of an obsessed and imaginative personality.

There may well be a further, and more curious, reason for the attraction of Greene's novels, one arising specifically from the fact that they treat of religion. Greene presents us with a view of the relationship between God and man in which the emphasis is almost entirely on the more dramatic aspects; the 'who sweeps a room as for thy sake' element is altogether lacking: "It was like a short cut to the dark and magical heart of the faith . . . to the night when the graves opened and the dead walked." This is only one aspect of religious belief, and to think it all is to have an inadequate view of religion. (I am concerned now, not with Greene's aims but with what may be the attitudes of those who read him.) It may be that exactly here lies an important part of the appeal of these novels. The audience for them is primarily one of unbelievers. To some unbelievers, I think, the more conservative, communal city-building features of faith are of little interest; if they were to become religious, they wouldn't go in for it half-way; they like their hellfire neat; they 'drink damnation down like brandy', to invert one of Greene's similes. The sort of excitement they derive from these books may therefore be, curiously enough, of the same order as that they find in the more 'existentialist' novels. Greene's kind of religion may be found interesting where the less melodramatic poetry of religion would be found dull. Consciously, these readers may think they inhabit a reasonable, ordered universe: but perhaps their taste in fiction betrays a subconscious unease.

1953

THE LONG WALK

The Poetry of W. H. Auden

1

MANY of us who began our adult reading during the Thirties will always think of W. H. Auden with a particular warmth, with the family sense we reserve for those writers who place their fingers on the pulse of a crucial period in our own lives, whose writings are interwoven with our intellectual and imaginative growing-up. We may differ in our judgments of his later work, but we agree in remaining grateful that at such a time he spoke about our common situation with intelligence and breadth, with urgency and energy and wit; that he spoke—to use a word he would probably find congenial—'memorably'. Auden's middle-class and private jokes were as puzzling to some of us as they were to foreigners; but we responded to his high spirits and confidence, his novelist's interest in the details of social life, the concreteness with which he captured salient features of the grey England of the raw suburbs and housing estates, the arterial roads and chromium-and-plastic cafés. With due scaling-down we can say of him what he said of Freud:

> *To us he is no more a person*
> *Now but a whole climate of opinion.**

We are not likely to forget the apt releasing power of such poems as 'Dover', 'Musée des Beaux Arts', 'Sir, No Man's Enemy' and 'A Shilling Life', or his vivid vigorous openings, or many scattered passages, such as:

> *What do you think about England, this*
> *country of ours where nobody is well?*

* All quotations from W. H. Auden's work are copyright, and are reprinted by permission of the publishers, Faber & Faber, London, and Random House Inc., New York.

THE LONG WALK: W. H. AUDEN

or,

The vows, the tears, the slight emotional signals
Are here eternal and unremarkable gestures
Like ploughing or soldiers' songs:

or,

May with its light behaving
Stirs vessel, eye, and limb,
The singular and sad
Are willing to recover.

Yet though Auden has held a special place in English poetic experience over four decades it is easy to feel the force of the argument that his illuminations are sometimes no more than heterogeneous surface-insights, and his technical skill more often showy than profound. Auden does occasionally employ fashionable clichés of tone and feeling: and he has been over-rated in some literary circles. Just as surely, he has been underrated in others. Both attitudes tell something about contemporary cultural conditions in Britain. They tell less about the merits of Auden himself.

Auden is still intellectually and technically open (this is not a polite euphemism for 'fickle') to a degree that is not evident in any of those who were once known with him as 'the poets of the Thirties'. His technical fluidity may be seen in his exercises in various poetic forms, especially since 1940. He has practised, for instance, in *terza rima*, the villanelle, the sestina and the ballade. From this point of view the long poems produced in the Forties are all aspects of the same formal search.

Yet this technical openness probably derives in part from a more fundamental quality, from an intellectual quixotry and eclecticism. Auden is something of an intellectual jackdaw, picking up bright pebbles of ideas so as to fit them into exciting conceptual patterns. He is evidently aware of this tendency and of one related to it; that is, of his inadequate submission to the 'this-ness', the immediate sensuous stuff, of life. More than once he refers with admiration to Rilke's

57

'acceptance', or insists that one must 'bless what there is for being', or that 'every poem is rooted in imaginative awe'. 'One must be passive to conceive the truth,' he says in 'Kairos and Logos'; and a fine metaphorical passage by Caliban in *The Sea and the Mirror* ('The shy humiliations . . .') treats the same theme.

We can probably carry this line of argument further. The intellectual unsteadiness seems to be a function of an even deeper force: of a profound desire to come to ordered moral terms with life, and a profound difficulty in doing so. *The Double Man* was the American title of *New Year Letter*. It is not one of Auden's best poems, though it has some moving lyric passages; it is nevertheless the fullest exposition of his philosophical problems. The American title was a peculiarly apt image for Auden's position at the time, and might still apply, though with less stress. Throughout his career, but with special force in the period before he became a professed Christian, Auden seems to have been an unusually divided man: searching for a belief towards which he could be truly humble, and finding humility difficult; questioning constantly the tensions within his own nature as both a fallen man and a creative artist. For Auden is primarily a purposive and moral writer. He is in the best sense a teacher, one who loves to influence others; on his weaker side he can be a somewhat gawky prose-moralizer. For him—the characteristic assertion indicates both a limitation and the source of much of his strength—'Art is not enough'.

So we may think of Auden in terms of one of his favourite images—that of the Wanderer, the man on a Quest. His poetry abounds in journeys over hills and across plains, in ascents of mountains and voyages across seas. The image appears in his very early adaptation of a Middle English poem, 'Sawles Warde':

> *But ever that man goes*
> *Through place-keepers, through forest-trees,*
> *A stranger to strangers over undried sea*

THE LONG WALK: W. H. AUDEN

Variations occur throughout the Thirties: in the Airman of *The Orators,* in poems such as 'Reader to Rider' and in the central characters of the plays *The Dog Beneath the Skin* and *The Ascent of F.6.* Later, the same figure appears in the group of Quest sonnets printed in the one volume with *New Year Letter,* in *The Sea and the Mirror,* in *The Age of Anxiety* and in the libretto of *The Rake's Progress.* It is the theme of Auden's first full-length book of criticism, *The Enchafèd Flood,* in which the sea and the desert are considered as complex images of man's spiritual wanderings.* Less sustained instances occur throughout all Auden's work, from the early 'mad driver pulling on his gloves' to 'A Change of Air' (in *About the House).*

During the last few years the Wanderer figure has not been quite so prominent. Before then we might have been justified in saying, with many qualifications, that Auden was himself the Wanderer; the Wanderer pursuing the two main groups of questions outlined above—about the 'double man' and, especially, about the double man as an artist.

Any one of a hundred passages could exemplify the first kind of question. The quotation below has been deliberately chosen at random from the *Collected Shorter Poems* so as to indicate the frequency of the theme:

> *In my own person I am forced to know*
> *How much must be forgotten out of love,*
> *How much must be forgiven, even love.*

---

* It would be a pity to allow the central claims of Auden's poetry to preclude any further mention of his critical prose. Here his strength is in freely ranging, synoptic, aphoristic reflections on the symbolic and philosophical implications of a work. During the last few decades this approach has been under suspicion in England and one can easily appreciate that it may lead to writing that is neither good literary criticism nor good philosophy. But in gifted hands (and Auden is often strikingly successful) it can be seminal and illuminating in a way which more closely controlled critical analysis usually cannot be. *The Dyer's Hand* collects a large number of literary critical and general essays; the earlier volume *The Enchafèd Flood* is more closely organized round a number of related themes.

The second question is raised most strikingly in Auden's elegies on other writers; as in these lines on Henry James:

> All will be judged. Master of nuance and scruple,
> Pray for me and for all writers living or dead;
>   Because there are many whose works
> Are in better taste than their lives; because there is
>   no end
> To the vanity of our calling: make intercession
>   For the treason of all clerks.
>
> Because the darkness is never so distant,
> And there is never much time for the arrogant
>   Spirit to flutter its wings . . .

Yet it is important to notice that the Quest is not undertaken for its own sake. That would be a romantic delusion, and Auden has never had much patience with the self-regarding romantic personality.* The Quest is for order, for pattern and meaning, in life.

The constant interaction of all the qualities we have briefly outlined—Auden's great technical skill (in particular his fine ear and sense of timing); his remarkably acute eye for revealing detail; his intellectual responsiveness, liveliness and range; his search for spiritual order—all these combine to produce his characteristic tones and themes:

> The earth turns over; our side feels the cold;
> And life sinks choking in the wells of trees:
> The ticking heart comes to a standstill, killed;
> The icing on the pond waits for the boys.
> Among the holly and the gifts I move,
> The carols on the piano, the glowing hearth,
> All our traditional sympathy with birth,
> Put by your challenge to the shifts of Love.

---

* Though he could be very interested in such a personality as a poet—like Byron.

. . .

Language of moderation cannot hide:—
My sea is empty and its waves are rough;
Gone from the map the shore where childhood played,
Tight-fisted as a peasant, eating love;
Lost in my wake the archipelago,
Islands of self through which I sailed all day
Planting a pirate's flag, a generous boy;
And lost the way to action and to you.

Lost if I steer. Tempest and tide may blow
Sailor and ship past the illusive reef,
And I yet land to celebrate with you
The birth of natural order and true love:
. . .

2

The Thirties

Few recent decades in English life have, retrospectively, so boldly defined a character as the Thirties. They seem now like a rising wave after a trough, a wave which preceded disasters.

In domestic affairs the keynote was struck in America, with the Wall Street crash of 1929. From the time this recession reached England until the rearmament boom of the decade's last years, unemployment was an ever-present feature of English life. This was the period of the 'Depressed Areas', of what Auden called 'the Threadbare Common Man / Begot on Hire-Purchase by Insurance', of 'smokeless chimneys, damaged bridges, rotting wharves and choked canals'. It was a period when shabby-genteel clerks could be found selling gimcrack Japanese household sundries from door-to-door. It was a grey and squalid period, especially for the millions directly affected by unemployment.

Internationally the starting-point lies earlier, but may be conveniently taken as Hitler's assumption of the German Chancellorship in 1933. Thereafter, as is clear now, there was a giant's march to the explosion of September 1939. The crucial mid-way stage was the opening of the Spanish Civil War in 1936.

For most young English people with left-wing interests this was a period of fervent activity, of Popular Front meetings, of milk for Spain and aid for Basque refugees, and of Victor Gollancz's Left Book Club publications. It was marked by a more than usually strong feeling that 'the old gang' were appallingly unaware of the changing world situation. It was, in Auden's phrase, a 'time of crisis and dismay'.

Yet in the apparent simplicity of its issues and in the dramatic quality of its detail (unemployed men standing idle under the lamp-posts at street-corners; the International Brigade; Guernica) it was a peculiarly heady period. It was in a certain sense enjoyable precisely because of its comparatively clear-cut moral situations and general all-hands-on-deck air. Such a period could call out the best qualities, as well as the more naïve enthusiasms, of concerned young Englishmen in all classes; and notably of that traditionally concerned group, the intelligent professional-middle-class at the Universities.

To this class Wystan Hugh Auden belonged. Born in 1907 in York, Auden was the son of a medical officer with wide general and literary interests. His mother was a devout Anglo-Catholic. Subsequently the family moved to Birmingham, and here Auden gained much of his first-hand experience of economic depression. Here too he probably first discovered the unfailing fascination which 'the soiled productive cities' have for him, the pull of the great urban sprawls of the commercial Western world (Pittsburgh, Manchester, Detroit, the Ruhr). "My heart has stamped on/The view from Birmingham to Wolverhampton," he said in a light poem he now rejects, and "Tramlines and slag-heaps, pieces of machinery/That was, and is, my ideal scenery." "Nothing is made in this town," he said of Dover, and the implication was plainly pejorative.

At Gresham's School, Holt, Auden talked first of becoming an engineer and read technological works, chiefly on mining and geology. But in his early teens, prompted by a friend, he began to write poetry. Hardy was his first master—an admirably humane man and a magnificently varied and idiosyncratic versifier who yet is rarely so completely successful as to discourage a young practitioner. At Christ Church, Oxford, Auden had reached the stage at which he could one day tell his tutor, with an impressive confidence, that only Eliot was worth the serious consideration of poetic aspirants. But this was one necessary moment in a poet's development and there were other influences, notably Anglo-Saxon and Middle-English poetry which have continued to fascinate Auden. At Oxford, too, Wilfred Owen and Edward Thomas were admitted to the accepted list of ancestors for his generation. Auden's friendship with Stephen Spender began (and had about it, typically, something of the English public schools' prefect-to-fag relationship); and his first links were made with others who were to become writers and publicists in what has variously been called the Thirties Group, the Pylon School and the Auden Group.*

After a stay in pre-Hitler Berlin there followed for Auden a short period of school-teaching, which he seems to have deeply enjoyed. He has, we have already implied, a strong teacher's sense, a mixture of charity and firmness, energy and fidelity. Meanwhile, his first volume of poems had been published in 1930 and been followed by *The Orators*, an acute, fantastic and vigorous squib. In 1936 he married Erika Mann. As the decade progressed he became more and more engaged, not only in his craft as a poet but in the time-

---

* Incidentally, the group were united more by common assumptions and written influence than by actual meetings. The best-known poets of the group, Auden, Spender and Day Lewis, did not all three meet together until the late Forties, at a cultural conference in Venice.

consuming borderland where political affairs and the practice of writing mingle. A largely light-hearted visit to Iceland with Louis MacNeice in 1936 was followed by visits to Spain in 1937, to China and the U.S.A. with Christopher Isherwood in 1938. A few months before the beginning of World War II Auden settled in America, and in due time adopted American citizenship.

Politics, Psychology, 'Love'

Centring the eye on their essential human element

Some critics argue that Auden is a peculiarly English poet, and that in leaving England he severed essential roots. The first suggestion is to a large extent true, in both more and less obvious senses. Local and family concerns are very dear to Auden; and his bedside book in New York was at one time a work on the mineralogy of the Lake District. More, the cast of Auden's mind has markedly been formed by some of the main elements in the English tradition. His is not a voice from the Middle West or from Central Europe: "England to me is my own tongue."

Yet does the second suggestion—that Auden has weakened his poetry by a physical removal—necessarily follow? Wherever he may live the bent of Auden's mind, the way he approaches the problems which interest him—his particular form of complicated cranky independence as well as his tough gentleness—will remain recognizably English. But the nature of these problems has something to do with the decision as to where he may best live. Auden's interest is in men in urban societies, in men now living through their perennial moral and metaphysical problems in megalopolitan settings. London or some large English provincial city might have provided such a setting; but England is small and domestically intimate, its cultural life demandingly homely. Auden needs a kind of anonymity within an urban mass, and this New York has provided (as well as providing sufficient money and the friendships Auden needs):

> *More even than in Europe, here,*
> *The choice of patterns is made clear*
> *Which the machine imposes, what*
> *is possible and what is not,*
> *To what conditions we must bow*
> *In building the Just City now.*

Auden is a socially unrooted poet who could be at home in any of the large urban centres of the Western hemisphere. Whatever he may have lost by leaving England was not central to these gifts: in America, he seems justifiably to feel, he has been at the chief pressure-point of forces which are changing the face of life in the West.

Auden's isolation in a crowd reflects a constant quality of his verse, a quality most plainly indicated in the early figures of the Hawk and the Airman (*The Orators*). The Airman was physically isolated from the messy close disorder of life below and, more important, was able from his post of observation to detect some pattern not visible to those immersed in the details of personal involvement. Similarly, Auden's is often an abstracting and generalizing intelligence. In some sense very difficult to define fairly we may say that he is emotionally detached from much of what he describes, that he has a 'clinical' quality.

Though Auden speaks to and for many in his generation his speech commonly lacks certain kinds of intimacy. There are important areas of experience, particularly those concerned with relations between the sexes, which he either does not touch or touches in a perfunctory or stereotyped or briskly impersonal manner (falling in love, married life, some forms of insecurity, the tragic, gay and dignified tensions in the day-to-day life of 'ordinary' people). At such points he is likely to move into a detached 'placing' of detail by the use of successive definite articles:

SPEAKING TO EACH OTHER

The boarding-house food, the boarding-house faces,
The rain-spoilt picnics in the windswept places,
The camera lost and the suspicion,
The failure in the putting competition,
The silly performance on the pier . . .

A poet's weaknesses are often peculiarly revealing. There are forms of emotional wobble in Tennyson, or of anger and enthusiasm in Browning, or of sensuous indulgence in Dylan Thomas, which both limit them and bring them closer to us. In Auden's poetry there are certainly struggles, but they are expressed through a continuous *argument* with the self rather than through the play of personal emotions. The 'I' is there, but is rarely at a loss with itself; it may be exploring its own weaknesses but always does so with an air of control, with the implication that certain areas are sealed-off and the limits of the struggle grasped. These are the roots Auden lacks and would have lacked even if he had remained in England.

This quality seems related to the fact that Auden's poems tend to be remembered not so much for their sensuous effects (apart from a few striking exceptions) as for the articulation of their phrasing and the pattern of their moral insights. His poems have little colour, smell or touch. He once said that he tends to think of them as 'squares and oblongs'; that is, as geometric shapes rather than as, for example, extended images. The bare shapes are the shapes of his dialectic. Similarly, his epithets usually have a conceptual rather than a sensuous relationship to the nouns they qualify; they comment rather than describe. Where several epithets are used they do not cumulatively describe their noun so much as set up an intellectual friction with the noun and with each other:

And the active hands must freeze
Lonely on the separate knees.

Auden does not say 'green slope' or 'grassy slope' but 'tolerant

enchanted slope'; a lover's head on his arm is caught, beautifully, as a moral pattern rather than a visual:

> *Lay your sleeping head, my love,*
> *Human on my faithless arm.*

Again, though Auden's similes are rhetorical, and often
boldly rhetorical, they usually gain their effect from the
yoking of an abstract idea to a vividly concrete fact, from a
vivid metaphorical personification of ideas:

> *Problems like relatives standing*

and,

> *Will Ferdinand be as fond of a Miranda*
> *Familiar as a stocking?*

And Auden's geography is almost always economic or
political geography; thus his poem about the Chinese port
of Macao opens—'A weed from Catholic Europe, it took
root'. Or his landscapes are symbols of human dilemmas.

A varied intelligence, a congenitally pattern-making mind
and a persistent moral drive: all these place the emphasis
in Auden's work firmly on man rather than nature, and on
man-in-the-city rather than man-in-the-fields. It was inevitable that in the Thirties Auden should pursue his psychological and social interests, should be purposively trying to
create an order in his experience:

> *Our hunting fathers told the story*
> *Of the sadness of the creatures,*
> *Pitied the limits and the lack*
> *Set in their finished features;*
> *Saw in the lion's intolerant look,*
> *Behind the quarry's dying glare,*
> *Love raging for the personal glory*
> *That reason's gift would add,*
> . . .

67

SPEAKING TO EACH OTHER

Who, nurtured in that fine tradition,
Predicted the result,
Guessed Love by nature suited to
The intricate ways of guilt . . . ?

The bent of Auden's political interests ensured that he was often thought, mistakenly, to be a Marxist. He did find much to admire in Marxist analysis; the argument that 'freedom is the recognition of necessity' alone would have won his interest. He did work, incidentally, for left-wing causes ('the expending of powers/On the flat ephemeral pamphlet and the boring meeting'). Of this kind of poem the most representative, whether by Auden or by any of the engaged poets of the Thirties, was 'Spain 1937' with its characteristic refrains:

> . . . *Yesterday all the past*
>
> . . . *Tomorrow, perhaps, the future . . .*
>
> . . . *But today the struggle . . .*

But for Auden this activity was inspired chiefly by his urgent search for spiritual order and moral responsibility. At bottom his attitude had more in common with that of some serious-minded conservative intellectuals than with that of the more progressive, 'free' and romantically expectant left-wing intellectuals of the Thirties.

And his psychological interest was deeper than his political interest. Why were so many out of love with themselves? How had we become a nation addicted to 'aspirins and weak tea'? At this stage Auden was predominantly interested in the plight of the specifically neurotic, of 'the lost, the lonely, the unhappy', of 'the malcontented who might have been', of the anxious and fear-ridden. The interest remains, but long ago widened into a concern with a more radical anxiety. In the Thirties Auden's reading of Freud and Groddeck, notably, encouraged a kind of modern myth-making, since both these writers communicate an unusual imaginative excitement in their presentation of richly suggestive concepts:

> *Sir, no man's enemy, forgiving all*
> *But will his negative inversion, be prodigal:*
> *Send to us power and light, a sovereign touch*
> *Curing the intolerable neural itch,*
> *The exhaustion of weaning, the liar's quinsy,*
> *And the distortions of ingrown virginity.*
> *Prohibit sharply the rehearsed response*
> *And gradually correct the coward's stance . . .*

The address to a negatively defined power was an early indication that politics and psychology were aspects of a more central interest, of Auden's concern with spiritual dilemmas of individuals beyond the reach of political and psychological reforms. This is a religious interest; and though it showed itself plainly only towards the end of the decade it had many earlier intimations. Particularly, Auden returns again and again to a single word, 'Love'—and uses it elusively:

> *O Love, the interest itself in thoughtless Heaven . . .*

and,

> *The word is Love*
> *Surely one fearless kiss would cure*
> *The million fevers . . .*

and,

> *Birth of a natural order and of Love . . .*

'Love' seems to have been an undefined but powerful third force, a quality both inside man and affecting man from outside, which both offered him hope and indicated the perennial and personal nature of his situation. The history of Auden's earlier mental journey is, roughly speaking, that of the gradual discovery of the potentialities of this word's meaning for him—from an unresolved assertion to a rich and complex ambiguity which embraces the idea of Christian love, of conscience, of charity and grace. When that moment was reached Auden was an avowed Christian. The more directly political and psychological interests had fallen into place and the first phase was over. It is easy to exercise hindsight in such matters. In Auden's development the lines are clear and expressed:

> *Perhaps I always knew what they were saying:*
> *Even the early messengers who walked*
> *Into my life from books . . .*
> *Love was the word they never said aloud*
> *. . .*
>
> *And all the landscape round them pointed to*
> *The calm with which they took complete desertion*
> *As proof that you existed.*
> > > *It was true.*

Public and Private Speech

There is a small body of Auden's very early verse whose qualities are different from those we normally associate with his poetry in the Thirties. These poems are dry and gnomic:

> *Love by ambition*
> *Of definition*
> *Suffers partition*
> *And cannot go*
> *From yes to no*
> *For no is not love, no is no . . .*

Since the impulse behind these poems is close to that which informs some of his poems of the Fifties, we are reminded once more of the coherence of his intellectual development. But in the Thirties Auden was more characteristically a poet of perceptive epigrammatic verse, of various kinds of conversational metre and of a number of remarkable lyrics.

THE LONG WALK: W. H. AUDEN

The epigrammatic manner clearly took force from Auden's purposively ranging mind and from his insistent rhetorical inclinations. The epigrams usually enshrine memorable social and psychological observation, sometimes not so much crisp as slick, but generally intelligent and pithy:

> *Steep roads, a tunnel through the downs are the*
> *approaches;*
> *A ruined pharos overlooks a constructed bay;*
> *The sea-front is almost elegant; all this show*
> *Has, somewhere inland, a vague and dirty root:*
> *Nothing is made in this town.*
>
> *But the dominant Norman castle floodlit at night*
> *And the trains that fume in the station built on the*
> *sea*
> *Testify to the interests of its regular life:*
> *Here live the experts on what the soldiers want*
> *And who the travellers are, . . .*

Poems such as this are among the more notable instances of the way in which the climate of the Thirties could affect a well-equipped poetic mind. There were other manners of 'speaking to the times' which said more for the earnestness of the poets' intentions than for their grasp of poetry's function. We may grant that society was 'sick' and that some poets urgently wished to contribute usefully. Yet by the nature of contemporary culture they spoke only to a small minority. How could they speak more widely? Could they in any proper way compete with the truly popular voices?

To this aspect of Auden's work belong the three plays he wrote with Christopher Isherwood and Louis MacNeice between 1935 and 1938. In some of their techniques for presenting social problems and for obtaining a sense of urgent participation from the audience they seem to have learned from the early 'epic theatre' of Bertolt Brecht. They made use also of hints from German expressionism, from popular

songs and variety and music-hall performances. The plays
were lively, intelligent and witty. To those, out of love with
a glossy commercial theatre, who saw them at Rupert Doone's
Group Theatre in London, they must have been exciting.
But they have the faults of their originating assumptions.
They are lively charades with passages of striking banality
and pert 'knowingness'. Their characters are not merely
'types'—that may be true of certain good plays. But they
are usually cliché-ridden or idea-ridden types, Freudian or
Marxist puppets. All of them have good lyrics and choruses,
but only *The Ascent of F.6* is now worth much attention. In
this play the 'Quest' theme, because it is more deeply probed,
inspires some scenes more searching and eloquent than any
in *The Dog Beneath the Skin*.

In his use of conversational metres at this time Auden
aimed at a laconic and loose-limbed, a dryly ironic or apparently off-hand tone of voice. The tone had begun to appear
by the middle Thirties, as in the unbuttoned, *in medias res*,
colloquially reflective opening of 'Musée des Beaux Arts':

> *About suffering they were never wrong,*
> *The Old Masters: how well they understood*
> *Its human position; how it takes place*
> *While someone else is eating or opening a window*
> >   *or just walking dully along;*
> . . .
> *In Brueghel's* Icarus, *for instance: how everything turns*
> >   *away*
> *Quite leisurely from the disaster; the ploughman may*
> *Have heard the splash, the forsaken cry,*
> *But for him it was not an important failure; the sun*
> >   *shone*
> *As it had to . . .*

For this manner (especially as it was adopted in his often
admirable symbolic sonnets) Auden took much from Rilke.
But the most important creditor was Yeats, whose conver-

sational metres Auden has saluted. Yeats's 'Easter 1916' begins:

> *I have met them at close of day*
> *Coming with vivid faces*
> *From counter or desk among grey*
> *Eighteenth-century houses.*

The echo can be heard (though the command is less) in Auden's '1st September 1939':

> *I sit in one of the dives*
> *On Fifty-Second Street*
> *Uncertain and afraid*
> *As the clever hopes expire . . .*

The conversational manner was predominant in *Another Time* (1940). Subsequently, it was influenced by Auden's experience in America, where the rhythms of colloquial speech seem more flexible than they are in England:

> *The sailors come ashore*
> *Out of their hollow ships,*
> *Mild-looking middle class boys*
> *Who read the comic strips:*
> *One baseball game is more*
> *To them than fifty Troys.*
>
> *They look a bit lost, set down*
> *In this unamerican place . . .*

Since this is essentially a relaxed manner it has sometimes encouraged Auden's characteristic technical faults, and become slipshod rather than relaxed, slick instead of laconic, informedly glib rather than finely allusive. At its best its shrewdly loose articulation has allowed it to carry very effectively the intelligent, unviatic, contemporary observations

73

Auden often wishes to make.

Most of the foregoing comments on Auden's style have had a bearing on his social and psychological interests. His lyrics exist much more in their own right, and spring from simpler but firm poetic roots. This is an aspect of Auden's work which his evident moral drive can easily lead us to underrate. Auden's admirable lyrics have been a continuous feature of his verse, from a fine group in the mid-Thirties which included such poems as 'O who can ever praise enough' to 'Deftly, Admiral' (*Nones*). We remember here also the quick and witty choral songs such as 'At last the secret is out', the comic and satiric poems such as 'O for doors to be open', the Nonsense Rhyme in *Nones* and the later 'Willow-Wren and the Stare'. The note which seems most characteristic and impressive in the lyrics is of a kind of stillness; not a passivity nor always the stillness of menace, but a held imaginative stasis where the spirit looks steadily and often tenderly at a still moment of experience. It is all, of course, as much a matter of sound as of sense:

> *Dear, though the night is gone,*
> *Its dream still haunts today . . .*

and,

> *Fish in the unruffled lakes*
> *The swarming colours wear . . .*

and,

> *Deftly, admiral, cast your fly*
> *Into the slow deep hover . . .*

and,

> *Now the leaves are falling fast,*
> *Nurse's flowers will not last;*

74

THE LONG WALK: W. H. AUDEN

Nurses to the graves are gone,
And the prams go rolling on.

Whispering neighbours, left and right,
Pluck us from the real delight;
And the active hands must freeze
Lonely on the separate knees.

3

'Original Anxiety'

Since 1940 Auden has moved around the American continent fairly consistently, chiefly as a lecturer and teacher at
universities and colleges. For some time he spent part of each
year on Ischia, the island off Naples. At present he has a home
in Austria. During his term as Professor of Poetry at Oxford
—it ended in 1961—he also spent part of each year in England. But for the past quarter-century Auden's most frequent
point of rest—his home-base during this time—has been
New York.

The move to America roughly coincided with the clear
appearance in Auden's poetry of a number of new influences.
If Freud and Marx were the most striking intellectual influences of the Thirties, then those of the Forties were Kierkegaard and Reinhold Niebuhr.

The exploration by the Danish 'existentialist' theologian
Søren Kierkegaard of 'original anxiety', the basic insecurity
of man which marks both his fallen condition and his possible
salvation, replaced for Auden—as a fruitful area of thought
and a seminal metaphor—the psychologists' more scientific
analysis of the nature of anxiety. "Psychotherapy will not get
much further until it recognizes that the true significance of
a neurosis is teleological," Auden now said.

Similarly, Reinhold Niebuhr's analysis of the moral dilemmas and social involvements of man submerged Auden's rather scrappy and qualified interest in Marxism.* His sense of continuous struggle in the will makes it easy to understand why he should be drawn to Niebuhr's form of Protestantism —Auden is in fact a Protestant Episcopalian today. We may assume that he would be in sympathy with this statement by Niebuhr: "The Catholic emphasizes the initial act of intellectual assent; the Protestant the continuous process of voluntary assent." Nor is Auden's awareness of society likely to allow him ever to become mystical or contemplative.

Such statements are bound to over-simplify; there are obviously many other interweaving lines of force. But these were the dominant and most revealing forces at this time. Auden quotes Kierkegaard repeatedly, in his poetry and prose; and some of his poems of the Forties are like versified paragraphs of Niebuhr.

Auden's social and psychological interests remain, but are related now to a central religious root. Man is seen as fallen yet free, and this is his paradox. He is bound by his 'creatureliness' yet always tempted to deny the limitations this imposes; he is free to exercise moral choice for good or ill. Hence his 'wilfulness', in both the senses of 'possessing free will' and 'prompt to disobey'. He works out his destiny here, historically, in time; his consciousness of time informs his awareness of guilt and of possible grace. This awareness marks man's unique situation and is the ground of his anxiety: "Anxiety is the inevitable concomitant of the paradox of freedom and finiteness in which man is involved," says Niebuhr.

Man is unfinished but forever has the possibility of 'becoming'. By contrast the animals and plants, which appear frequently in Auden's poems as images of unawareness, are perfect, finished and for ever unpromising, unconscious of identity, of time and of choice:

* Niebuhr was, from 1930 to 1960, Professor of Applied Christianity at the Union Theological Seminary, New York; the most accessible exposition of his outlook is in the two volumes of Gifford Lectures, *The Nature and Destiny of Man* (1941).

THE LONG WALK: W. H. AUDEN

Let them leave language to their lonely betters
Who count some days and long for certain letters;
We, too, make noises when we laugh or weep,
Words are for those with promises to keep.

And elsewhere,

The hour-glass whispers to the lion's paw,
The clock-towers tell the gardens day and night,
How many errors time has patience for,
How wrong they are in being always right.

So far this description might seem to suggest an anxiety-ridden outlook which could easily become querulous or nagging. Auden is never querulous and rarely nags; both his purposiveness and sense of humour relieve him. "Accept the present in its fullness," he says in a characteristically firm passage. Man is a social creature, and one sign of an individual's growing spiritual maturity is the decision not to try one of the many forms of escape from this commitment, but to stay where he is, soberly and steadily to work out his destiny with the intransigent material of human relations. To work for *civility*, and to build the Just City—these are favourite phrases of Auden's. The building of the Just City can never be completed, he adds, but could not be even an aspiration were there not outside man an order of which his dream of the Just City is a reflection.

In all this, 'Love' is still often invoked by Auden, though now with a more complex sense of its difficulty and also of its ineluctability:

O let none say I love until aware
What huge resources it will take to nurse
One ruining speck, one tiny hair
That casts a shadow through the universe.

Auden's general approach is well illustrated in a vigorous and hortatory post-war poem, 'Memorial for the City'. The

theme is the destruction of traditional European values as
they are expressed in the ancient city-architecture of the
continent, and the now more plainly exposed dilemma of
fallen man immersed in time:

The steady eyes of the crow and the camera's candid eye
See as honestly as they know how, but they lie.
The crime of life is not time. Even now, in this night
Among the ruins of the post-Vergilian city
Where our past is a chaos of graves and the barbed wire
    stretches ahead
Into our future till it is lost to sight,
Our grief is not Greek: as we bury our dead
We know without knowing there is reason for what we
    bear,
That our hurt is a desertion, that we are to pity
Neither ourselves nor our city;
Whoever the searchlights catch, whatever the loudspeak-
    ers blare,
We are not to despair.

In a later poem, 'The Shield of Achilles', Thetis, the
mother of Achilles, looks over the armourer Hephaestos's
shoulder at the decorative scenes on the shield. Here is time
and event, but without the sense of sin or the hope of redemption; a world which is, in the most terribly exact sense,
meaningless:

A ragged urchin, aimless and alone,
    Loitered about that vacancy, a bird
Flew up to safety from his well-aimed stone:
    That girls are raped, that two boys knife a third,
    Were axioms to him who'd never heard
Of any world where promises were kept.
Or one could weep because another wept.

The altered emphasis in Auden's preoccupations often

brought with it a greater leanness. He seemed and seems less attentive to the rich muddle of life. But we may be disproportionately fascinated, as well as seriously concerned, with the sheer detail of experience. In some ways Auden's approach in the Forties and early Fifties was more austere than it used to be, closer to the kind of promise made in his earlier poems. And in seeking to express this new pattern of interests he developed some sinewy and complex verse of great power and interest.

Symbolic Landscape and the Long Line

For a few years after his arrival in America Auden seems to have decided that he would, predominantly, write long poems (poems occupying all or most of one volume), whose structural complexities would embody a variety of materials, tones and intellectual approaches. More recently his collections have been of shorter poems, ranging from lyrics to what might be called longish short poems (of from sixty to a hundred lines), and it does seem as though for the present the experiments with really long poems are finished.

Of the four long poems Auden produced between 1941 and 1948—*New Year Letter, The Sea and the Mirror, For the Time Being,* and *The Age of Anxiety*—the first is poetically the least interesting though, as we noted earlier, it has some moving lyric passages and is almost everywhere lively; and the Quest sonnets which complete the volume are more than good derivatives from Rilke. The title-poem draws to its close, all argument put aside, with a joyful invocation to God:

> *O Unicorn among the cedars*
> *To whom no magic charm can lead us,*
> *White childhood moving like a sigh*
> *Through the green woods unharmed . . .*

The Sea and the Mirror is subtitled 'A Commentary on Shakespeare's *The Tempest*', and is chiefly about the rela-

tions between art, the artist and society. For each character
Auden produces a different verse-form, often highly elaborate. The result is sometimes merely curious, though the performance is technically brilliant; yet some parts (Alonso's
address to Ferdinand; Miranda's villanelle) are not only brilliant but more deeply evocative.

For the Time Being, a Christmas oratorio dedicated to
the memory of Auden's mother, is more emotionally harmonious than the other long poems, probably because of the
greater simplicity and firmness of his theme—belief and
hope, though in sin and humility. Here, not surprisingly, is
to be found the peculiarly 'still' lyric note we remarked
earlier:

> *Let number and weight rejoice*
> *In this hour of their translation*
> *Into conscious happiness*
> *For the whole in every part,*
> *The truth at the proper centre . . .*

The Age of Anxiety is brilliant, perverse, disjointed, a
'baroque eclogue' with all the extraneous ornamentation and
deviousness such a sub-title implies, a structural experiment
that does not succeed. Yet even here, in a metre drawn from
Anglo-Saxon verse, a few sections achieve an unusual gaunt
beauty. A tired clerk in a New York bar nostalgically describes childhood in a city which might just as well have been
Birmingham or Dortmund:

> *. . . how fagged coming home through*
> *The urban evening. Heavy like us*
> *Sank the gas-tanks—it was supper-time,*
> *In hot houses helpless babies and*
> *Telephones gabbled untidy cries,*
> *And on embankments black with burnt grass*
> *Shambling freight trains were shunted away*
> *Past crimson clouds.*

THE LONG WALK: W. H. AUDEN

Perhaps in the last three of these long poems Auden was tackling his own form of a problem similar to that of T. S. Eliot in 'The Waste Land' (though aspects of the same problem in its contemporary form can be seen at least as far back as Browning's *The Ring and the Book*): how to achieve a form which would embody the detail of social dilemmas, the diverse pressures of moral problems, and the necessary changes of tone, angle and level of suggestion—in a shape organic to the theme. Auden does not succeed: *For the Time Being* is comparatively harmonious but not really complex; *The Sea and the Mirror* is complex and in a sense unified, but gains its unity chiefly from the assumed background of *The Tempest*.

In his shorter poems Auden continues to use several kinds of conversational metre, and seems still to regard some of this verse as a sort of 'public' utterance, though now to a public accepted as small, and sympathetic by predisposition. This is an aspect of what Auden has called 'unofficial poetry' and 'comic' art:

> From now on the only popular art will be comic art . . . and this will be unpopular with the Management. . . . It is the law which it cannot alter which is the subject of all comic art. . . .*

Cheerful and debunking comic art can help to preserve self-respect in increasingly 'generalized' societies. Against 'the lie of Authority' a poet, as one of the few individuals—by profession—in modern society, will set the idea of the personal life.

Auden seems to have a more deliberate and prescribed purpose in his later use of the conversational voice than he had earlier. He seems to be aiming not at a widely-acceptable demotic speech but at a low-temperature verse of intelligent observation and comment:

* 'Squares and Oblongs', *Poets at Work* (1948).

81

SPEAKING TO EACH OTHER

[We] would in the old grand manner
Have sung from a resonant heart.
But, pawed-at and gossiped-over
By the promiscuous crowd,
Concocted by editors
Into spells to befuddle the crowd,
All words like peace and love,
All sane affirmative speech,
Had been soiled, profaned, debased
To a horrid mechanical screech:
No civil style survived
That pandemonium
But the wry, the sotto-voce,
Ironic and monochrome . . .

Verse such as this can encourage its own snobberies and is no doubt not meant to seem particularly important. It is 'occasional' verse in a valid sense—verse written for and commenting on specific occasions—and within these limits is usually acute and enjoyable. Inevitably, it retains some of the faults of its kind: it is sometimes slapdash and unmuscular, a versified *New Yorker* journalese which may be observant and intelligent but is too brittle to cut deep.

In his imagery Auden turns instinctively to landscape: he commonly speaks of 'villages of the heart', 'our landscape of pain', 'suburbs of fear' and so on. We may say roughly that he has two distinctive kinds of natural imagery: that in which landscape is an illuminating backcloth to some human social activity, and that in which landscape is a symbol for an inner dilemma in human personality. Again speaking generally, we may say that the first predominates in Auden's earlier poetry, and the second later. Nowadays the great industrial cities of America may occasionally provide the first kind of imagery; and the Apennine backbone of Italy, dropping to its coastal plains, may provide the second. But the scenery common to the Northern and Midland Pennines of Auden's childhood and youth continues more than any other to be drawn on for both types of imagery. The lusher scenes of southern England—or the hollyhocks and lawns of Tennyson's rectory gardens—have little appeal for him.

In the Thirties Auden was more likely than now to invoke the densely-packed, intensively worked-over, huddled and smoky Industrial Revolution landscapes of the Pennines, the grim and uncompromising little towns of the foothills and valleys or the great black sprawling cities on the plains below. He did write also of the bare stark uplands then, but was still likely to speak of them, with their abandoned workings and derelict mines, as illustrations of the same direct social interest; to use them as backcloths. And of course he loved them, and still loves them, in and for themselves:

> *Always my boy of wish returns*
> *To those peat-stained deserted burns*
> *That feed the Wear and Tyne and Tees.*

During the Fifties landscape became for Auden more and more a means of visually symbolizing the spiritual conflicts in man, and to this need the involved geometry of the upper hills speaks best. As in so much, Rilke had guided Auden to what he sought here:

> One of the constant problems of the poet is how to express abstract ideas in concrete terms. . . . Rilke is almost the first poet since the seventeenth century to find a fresh solution . . . (he) thinks of the human in terms of the non-human . . . one of (his) most characteristic devices is the expression of human life in terms of landscape. It is this kind of imagery which is beginning to appear in English poetry.*

Certainly Auden's use of landscape in the Fifties expresses his characteristic urge to draw meaningful patterns from experience. But it is important to recognize that the landscapes are not being wrenched into the form of symbols. They speak

---

* From a review of the *Duino Elegies, The New Republic*, 6 September 1939.

to him—have indeed always spoken to him, though not always
so clearly—as symbols, as 'sacred objects'. They spoke to him
before he could consciously decipher their language:

> *. . . There*
> *In Rookhope I was first aware;*
> *Of Self and Not-Self, Death and Dread:*
> *Audits were entrances which led*
> *Down to the Outlawed, to the Others,*
> *The Terrible, the Merciful, the Mothers;*
> *Alone in the hot day I knelt*
> *Upon the edge of shafts and felt*
> *The deep* urmutterfurcht *that drives*
> *Us into knowledge all our lives . . .*

The process is not a fitting of pictures to ideas, but is part
of Auden's natural manner of establishing relations with the
outside world, of establishing 'the relations of man—as a
history-making person—to nature':

> *Whenever I begin to think*
> *About the human creature we*
> *Must nurse to sense and decency,*
> *An English area comes to mind,*
> *I see the native of my kind*
> *As a locality I love . . .*

Since the war Auden has much more closely exercised this
interest in symbolic landscape, especially in what I have described as longish short poems. The sequence began notably,
with a remarkable poem, 'In Praise of Limestone', and was
continued in the seven 'Bucolics' in his book, *The Shield of
Achilles* (1955). The symbolic landscape and the long line
which usually accompanies it combined to make the most
interesting post-war development in Auden's work.

Auden will muse before a large and varied landscape and
seek to evoke from within it his sense that it symbolizes an

extensive pattern of human dilemmas. In the following passage the people who remain within the gregarious life of the
valleys are contrasted with the exceptional few who go elsewhere:

> *Adjusted to the local needs of valleys*
> *Where everything can be touched or reached by walking,*
> *Their eyes have never looked into infinite space*
> *. . .*
>
>   *That is why, I suppose,*
> *The best and worst never stayed here long but sought*
> *Immoderate soils where the beauty was not so external,*
> *The light less public and the meaning of life*
> *Something more than a mad camp. "Come!" cried the*
>   *granite wastes,*
> *"How evasive is your humour, how accidental*
> *Your kindest kiss, how permanent is death." (Saints-to-be*
>   *Slipped away sighing.) "Come!" purred the clays and*
>   *gravels.*
> *"On our plains there is room for armies to drill; rivers*
> *Wait to be tamed and slaves to construct you a tomb*
> *In the grand manner; soft as the earth is mankind and*
>   *both*
>   *Need to be altered." (Intendant Caesars rose and*
> *Left, slamming the door.) But the really reckless were*
>   *fetched*
> *By an older colder voice, the oceanic whisper:*
> *"I am the solitude that asks and promises nothing;*
> *That is how I shall set you free. There is no love;*
> *There are only the various envies, all of them sad."*

Here Auden is using his long line and verse-sentence,
which have themselves some of the qualities of his second
kind of landscape. The lines are syllabically-counted (13 : 11
syllables, with elision of all contiguous vowels and through
'h'). They have a sinuous, following-through, flexible though

connected movement; they follow the ideas suggested by the panorama, varying pitch easily as Auden turns to a new aspect or alters his angle of approach or branches into a side-consideration. They hold always to the main thread of the thought, though directed from moment to moment by its sinuosities and qualifications.

The intention differs from that which produced the curt epigrammatic line of the mid-Thirties and probably owes most, in so far as it is indebted to Auden's earlier practice, to the conversational verse of the later Thirties. The long verse-sentence is unusually free from the more obvious demands of line-endings (as, for instance, Auden's laconic sonnets necessarily were not). It is less immediately restricting than the three- or four-iambic line of Yeats—though that line was so magnificently varied in Yeats's hands that its apparent limitations turned to real advantage. Auden, we know, immensely admires the Yeatsian line and has sometimes used it. But a longer and more loosely-articulated line seems more natural to him.

Like most of even the valuable developments in Auden's verse this line is frequently marred—in this case by jarring and artistically unjustified changes of tone and attitude, and especially by a tiresome over-insistence on remaining unbuttoned. We see the point, in the passage quoted above, about 'Intendant Caesars . . . slamming the door' (it echoes an assertion by Joseph Goebbels), but the combination is intellectually pert.

At its best the long verse-sentence has a beautifully easy spoken note, an attractive mixture of colloquialism and serious observation, of wit and moral concern—all managed with a verbal and aural skill which few living poets can approach. The shape and movement of the poem acts out, as it were, the tense dialectic of the poet's will, mind and heart. In the following passage Auden opens on a typical landscape, limestone hills above the wide plains and their towns. The landscape is both actually and symbolically moving to him:

THE LONG WALK: W. H. AUDEN

If it form the one landscape that we the inconstant ones
  Are consistently homesick for, this is chiefly
Because it dissolves in water. Mark these rounded slopes
  With their surface fragrance of thyme and beneath
A secret system of caves and conduits; hear these springs
  That spurt out everywhere with a chuckle
Each filling a private pool for its fish and carving
  Its own little ravine whose cliffs entertain
The butterfly and the lizard; examine this region
  Of short distances and definite places . . .

So the complex interplay of human motives for which this
landscape speaks begins to be developed. The poem closes
on a view in perspective of the statues man makes out of this
same rock, and farther back—picking up again the wider
panoramic view of the opening—of the rock in its aboriginal
landscape:

. . . In so far as we have to look forward
  To death as a fact, no doubt we are right: But if
Sins can be forgiven, if bodies rise from the dead,
  These modifications of matter into
Innocent athletes and gesticulating fountains,
  Made solely for pleasure, make a further point:
The blessed will not care what angle they are regarded
    from,
  Having nothing to hide. Dear, I know nothing of
Either, but when I try to imagine a faultless love
  Or the life to come, what I hear is the murmur
Of underground streams, what I see is a limestone land-
    scape.

This kind of poetic activity is less gregarious and less intellectually extensive than that normally associated with Auden's
work in the Thirties. But it emerged naturally from the broad
lines of his intellectual and poetic development over twenty-
five years.

4

Lost of course and myself owing a death

Marking Time?

A fine passage in 'The Shield of Achilles' marks one of the last occasions on which Auden has used a confident public rhetoric:

> *The mass and majesty of this world, all*
> *That carries weight and always weighs the same*
> *Lay in the hands of others; they were small*
> *And could not hope for help and no help came:*
> *What their foes liked to do was done, their shame*
> *Was all the worst could wish; they lost their pride*
> *And died as men before their bodies died.*

Increasingly since then, and during the last seven or eight years in particular, Auden's poetry has been more closely contained, more quietly ruminative. Technically it is as brilliant as ever, inventive, witty and extraordinarily skilful. But there is hardly any larger formal experiment. The predominant tones and manners are occasional, domestic, relaxed and idiomatic rather than more largely thematic or public.

The audience envisaged today is, more often than not, a small group of good friends. Sometimes there is even—though partly with the tongue in the cheek—a prim, keep-your-distance manner towards outsiders. Catching familiar notes in these late poems one realizes sharply that much of Auden's poetry right from the beginning has addressed itself to, found its voice in, a small, known, domestic group of friends. It seems, at first glance, ironic that Auden's reputation in the Thirties should have been so much that of 'the conscience of his generation', which seems to imply adopting a more public intellectual stance. But the reputation was fairly gained; the two qualities do not conflict.

Today poetry seems less absorbing and important to Auden than it used to be. The stress falls less on poetry as a way to 'truth', more on poetry as verbal artifice expressing celebration, awe or piety before experience. Poetry has been put in its place as, in the last resort, a side-occupation or exercise. Worthwhile, of course:

> ... *After all, it's rather a privilege*
> *amid the affluent traffic*
> *to serve this unpopular art*

but still, as the tone of the above quotation conveys, a marginal matter, secondary to the real questions of faith and the effort to serve God. That effort does not demand melodramatic, rhetorical or histrionic responses. We do best if, without underestimating the actual melodrama of experience, we work quietly and as well as we can, trusting in God and his grace. The times may tempt us to do otherwise, and especially tempt writers to assume roles beyond their competence; these voices have to be quietly ignored.

The practice of poetry is still an activity of the moral will, a serious arguing but a cheerful one. He can write:

> *... wherever*
> *The sun shines, brooks run, books are written*
> *There will also be this death ...*

But also, just as characteristically, he will write:

> *After so many years the light is*
> *Novel still and immensely ambitious.*

Yet most of the time poetry now may have to be a form of 'dry farming' as Auden calls it. Whether he is only marking time, tuning up some of the quieter instruments of his verse, or whether this is the place he will finally give to poetry, no one can yet say. At its best Auden's poetry of this kind is both warm and dry, exceptionally elegant, civil and agreeable. It is not at these times at all frivolous or trivial; its basic seriousness as well as its sober lightness of tone are caught well in the last lines of the last poem in his most recent volume:

> *. . . about*
> *catastrophe or how to behave in one*
> *I know nothing, except what everyone knows—*
> *if there when Grace dances, I should dance.*

But we need, before ending, to place this tone—Auden's arrival at this curiously provisional-sounding tone—against the larger questionings from which it seems to have emerged.

Divided Aims: The Game of Knowledge

> *Can I learn to suffer*
> *Without saying something ironic or funny*
> *On suffering?*

Auden's work since the war expresses some striking tensions and divisions; expresses them with unusual directness. The tensions seem to be of three main kinds, each a matter of uncertain relationships: between Auden and his audience; between the artist and the moralizer; and between the artist and the believer.

Especially until the early Sixties, Auden is still often unsteady in tone and taste; the excellent parts have still to be sifted from much that is clever-clever (a poem such as 'Homage to Clio' shows this as well as any). To say this is not to be academically portentous or to forget that, now as always, a part of Auden's pertness arises from a deliberate wish to flout all conceptions of artistic decorum. This particular quality is not a tough or quirky comedy so much as something would-be funny. Several kinds of instance could be named: the raiding of the dictionary for words which are not merely odd but unhelpfully odd; that overworking of pat endings which has persisted since the early sonnets; the drop into an affectedly colloquial manner; the showy manipulation of conceits; in short, a recurrent bright technical flurry.

These characteristics seem due in part to Auden's unsureness about his exact audience, his lack of relation to a known and fairly homogeneous group whose attitudes he habitually appreciates. He has, we know, a considerable capacity for friendship; and he is not without a good circle of admirers among poets—indeed, he has been a strong influence on American poetry for many years. He is yet in one sense isolated, and this is partly the result of the move discussed earlier and defended.

There is no need to retract that justification. But we need to see as sharply as possible the problems it presents Auden. The difficulty of knowing just to whom he is speaking has sometimes led him to solitary verbal pirouettes or to new versions of the 'private joking in panelled rooms' of which he accused himself in the Thirties. At such times the audience seems to be either a very small 'in-group' or almost hypothetical—the audience of the brighter weeklies, say, which is not really any of us but is parts of many of us on both sides of the Atlantic, and which is intellectually fashionable.

But occasionally Auden can speak steadily as well as wittily and intelligently to an audience composed, we may imagine, of what he calls 'ironic points of light'; of people whose irony does not preclude charity, who are interested in both poetry and moral ideas, who are on the whole unambitious and who try to steer between righteous indignation, contempt and self-surrender. No doubt this is a small audience, scattered and hard to find. But it exists, and Auden's career particularly qualifies him to seek it:

> *O every day in sleep and labour*
> *Our life and death are with our neighbour,*

91

SPEAKING TO EACH OTHER

And love illuminates again
The city and the lion's den
The world's great rage, the travel of young men.

In his vividly metaphorical, alert and companionable conversational verse and in his landscape poetry Auden can
sometimes reach out to the kinds of audience he may now
particularly address. 'In Praise of Limestone' is a fine poem
and yet a poem severed from local cultures. Its unrooted,
engaged intelligence sees, and sees through, the landscape.
The more recent 'Whitsunday in Kirchstetten' rediscovers
the sense of locality, and is companionable in a way which
recalls some of the poems of friendship in the early Thirties
(such as 'Out on the lawn I lie in bed') but is less parochial.

Auden's second area of tension lies in the uneasy relationship between the purposive moralist and the creative artist—
the artist who is not concerned to wrest statements from
experience directly but works in the intuitive knowledge
that, to use Yeats's phrase, 'words alone are certain good'. He
is able to quote with obvious approval, "the value of art lies
in its effects—not in beauty but in right action"; but he can
also refer to 'the devil's subtlest temptation, the desire to do
good by (your) art'. There need be no real contradiction
there. Yet for a personality such as Auden's there is likely
to be a powerful tension until the exact ways in which each
statement may be true have been resolved.

The work of resolution leads directly into what we are
calling Auden's third problem. Around this whole area he has
exercised his mind considerably for many years, and it was
entirely typical that he should devote his Inaugural Lecture
as Professor of Poetry at Oxford to aspects of it. The core of
the question is the relation of the poet and his work to himself as a man (fallen, free, bound and wilful) and so to God.
Its main divisions are: what are the dangers of artistic vocation? What are the justifications?

The theme of the spiritual dangers in the life of an artist
has engaged several important contemporary writers, notably

Eliot and Mann. There are striking similarities between the theme of Mann's short story 'Death in Venice' and the long second part of Caliban's vivid parody of the later Henry James (and also the whole concept of Prospero) in *The Sea and the Mirror*. If man's life is a constant struggle in the will, how far is the artist tempted—because he is a sort of creator—to abrogate this responsibility? to get, so to speak, between himself and God? "The artist up to his old game of playing at God with words", quotes Auden from Kierkegaard, and adds a note from the same source about the need to "get out of the poetical into the existential".

Auden had, therefore, to define to his own satisfaction the justification of art. His most typical single phrase from many on the subject asserts that poetry is 'a game of knowledge'. First, poetry (and all art) is a *game*. It is a form of magic (the naming of 'sacred objects') and of fun ('the joke of rhyme'), a release for writer and reader, inspired first not by a desire to do good or acquire fame but by a love of 'playing around with words'. Also as a game, it is not finally real or serious as 'theology and horses' are; it 'makes nothing happen'. Again like a game, it has fixed rules (patterns, rituals, ceremonies, forms, 'necessities') which the players must obey if they are to enjoy. But also pure luck ('the luck of verbal playing') has a part; something is simply 'given' (grace?). "Only your song is an absolute gift," Auden says of the composer, and intends the line to carry the ambiguities of both the idiomatic and the philosophic meanings. The practice of art is for Auden yet another example of the fruitful paradox of freedom and necessity.

Yet poetry is a game of *knowledge*. It is in a certain sense concerned with knowledge, and its magic is meaningful. The knowledge is, though, a product of the play and comes by indirection, as in the serious absorbed play of a child. Aesthetic patterns and resolutions are not metaphysical patterns and resolutions ('Analogy is not identity'), but can analogously point towards them: "And the hard bright light composes/A meaningless moment into an eternal fact." In art's harmony and ritual are mirrored the possibility of a greater order outside man's power; both demand "an acknowledgment that there are relationships which are obligatory and independent of our personality".

So poetry can help to 'direct us to ourselves', can 'persuade' us to a form of 'moral rejoicing', can point through man's 'lying nature' to 'love and truth'. At this stage we realize that this is the fullest expression of Auden's continuing urge to irradiate daily human activity with mythical meaning, and of his questioning of the relation between art and moral purposes. So perhaps one may after all say that to the artist, in a special sense, 'analogy *must be* identity'; that the tense play of ambiguities which make up a poem is indeed part of the poet's 'being'.

1957; revised 1966

FINDING A VOICE

A Matter of Rhetoric: American Writers and British Readers

THE attractive and foreign quality I'm thinking of can be heard in this, the final paragraph of *The Great Gatsby**:

> And as I sat brooding there on the old, unknown world, I thought of Gatsby's wonder when he first picked out the green light at the end of Daisy's dock. He had come a long way to this blue lawn, and his dream must have seemed so close that he could hardly fail to grasp it. He did not know that it was already behind him, somewhere back in that vast obscurity behind the city, where the dark fields of the republic rolled on under the night.

Rather inflated, an Englishman might say. It has a kind of rhetoric (I am using the word only descriptively) which suggests it is American rather than English. This is not simply the rhetoric of 'the American dream', though certainly that does inform it. The passage is rhetorical in the face of its own emotions, wondering and uncautious and unprescribed. It is not as sure as Turgenev, yet it does recall something of his vibrant acceptance before the feelings. The tone is very rarely found in the English novel, particularly in this century; think, for instance, of Fitzgerald's contemporaries in England, Huxley and Waugh. Or compare Fitzgerald's note with Angus Wilson's in *Anglo-Saxon Attitudes*—a nicely apt title:

> Gerald Middleton was a man of mildly but persistently depressive temperament. Such men are not at their best at breakfast, nor is the week before Christmas their happiest time. Both Larwood and Mrs. Larwood had learned over the years to respect their employer's melancholy moods by

* By F. Scott Fitzgerald, London: Bodley Head; New York: Scribners.

95

remaining silent. They did so on this morning. The house in Montpelier Square was as silent as a tomb.

There is a confident coolness of tone, a thoroughly assured sense of the way syntax shall be made to denote just this kind of quality, this sort of attitude; there is a sense of closely prescribed and regulated communion between the author and his readers in their approach to the emotions and the way they will express them.

Something of this can be found in certain American writers, in several nineteenth-century novelists right up to James, and in some today. But this is to say that there are exceptions, and that is always so.

The coolness, the lack of untidiness or strain, in the passage from Angus Wilson quoted above arises largely, I suggested, from the assumption of a firmly established relationship between the writer, his readers and certain modes of feeling and expression. The denotations of the verbal currency for feeling are pretty exactly known. Socially, it is a remarkably assured writing.

It is the writing of a class, of the sensitive English middle-class who know or knew their place and their value both intellectually and socially. Whatever the present changes in English social patterns—I think we shall be able to see in another generation that they have been major changes—the English novel is still largely class-based. It belongs to the self-possessed and firm, the cultivated and kindly, intelligent middle-class. It is difficult for anyone writing outside the class modes not to be defiantly strident (as in the proletarian novels of the Thirties) or fiercely experimental, since the establishing of a ground from which to work demands a re-assessment of tonal range and so of style. Apart from Joyce, and his Irishness makes the crucial difference, the only outstanding achievement among these exceptions was made by D. H. Lawrence, whose *Sons and Lovers* is still the only considerable working-class novel we possess—one that is organic, unpolemical and unpatronizing—and who went on in his next novels to explore emotional alignments and formulations which included but passed beyond class.

I am not suggesting that the English novel simply cuts out whole areas of emotional experience; that might be only another way of saying that we go to the American novel for 'real toughness'. One recalls what an English critic called the 'regulated hatred' of Jane Austen or the murderous novels of Ivy Compton-Burnett. We may express our emotions tightly, but in the best novelists they can have great resonance; the 'regulation' is the crucial quality.

At the back of the class connections lie the qualities which have made that class—restraint and understatement, obliquity used as an emotional check. How often does a man 'break down' (the manner in which the phrase is used is significant) and cry in an English novel? One goes to the Russians—or the Americans—for that. It is ironic, for in its context the plea has an oddly academic ring, that E. M. Forster should be the modern novelist who most often asks the English middle-classes to release 'the tender core of the heart'. Very near the beginning of his career, in *The Longest Journey*, he made Rickie tell Agnes, who was meeting Gerald's death with a stiff upper-lip, that she must 'mind', must mind deeply. Yet the core of the heart is not simply tender; it is terrible and tragic and splendid and grotesque and comic. But again it was Forster who noted that the English novel was rarely 'prophetic'; the 'prophetic' novel of Dostoevsky, of Melville, can hardly grow in such a soil. Emily Brontë was what biologists call a 'sport'. Dickens was something of an exception also; in part his tonal unsteadiness reflects his unsteady relation to the modes of the class for which he wrote. On one side, his emotional links were with Dostoevsky and Melville rather than George Eliot. Conrad was probably the last major figure who showed a similar rift: but he was a foreigner who had inherited a larger manner of emotional expression.

So remarkable a homogeneity of tone could only arise, presumably, in a well-articulated, hierarchical and traditional society. The quality is so pervasive that one can make a fair guess by ear, whatever the overt dramatic situation, that this is an English book, this is not. Here in a very dramatic scene, the first paragraph of William Golding's *Pincher Martin*. It opens on a solitary, shipwrecked sailor clinging to a rock in mid-Atlantic, desperately holding on to a life as good as lost:

> He was struggling in every direction, he was the centre of the writhing and kicking knot of his own body. There was no up and no down, no light and no air. He felt his mouth open of itself and the shrieked word burst out. "Help!"
>
> When the air had gone with the shriek, water came in to fill its place.

And this is the opening of Saul Bellow's *The Adventures of Augie March:*

> I am an American, Chicago born—Chicago, that somber city—and go at things as I have taught myself, free-style, and will make the record in my own way: first to knock, first admitted . . .*

It may be that the necessarily more direct tone of such a first-person narrative weighs the issue to the side I wish (though I suspect the American novel uses first-person narrative more than the English—from "Call me Ishmael" up to "I am an invisible man. No, I am not a spook" and "If you really want to hear about it the first thing you'll want to know is where I was born, and what my lousy childhood was like"—and this could support my general point). But since my main concern is with tone and style, here as a reinforcement is an English first-person opening, George Orwell's *Coming Up for Air:*

> The idea really came to me the day I got my false teeth. I remember the morning well. At about a quarter to eight I'd nipped out of bed and got into the bathroom just in time to shut the kids out. It was a beastly January morning, with a dirty yellowish-grey sky. Down below, out of the little

---

* For a fuller use of this opening, see 'A Question of Tone', later in this volume.

square of bathroom window, I could see the ten yards by five of grass, with a privet hedge round it and a bare patch in the middle, that we call the back garden.

Most striking in the passage from Golding is what might be called the 'sub-classical' quality of the language, the verbal abstracting. He need only string this epithet and this verb along his syntactical necklet and his readers can be trusted to do the rest. He scarcely even bothers with a metaphor.

Orwell is writing outside his own class, about a dingy lower-middle-class life, and certainly not writing in a 'literary' way. But the tightly-sure phrasing of the sentences, the ability to imply a whole nipped-in field of social sarcasm in the simple fall of a sentence (as at the end of the extract), belong to the world of the English socio-linguistically-sure novelist.

Bellow's tone suggests a more open and fluid society. He assumes he must create his own emotional pitch as he goes along, identify it and establish it with his readers.

I mentioned earlier a pair of exceptions to the characteristic English range, but one was working-class and one Irish. There are certainly a few from within it, though I do not think they weaken the argument. Those works of Joyce Cary which come to mind are *tours de force*, efforts to achieve a direct sinewiness within the established modes; and so somewhat artificial. Graham Greene's brilliantly presented caricatures of the emotions acquire their force precisely from the understatement and obliquity of most English writing; for the understatement is intermittently inverted into a huge inflating, and the obliquity becomes a wry, dry sin-and-bitters. And the 'declassed' novels of Kingsley Amis? One need only compare *Lucky Jim* or *That Uncertain Feeling* with *The Adventures of Augie March* to realize that they are variants of the traditional mode, in both their manner of debunking and their sentiments.

All this may help to explain why some English readers feel more responsive to American than to English novels. The English novel usually presents itself in the tones (and often the properties) of a group. Here one realizes again, sharply, that when an English reader not of the cultured middle-class seeks to 'become cultured' he is led to acquire a culture of a peculiarly defined kind. He is led to adopt the traditional ways of feeling of a particular social group. It is easy for such a reader—one, say, from a provincial grammar-school—to feel out of place, even though he may also admire. There is likely to be some loss, whatever the gains.

What appeals to him in American fiction, I should guess, is a more demotic tone and a more flexible emotional range. It may be true that, in general, American novelists do not have the stylistic 'finish' of, say, Sansom, Newby or Hartley. By contrast, many American novels are coarse-grained. But if this is the danger of American rhetoric, that of English sensibility is well-bred debilitation.

1957

Art and Sex: The Rhetoric of Henry Miller

Henry Miller's *Tropic of Cancer* uses freely a greater variety of four-letter words than *Lady Chatterley's Lover* and uses them in a different way. Perhaps the prosecutors in the *Lady Chatterley* case, in 1960, did more than they knew. They took so crude a line against a book which obviously sought to be 'moral' that they led the defence witnesses to spend almost all their time underlining, and probably over-stressing, this 'moral purpose' rather than in arguing the book's right to publication as a work of art. Were a prosecution to be mounted over *Tropic of Cancer* the defence could suffer if the arguments used to defend Lawrence were turned against Miller. *Tropic of Cancer* can hardly be called 'moral' in any sense likely to be intelligible in a court of law. Nevertheless, it is the work of a genuine if disordered and distorted artist.

It is, to begin with, a valuable document from and of the Twenties, of the American expatriates' Paris. Not the Paris of Hemingway's or Scott Fitzgerald's fugitives from Main Street or Manhattan, nor of Orwell's rock-bottom down-and-outs, but the Montparnasse of penniless writers and artists. It is a bug-ridden and sex-ridden, smelly, scrounging, boozing, fantastic, uncalculating free-masonry of odd characters—real artists and shams—of all types and colours. Since the book is professedly more an autobiography than a novel—a portrait of the artist just before he ceases to be a young man—one might have expected it to be heavy with Henry Miller's own presence. In fact he keeps himself well in the background and shows a generous and sympathetic interest in other people.

But he is, more even than the rest, determined to 'get out of harness and out of step'—in flight from machine-tooled America, from modern society as a whole, from every political concern, from 'the men of science', from all abstractions and concepts, from what he regards as the meaningless or bogus moral imperatives of social man. So Paris, which is old, weathered, human, splendid, and miserable, is where all the ladders start: "Here all boundaries fade away and the world reveals itself for the mad slaughter-house that it is." Given such an outlook, the only meanings left for Miller are to be found in art and sex and these are the book's two subjects. The two become inextricably interwoven; some of the descriptions of fornication and those of literary exertions could be transposed without a noticeable difference.

For a number of reasons—because all formalities are suspect, and probably because Miller is naturally this kind of artist—his models are 'the great imperfect ones', notably Whitman; the formalists, such as Turgenev and Joyce, are on the enemy's side. It follows that Miller is often prolix, grandiose, hyperbolic, and histrionic; perhaps he can only get up steam for his more successful passages if he has burned up a lot of waste matter. At his best—and the good parts are very good indeed—he has a fine cumulative sweep and energy, a striking sense of the grotesque and pitiful at once, and an exceptional capacity to communicate a sense of place and situation.

As to the 'sex'—that really is a puzzle. I doubt if the book is aphrodisiac. For one thing, as others have said before, the sexual descriptions are often curiously comical; for another, they are not really funny at all. They are comical in that almost everyone approaches sexual activity with a touch of the buffoon. But this is not the grown-man's sexual comedy of Chaucer or Rabelais; it is boyishly surprised at a wide-open world of easy laws, and can't get over the shock. The men go around collecting women to take to bed with the excitement of boys collecting cigarette cards. This may be an 'apocalyptic' world, but it is naïvely apocalyptic in comparison with the world of Dostoevsky, whom Miller cites with admiration.

Yet the insistent need to fornicate is, underneath, not at all comical or light-hearted. It seems more like a blind search. In a world where so much has been written off—perspectives back and forward in time, all proffered moral standards—in such a world what remains worth doing? One thing—trying to be an artist. But what do you celebrate in your art? You celebrate the only 'real' thing left—the act of sex. One cannot call it the act of love or speak of 'relationships'. You may behave kindly to the women you enter, but they are not persons to you; and they bore you when they talk about being 'in love'—since that is to use an abstract concept, and suggests continuity and commitment. The sexual passages in this book are not, we might say, about women at all. The men are alone even when they are fornicating. They are blindly burrowing through to what seems the only reality; this, at last, is home . . . this utterly private, naked travail by forked and unaccommodated man.

Nevertheless, all goes along at a spanking pace for about three-quarters of the book. Then the air turns chiller. After forty pages of—sometimes rather flat—disquisition on life and art the narrative is picked up again as Miller is efficiently dispatching one of his friends back to America, to save him from marriage to a tart who has turned awkward. For him, at least, the dream of living only in the present is over. Miller remains, brooding over the beautiful Seine; but it is plain that for him too a phase is ending. The last pages sound like a farewell to one aspect of the Twenties, to one view of art, and to one kind of response to the complexity of experience.

1963

Lawrence's Voices

The most brilliant attack on Lawrence's poetry for its 'failure to employ the formal devices of art' is, without much doubt, R. P. Blackmur's famous essay 'D. H. Lawrence and Expressive Form'. And the best short defence of Lawrence's formal flexibility, seen as the servant of his effort after truth to feeling, is A. Alvarez's 'D. H. Lawrence: The Single State of Man'. The two main opposing positions in a literary argument are not often so compactly and well put.

But probably this approach—through the old free-or-formal argument—ought to be ignored for a time; other approaches are likely to be more profitable. It might be useful to listen more to tone in Lawrence's poetry. In poetry, Lawrence's expressive problems were centred as much on manner as on structural means, as much on finding a voice as on questions of form. We do not talk enough about Lawrence's poetic voices because we have not listened to them closely enough.

These voices cover a wide range and at each end of the range seem very different from one another. But when they succeed they have this in common: behind them all is the pressure of Lawrence's search for honest, direct, and peculiarly naked expression. To read these poems* again, especially the earlier ones, is to realize how much Lawrence forced himself

---

* *The Complete Poems of D. H. Lawrence* (London: Heinemann; New York: The Viking Press, 1964). All quotations are by permission of the publishers.

to be *exposed* to his experiences, how consistently he refused
to accept second-rate compromises or comfortable near-truths.
The pulse behind his voice, behind all his best voices, is
the pulse of this effort.

This is not one of Lawrence's true voices:

> *The voice of my education said to me*
> *He must be killed,*
> *For in Sicily the black, black snakes are innocent,*
> *The gold are venomous.*

The tone there is imposed, rather breathily self-conscious,
high-pitched and prosy at the same time. Lawrence may, of
course, have meant to set a high-collared, educated voice
against the deeper voices which spoke through the snake.
But the rest of the poem doesn't support this idea.

At one end of his range of effective voices Lawrence
embodies some elements from his working-class background.
At its best, this voice has a quick, resilient intelligence; it
is quirky, irreverent, and eager:

> *Imagine that any mind ever thought a red geranium!*
> *As if the redness of a red geranium could be anything but*
> *a sensual experience*
> *and as if sensual experience could take place before there*
> *were any senses.*
> *We know that even God could not imagine the redness of a*
> *red geranium*

Perhaps one would expect to find such tones more often
and more surely used in the poems written before Lawrence
had moved far from home. But in fact we find only odd
touches, occasional passages, in which this kind of voice gets
through for a while; and then the restrictions of form or
emotional uncertainty hide it again. Some of the dialect
poems—especially 'Whether or Not'—show the tone beginning to appear if you listen, so to speak, below the dialect

itself (the use of dialect has little to do with the timbre of
a voice); and the 'Hymn to Priapus' is an extraordinary
mixture of manners derived from other writers and individual intonations. Many of the early poems seem baffled and
half-throated; others are impressive, but for qualities different
from those I am concerned with. Later, this kind of voice
found itself in, particularly, the 'Creatures' and 'Reptiles'
groups in *Birds, Beasts and Flowers* and in some of the
Pansies. And sometimes it became a knowing sneer, but this
was not common.

At the other end of the range of voices is Lawrence's
prophetic or mystical voice. Neither adjective really suits,
but it is hard to find a better. This is, on the whole, a voice
rinsed clear of evident local associations, a kind of quiet
brooding over the mystery of human life and death:

> *Not every man has gentians in his house*
> *in soft September, at slow, sad Michaelmas.*
> *Bavarian gentians, big and dark, only dark*
> *darkening the day-time, torch-like with the smoking*
> *blueness of Pluto's gloom,*
> *ribbed and torch-like, with their blaze of darkness*
> *spread blue . . .*

Almost inevitably, one mentions 'The Ship of Death' here,
though that poem is over-used in studies of Lawrence's poetry.
Still, it is a lovely poem, the culmination of the resolved
gentleness one finds in many of the *Last Poems*. When the
prophetic voice fails, one hardly needs to say, it is inflated
and over-insistent. In the earlier poems it sounds like mis-
transplanted Whitman; later, it tends to be shrill.

There were elements in Lawrence's working-class background which helped him—once he had discovered their
strengths and limits—to explore parts of the emotional life.
I am suggesting that the effort to draw on these elements
showed itself, in part, as a search for tones true to their
native temper. To the prophetic strain little in Lawrence's

background gave immediate access, unless it was the chapel tradition; and that did not show him how to speak in that strain in the ways he wished. But probably the links between the 'working-class' voice and the mystical are deep-seated, for they seem to help validate each other.

All this Lawrence had to try to work out, in a confused cultural situation. Like the other outstanding nonconforming, puritan, idealistic British 'voice' of this century—George Orwell—Lawrence's effort at saying what he had to say meant that he had to reject most tones—social or literary, or more likely a mixture of both—which were offered him. This type of effort is not required of all writers; nor is it necessarily harder than the efforts other kinds of writers have to make. It seems especially to affect those—such as Lawrence and Orwell—whose lives and art are peculiarly interdependent, who want to 'live-out' their beliefs, whose 'personalities' are not easy to separate from their art.

1964

Walking the Tightrope: *Animal Farm*

Reading *Animal Farm** is like watching a man walking a tightrope—and on the whole find his balance so well that he can pause and play briefly on the way. By casting the book in the form of an animal allegory Orwell was able to acquire a peculiar poise, a poise difficult for any writer but for Orwell exceptionally difficult. He managed to hold the poise for the 80-odd pages the book runs. I wonder whether he could have held it much longer. In the last paragraph, as though relieved to be released from the strain, he slides down the rope to solid and literal earth so sharply that—even though we have had a succession of shocks throughout the book—we are startled.

The tension, it seems to me, is between Orwell's tenderness and his terror, between his knowledge that we can some-

* By George Orwell, London: Secker and Warburg; New York: Harcourt Brace and World.

times be loving to each other and his knowledge that we can at least as often be vicious and brutal, between his respect for the meek and innocent and his conviction that those kinds of people always get trampled on, between his faith in a few moral imperatives—such as charity and honesty—and his realization that life is too muddy, too much a matter of endlessly unfolding ambiguities, for simple assertions like those to be of much use, between his pity and sympathy for human beings and his fastidious withdrawal from close human contacts, between his nostalgic vision of a pastoral simplicity which might somehow be regained and his fear that what we are really heading for is something more like the world of *Nineteen Eighty-Four*.

By making *Animal Farm* into a particular kind of moral fable Orwell was able to hold these elements in suspension. He needed a form which distanced his terrible and haunting subject and yet got its moral home. That subject is the corruption of Stalin's regime. Point by point, Orwell drives home exact parallels with his interpretation of post-Revolution Russian history. He was a socialist, a special sort of English socialist; he attacked Stalinism so strongly because he was outraged at Stalin's betrayal of the human imperatives of socialism. More generally, Orwell's fable is about the way revolutions go bad on themselves, about the apparently inevitable progression from corruption to revolution to corruption, and about all the attendant evils—the endless double-talk, the rewriting of history, the murderous struggles for power by individuals, the appalling mass purges and the rehearsed treason trials.

Yet most of the book is limpidly tender. Almost all the animals—the pigs are the great exception—are lovable:

> The two carthorses, Boxer and Clover, came in together walking very slowly and setting down their vast hairy hoofs with great care lest there should be some small animals concealed in the straw. . . . The two horses had just lain down when a brood of ducklings, which had lost their mother, filed into the barn, cheeping feebly and wandering from side

to side to find some place where they would not be trodden on. Clover made a sort of wall round them with her great foreleg, and the ducklings nestled down inside it and promptly fell asleep.

Clearly, this distancing makes the cruel episodes all the sharper and heightens the real meaning behind the allegory. It does more than this. It allows play within controlled limits to Orwell's direct and unaffected tenderness. The frame permits a closeness of detail which becomes an expression of love. "Most of the good memories of my childhood and up to the age of about twenty are in some way connected with animals," Orwell once said.

It is easier to be tender to animals than to humans. Orwell hated human beings to be exploited, and felt sorry for those who were. He also hated the foolishness and self-indulgence which makes some human beings almost willing to be exploited. Animals don't have the responsibility of free will, so you can pity them more purely.

This neatly defined shape also gave Orwell a freedom for verbal inventiveness which he didn't have in quite that degree in his other books. Within this defined ground he could carve out those epigrams which are among the best things in the book—such as the seven animal commandments and the variations he plays on them. Best of all is the transmutation of the 7th commandment as the pigs grow more and more dominant, from 'All animals are equal' to 'All animals are equal, but some are more equal than others'.

The form also gave a special kind of play to Orwell's moral earnestness. He may, as I've said, have felt strongly the weight of great, basic moral imperatives. But he knew at least as well as the rest of us that human beings who recognized no ambiguities would be near idiots, as simple as Boxer the horse. The point is that here the moral questions are being played out by animals. So being deceived and suffering loss seems poignant and childlike, and gives us no grounds to exclaim: "But they *ought* to have seen what was afoot!"

All these qualities—and Orwell's rural nostalgia—coming

together in the one fable give *Animal Farm* the feeling of something small, neat, complete, something that can be held in the hand; they released Orwell's clear, easy, narrative flow. The book reads as though it had written itself. But it is shot through with cruelty—of a kind made all the more powerful because it too, horribly enough, belongs to that setting. For much of the time *Animal Farm* seems a gentle, anthropomorphic farmyard fable; its cruelties belong to the other side of that world, to the butcher's knife and the knacker's yard:

> The three hens who had been the ringleaders in the attempted rebellion over the eggs now came forward and stated that Snowball had appeared to them in a dream and incited them to disobey Napoleon's orders. They, too, were slaughtered. Then a goose came forward and confessed to having secreted six ears of corn during the last year's harvest and eaten them in the night. Then a sheep confessed to having urinated in the drinking pool—urged to do this, so she said, by Snowball—and two other sheep confessed to having murdered an old ram, an especially devoted follower of Napoleon, by chasing him round and round a bonfire when he was suffering from a cough. They were all slain on the spot. And so the tale of confessions and executions went on, until there was a pile of corpses lying before Napoleon's feet and the air was heavy with the smell of blood, which had been unknown there since the expulsion of Jones.

The domestic, English farmyard setting makes more terrible the realities of the public, totalitarian cruelties which are allegorically represented there. Farmer Jones got rid of his old dogs by tying bricks round their necks and throwing them in the nearest pond. Napoleon's men carry out purges with the emotionless efficiency of horse-knackers. When Napoleon (Stalin) wanted to show his contempt for Snowball's (Trotsky's) plans for the new animal state he

> walked heavily round the shed, looked closely at every detail of the plans and snuffed at them once or twice, then stood for a little while contemplating them out of the corner of his eye; then suddenly he lifted his leg, urinated over the plans, and walked out without uttering a word.

The power of that passage comes from its closely observed, particular, human individual's heartlessness.

In this world, evil is universal and deep-seated. Only pity and charity oppose it, but pity and charity are small, full of self-mistrust, and likely to stretch out their necks for the block which the pigs of this world—with fierce tusks and unbridled appetites—prepare for them. At the end of *Animal Farm* the world of fable dissolves and changes. We see, nakedly, the real world of cruelty and greed beneath all the stories we tell our children and ourselves:

> But as the animals outside gazed at the scene, it seemed to them that some strange thing was happening. What was it that had altered in the faces of the pigs? Clover's old dim eyes flitted from one face to another. Some of them had five chins, some had four, some had three. But what was it that seemed to be melting and changing?
>
> . . . .
>
> Twelve voices were shouting in anger, and they were all alike. No question, now, what had happened to the faces of the pigs. The creatures outside looked from pig to man, and from man to pig, and from pig to man again; but already it was impossible to say which was which.

c. 1964

GEORGE ORWELL

and The Road to Wigan Pier

T HE *Road to Wigan Pier* has been disliked by almost all commentators on Orwell. Tom Hopkinson calls it his worst book and Laurence Brander 'his most disappointing performance'.

Disappointment began when the typescript reached the desk of its publisher, Victor Gollancz, who had commissioned the essay. He had good reason to be surprised, for this must be one of the oddest responses to a commission which even the Left Book Club inspired. The club was intended to mobilize and nourish socialist thought. With his co-editors John Strachey and Harold Laski, Gollancz selected each month and issued to club members, under the imprint of his own publishing house but in distinctive limp orange covers, a book designed to promote socialism. He had asked George Orwell to write a 'condition of England' book, a documentary on the state of the unemployed in the North, a book of descriptive social analysis. What he got was a book in two halves, neither what he had asked for. The first half seems to be roughly on the contracted subject but approaches it most idiosyncratically. The second half is partly cultural autobiography, partly opinionation about socialism by a man who had at that time a patchy idea of its nature. *Wigan Pier* duly appeared in March 1937 but with a preface in which Gollancz, though doing his best to be fair and appreciate fully what he had been offered, showed his disagreement on every page.

In the mid-Thirties socialism was fairly new to Orwell, and *Wigan Pier* was his first directly political book. Nor was he much known, so that the club editors were to some extent chancing their collective arm. Orwell had published his first book, *Down and Out in Paris and London* (social observation but not directly political writing), four years before. He had followed it at yearly intervals with three novels (*Burmese Days, A Clergyman's Daughter, Keep the Aspidistra Flying*), all interesting but the first probably the best. When the Gollancz commission came he was living in London and working as a part-time bookshop assistant. He gave this up at the end of January 1936 and spent February and March in the North of England, gathering material. In early April he took over The Stores, Wallington, Hertford-shire and in early May began writing *Wigan Pier*. He married in June, sent the manuscript of *Wigan Pier* to his agent in mid-December and a few days later set off for Spain where the Civil War had been going on for almost six months. At the end of December he enlisted in the militia of the POUM (Workers' Party of Marxist Unification). That he joined the POUM rather than the International Brigade was 'partly an accident' but an accident he came to be glad about since it brought him 'into contact with Spaniards rather than Englishmen and especially with genuine revolutionaries'. The relentless enquiry which had led him from filthy work in Paris kitchens to London dosshouses and the Brookers' tripeshop-cum-boarding house finally brought him to the front near Huesca where, luckily for him, he got a bullet in the neck and so—with some difficulty—came home. He was back at Wallington by mid-1937.

It was not a pilgrimage for which anything in Orwell's background gave a prior hint. He was born Eric Blair (the 'Orwell' came from a river near which he once lived in Suffolk). With his characteristic effort at precision in matters of class Orwell called himself in *Wigan Pier* a member of 'the lower upper middle classes'. His point was that his father was a public servant, not a landowner nor a big businessman; so, though he had the rank, status and tastes of a gentleman, his salary was modest. He was, in fact, a minor official in the Indian Customs service and Orwell was born in Bengal, in 1903. He was, as was usual, sent to a preparatory school in England, a school which he described with great bitterness in the essay 'Such, Such were the Joys'. From there he won a scholarship to Eton which he also wrote about, though with less bitterness. When the time came to leave Eton Orwell was unsure of his plans and in particular unsure about whether or not he should try to go to Cambridge. A tutor, for reasons we do not certainly know, suggested he should take a job abroad. Orwell joined the Indian Imperial police and served for five years (1922–1927) in Burma. In some respects the central character of *Burmese Days*, Flory, is Orwell himself.

It is plain, from *Wigan Pier* and from many of Orwell's other writings, that he was much of the time trying to cast off his class. But he always respected certain virtues of that class, such as fairmindedness and responsibility, And in some deep-seated ways Orwell was characteristic of his class and didn't himself always realize how much this was so. To begin with, he had a kind of fastidiousness (which is not the same as gentility) which never deserted him and which much of the time he was fighting. But it was there. It was reinforced by his phenomenally sharp sense of smell: he could *smell* his way through complex experiences. Thus, he remarks in *Wigan Pier* that at first he found the English working-classes physically repulsive, much more repellent than Orientals. Look, too, at a tiny but characteristic moment in this book. He constantly drove himself into extreme and unpleasant situations and could describe them with exactness. One of the best passages in *Wigan Pier* is the description of work down the mine. It is terribly hard and grimy work, and Orwell wanted his readers to know this. In the course of his description he says that he suddenly put his hand on 'a dreadful slimy thing among the coal dust'. Orwell uses that word 'dreadful' frequently, and usually means by it something which really inspires horror. So one wonders what it will prove to be this time—perhaps a dead rat? In fact it is a quid of tobacco spat out of a miner's mouth. For a man who had subjected himself to the trials Orwell had endured, this hardly seems a 'dreadful' thing. The phrase unintentionally acts as a sudden shifter of perspective: used in that way, it comes out of the vocabulary of the class which Orwell's journeys were a way of escaping from. Inevitably, in describing this little incident in full I have given it too much weight. But it is an accurate small pointer to a quality Orwell never lost and which was partly socially-acquired (but not wholly; he was also by nature fastidious).

At other times (and this quality can be seen in Part 2 of *Wigan Pier* and, most notably, in the essay 'England Your England') Orwell revealed a particular toughness in manner, a sort of anti-intellectual pugnacity which reminds you of a no-nonsense upper-class colonel. This from a man who could, a few chapters earlier in *Wigan Pier*, talk so warmly and gently about working-class interiors. The two characteristics do not blend: they remain throughout Orwell's short life a contradictory mixture.

More important, to this tracing of Orwell's deep-seated connections with his class, he was one of the latest in a long and characteristic English line: those dissidents which a system in so many ways designed to reproduce its own kind has always managed richly to produce. In this aspect of his character Orwell joins hands, among men of this century, with Lawrence of Arabia. They went in different directions, geographically and intellectually; but in their tempers they had much in common.

All these tensions finally brought Orwell out of the Indian Imperial Police and sent him on the first phase of his journey to the lower depths. He had to go, that is certain. But why? There are easy answers and hard answers to this question, and all probably have some truth in them. But to establish anything like a satisfactory order of reasons would require a fuller study of Orwell—not only of his works but of his life —than we have had so far (or than we are likely to have if his wishes are respected, since he asked that there should be no biography).

In trying to touch bottom, Orwell most obviously was reacting against imperialism and his own guilt as a former agent of imperialism. He came to regard it as evil. Not just because one side was a tyrant to the other: not all the British rulers were tyrannical, and Orwell was as likely to dislike a Buddhist priest as a British colonial policeman. He believed that imperialism was evil because it distorted the moral character of both the oppressor and the oppressed.

So when he came back to an England in the grip of a slump, with millions unemployed and therefore many more millions directly affected by unemployment, he felt that he knew what he had to do. He had to associate himself with the oppressed half of England rather than with his own kind by birth and training. He had to feel for himself the pressures the poor felt, and suffer them; he had to get to know the victims of injustice, had to 'become one of them'. He had to try to root out the class-sense within himself. He did not have a romantic idea of what that last duty meant; he knew it always means trying to root out a part of yourself.

But that explanation, though it contains some of the truth, is not the whole. The whole truth is more varied. To touch bottom for Orwell was a very complicated release indeed, a shedding of guilt but also a positive test to which he was impelled. Phrases like the following occur throughout his work and are typical of an important characteristic of the Orwellian stance: 'It had to be done', 'There was nothing else for it', 'It is a kind of duty'. They are brave phrases; they are also the phrases of a very vulnerable and obsessively driven man, a man with at times a burning sacrificial egoism. As so often with writers, Orwell's use of language, the words and images he instinctively chose, show this more surely than his actual statements. Describing his first trip to the rock-bottom poor, the fear and then the relief when a down-and-out lumbered straight at him—and then embraced him and offered him a cup of tea, he says: "I had a cup of tea. It was a kind of baptism". It is the image which stands out.

By nature Orwell was a lonely man. He wanted to belong to a coherent society; he longed for a sense of communion. But he could never quite believe in the eventual good effect of any man-made groups. "No one who feels deeply about literature, or even prefers good English to bad, can accept the discipline of a political party," he said in his introduction to the first volume of *British Pamphleteers* which he edited with Reginald Reynolds. He could just as characteristically have said "No one who feels deeply about *life* . . . can accept . . ."*

It may be that, more deeply than he knew (and this is ironic since he so much distrusted intellectuals who did not belong), Orwell was temperamentally an isolated intellectual. He was always seeking out the lepers of life, yet he shrank instinctively from physical contact. Christian critics of Orwell will of course carry their interpretation of his 'metaphysical loneliness' further. In his full-length study of Orwell Mr. Christopher Hollis, who is a Roman Catholic, sees him as a deeply religious man who, for reasons both temperamental and cultural, could not accept any religion; sees him as a believer without a religion, a man full of convictions, full not only of a moral sense but of metaphysical assumptions (without them in the background his convictions, to Mr. Hollis, would be meaningless).

Certainly much of Orwell's passion was inspired by a very un-material sense of man; and at key moments his language often moved into the metaphors of religion. This can be seen in the baptism image just quoted. Just before Gordon Comstock and Rosemary, in *Keep the Aspidistra Flying*, decide to marry rather than get rid of their unborn child by abortion Orwell says, of Gordon: "He knew it was a dreadful thing they were contemplating—a blasphemy, if the word had any meaning." In its image and in its doubling back upon itself at the end that sentence nicely catches the 'religious' feeling of Orwell and the dry metaphysical unexpectancy. He was an intensely moral man. He knew in his

* In a chapter of *Culture and Society* Raymond Williams discussses Orwell's representative importance as a modern intellectual, representative of 'the dissociation between the individual and society which is our deepest crisis'. The argument is interesting and subtle and should be read. But this condition may well be, as Mr. Williams recognizes, as much a matter of individual temperament as of the climate of the age; Orwell's attitude was at least as much personal as representative.

bones, to quote a phrase he noted as evidence of the natural religion of many working-class people, that 'we are here for a purpose'. But he could settle in no church and with no formal religion.

Though he found membership in organized groups difficult Orwell had an exceptionally strong feeling that we are members one of another, that we belong to each other, that all men are brothers. No one ever needed to remind Orwell that he should not send to find for whom the bell tolls; he knew. During the war, it is said, he and his first wife deliberately went short on their rations (Orwell thought this hastened his wife's death) so that there would be more for other people. The remarkable fact here is not that they went short; others did that. But most went short so as to help someone known to be in need, someone identified—an old lady down the road or a local hospital. The Orwells went short so that there would be 'more for others', and this is both a saintly and an intensely familial act. It conceives the whole nation as one family. It doesn't calculate or assume that if you let yourself go short some official will make away with what you have saved, or someone else down the road will waste it anyway, so why bother. Orwell had a rooted sense of Britain as a family, as a continuing community (he was, to use one of his own distinctions, a patriot but not a nationalist). "England is a family with the wrong members in control," he said in an epigram which neatly catches his attitude: it assumes that we are a family, and it grumbles about the way the family is being run. This doubleness is itself very much a family attitude, a basic acceptance and a readiness to criticize in a way we would not be happy to accept from outsiders.

These impulses seem to have been moving the man who set out North to fulfil Victor Gollancz's commission. No wonder the result was a surprise. The North of England was stranger to Orwell than Burma. Not only had he spent many years out of England; he was by class and domicile a stranger to the heavy industrial areas of the North. They hit him hard, and the harder because he saw them at the worst time, at the bottom of the slump. He set out to recreate as vividly as he could the shock of this world of slag heaps and rotting basements, of shabby men with grey clothes and grey faces and women looking like grandmothers but holding small babies—*their* babies, all of them with the air of bundles of old clothes roughly tied up; the world of the Means Test and of graduates nearly penniless and canvassing for newspaper sales. This is the Thirties all right, for many in the working-classes a long-drawn-out waste and misery which only the preparations for the war of 1939 ended. We may qualify Orwell's accounts but would falsify our own history if we tried to qualify it out of existence. These things happened not long ago in this country (as they are happening in many other countries now); and it matters—matters, as Orwell would have been the first to admit, far more than simply the need to get his record right—that we should take their emotional measure.

The qualifications are many and critics have not spared them. Orwell, as John Beavan points out, picked out the most depressed of the working-classes. The respectable working-class figure hardly at all in his pages. He chose the miners and, more, the unemployed miners, people on Public Assistance, the unemployable and the shabbily itinerant, the kind of people who land up at the Brookers'.

All these qualifications are true. So is the charge that Orwell sometimes sentimentalizes working-class life. His famous description of a working-class interior *is* slightly idealized and 'poetic'. His account of working-class attitudes to education is oversimplified, and has a touch of the noble savage.

Before we look more closely at these charges we could add some others not so evident. Orwell's picture of working-class life, even of that good side typified in a working-class interior, is too static, is set like a picture caught at a certain moment. It becomes in part a nostalgic looking back (and for Orwell himself probably also suggested an unanxious calm, free of status-striving, which was a balm to him). In general his portrayal of the working-classes in *Wigan Pier* has not sufficient perkiness and resilience, is a bit dispirited. One can see why, given the kinds of people he chose to describe. Still, he did offer it as a picture of 'the working-class'. Later, in his last full-length work, *Ninety Eighty-Four* (in all but this a terrifyingly hopeless novel) Orwell was to say 'if there is hope it lies in the proles'. But from the 'proles' of *Wigan Pier* we would not get much hope of resistance and rebirth. There is just a hint now and again of a related quality, the ability to soldier on, to stick together and bear it, that basic stoicism which Orwell himself possessed and which may have been one of the reasons why he found the disposition of working-class people so immediately attractive.

When all has been said, Orwell's picture, though not the whole truth, was truer than almost all the documentary material which came out of the documentary Thirties. It was true to the spirit of its place and time and (with the reservations noted) its people. It was true to the spirit of the misery:

> And this is where it all led—to labyrinthine slums and dark back kitchens with sickly, ageing people creeping round and round them like black beetles. It is a kind of duty to see and smell such places now and again, especially smell them, lest you should forget that they exist; though perhaps it is better not to stay there too long.

Orwell's picture was true too to the spirit of some of the good qualities in this environment. He was not foolish when he said that he felt inferior to a coal-miner, though he has been called silly; within the terms defined in that first part of *Wigan Pier* he was talking humane good sense then. He may have sometimes sentimentalized working-class interiors. But fundamentally he is not wrong to praise them. It demanded, especially then, a particular sort of insight and hold on truth to be able to speak about the 'sane and comely' home life those interiors represented. And it is not at all foolish— as some have called it—but it is sensible and humane, to say that the memory of working-class interiors "reminds me that our age has not been altogether a bad one to live in".

It is important to be sure of our own motives here. Some writers on Orwell, sympathetic though they are to much of his work, have tried to shuffle off this side because it makes them uncomfortable. But he knew what he was about. It is no accident that again and again in this book he directly addressed himself to people of his own class. The 'old ladies living in retirement at Brighton' are representative of a great many other figures, of politicians and businessmen and writers and rentiers and university lecturers. It was to these above all that Orwell was speaking. He was trying to correct that conveniently distant vision of other people's problems, that face-saving view of slum life and slum dwellers, which the training of his class offered him; he was insisting that people do hate living in slums (remember, in *Wigan Pier*, the sight of a young woman poking at a blocked waste pipe which printed itself on his memory as the train carried him South again), that even if some have become so dispirited as not to seem to mind, or have adapted themselves, it is still rotten—rotten for them and rotten for what it does to the souls of those of us who are willing to let other people live like that. These attitudes die hard and they are not dead yet.

In the beginning of its second half *Wigan Pier* is auto-biographical about the sense of class. Inevitably, Orwell has been accused of exaggerating, of carrying on wars already dead. He did exaggerate; this was rough polemical writing. But it is important to say, and say firmly, that Orwell's sense of the importance and pervasiveness of class in Britain was sound, sounder than that of most of those who criticise him for it. He feels the smallness of small snobbery accurately. He grasps the rooted nature of class feeling and the immense effort needed to grow out of it. To believe that it can be easily shaken off is one of the continuing self-deceptions of the British. Orwell was right to stress the subtle pervasive force of class, the way in which it cuts across and sometimes surmounts economic facts.

The professedly socialist parts of the book which follow

are not so easily defended. The comic-grotesque gallery of cranks whom Orwell attacked—pacifists, feminists, fruit-juice drinkers, Quakers, birth-control fanatics, vegetarians, nature-cure quacks, nudists, 'nancy poets'—these were to him the left-wing intelligentsia, the literary intellectuals, the middle-class socialists. Towards them all he was intemperately violent.

Of course, there is some truth in what he says. A man with Orwell's insight could not fail to score some shrewd hits. But at bottom his attack was probably inspired as much as anything by his puritanical mistrust of self-indulgence, physical or mental. His great antagonism to the left-wing intelligentsia was founded in his feeling that they were intellectually and imaginatively self-indulgent. He sombrely hated what seemed to him moral shallowness. He thought them prim and out of touch with decent ordinary life. He thought they wanted to have things both ways, to get socialism on the cheap whilst remaining undisturbed in their fundamental attitudes and habits. He thought they wanted to remain dominative or at least distantly paternal in their attitude towards the workers rather than to recognize the need for a radical change of outlook. In his view, they thought they could remain vaguely international in their socialism without facing the full implication of their beliefs (which Orwell had proved in action he *was* ready to face). They thought they could be true socialists and yet keep their prosperity, though that was founded on the subjection of millions of coloured people; "We all live by robbing the Asiatic coolies". For Orwell, responsibility, responsibility in action, existed all the time, was heavy and had to be obeyed.

All this is useful. But Orwell did not leave it there. He was grossly unfair to his victims. At one moment he was asserting that working-class habits are better than middle-class and seemed to be mocking the middle-classes and urging them to drop their middle-class habits. At another moment he was warning them not to dare try. At yet another time he was telling them that they cannot drop their middle-class habits anyway because they are too ingrained. At still another time he said that he could not drop middle-class habits himself. It is a confused, harsh and one-sided attack and omits altogether the history of good and self-forgetful action which many middle-class socialists have shown. On the other hand, Orwell idealized some working-class socialists and omitted to criticize—it would have been easy to do so—the limitations of, for example, some professional trade union politicians.

More than all this, his attack purported to be an attack on the main body of socialists. As such it is fantastically inadequate. The left-wing intelligentsia are only a small part of the labour movement, though a valuable part. Outside them there is a complicated range of other people and groups; unions, co-operatives, local branches, chapels, friendly societies, and the like. All these and many other groups and individuals make up the texture of British socialism.

Something similar could be said about Orwell's attack on machine society which also runs through this part of the book. He had a continuing fierce suspicion of the emergence of a beehive state, a rage which later lay behind his two most famous books—*Animal Farm*, where it was held under pressure in an apparently unimpassioned allegory, and *Nineteen Eighty-Four* in which it erupted into terror (but by then Orwell was a sick and indeed dying man). His tirades in *Wigan Pier*, though sometimes pointed, have nothing like the edge and force of D. H. Lawrence's. One may agree with him because one has long accepted a particular point (without being clear what next can be done about it), but Orwell did not often illuminate the issues. Here, as in some other places, one has to be on guard not to be carried away by him. He had such an honest voice, as we all say; he so often said, outright, things we have all wanted to say and been inhibited from saying, that we are in danger of being swept away. We have sometimes to distinguish between sentimentality and hysteria on one hand and a just rage and pity on the other.

Wigan Pier, more than any other book of Orwell's, shows a host of contradictions in his thinking—between an absolutist and a tolerantly gentle man; between a resilient man, out to get things done by communal action, and a dark and solitary despairer; between one who urged the need for revolutionary changes in our thinking and a man with a deep-seated sense that things would always go on much as they always had ("Every revolutionary opinion draws part of its strength from a secret conviction that nothing can be changed", he says in *Wigan Pier,* and elsewhere: "On balance life is suffering, and only the very young or the very foolish imagine otherwise"); between a pessimist and an optimist who believed in the eventual triumph of ordinary good sense. These things came together in his interest in working-class people. His pity for their condition made him want to bring about improvements for them; his basic, stoical acceptance and unexpectancy made him—with one part of himself—not really believe in the efficacy of change and made him also admire, with a peculiarly close natural feeling, the stillness of working-class interiors. It is useful to follow a reading of *Wigan Pier* with *Homage to Catalonia,* a more variously spirited book and surer of itself. By then some of the things unproved for Orwell at the time of *Wigan Pier,* especially about his capacity to live up to his own convictions, had been proved.

There is a danger at this point of making *Wigan Pier* sound too faulty, too unfinished to be worth much attention. This would be a mistake. It has some impressive parts and is, as a whole, unforgettable. When we are trying to explain this we usually say that it is because of Orwell's exceptional honesty. What does 'honesty' mean here? And is honesty enough to make a memorable writer, whatever it may imply for a man as a man? I think honesty means here a certain way of seeing and the possession of the power of showing what it is you have seen. It means a certain manner and quality of perception, and a style which isolates it. It means an eye for telling gesture and incident—the ability to notice that the mines' offices had a rubber stamp which said simply 'Death stoppages'; realizing that, you know unforgettably how much the risk of death is accepted in mining. It means the sense of detail and verisimilitude which allowed Orwell to create atmosphere in much the same way as Defoe and Cobbett. We do not easily forget the exact description of the 'fillers'' work at the coal-face, or the budget of a family on P.A.C., or the 'scrambling for the coal' on the slag-heaps, or Mr. Brooker's dirty thumb finding its way into everything.

We mean also, by Orwell's 'honesty', his training himself to get rid of the expected, the social-class, response. You can almost feel him disciplining himself to the point at which, when he looks up and says 'What different universes different people inhabit', such an obvious remark seems to have the fresh validity of a self-forged truth. He tests on himself, bites between his teeth, the kind of socially conventional coinage which most of us accept; he tests it by talking flat out about the smell of working-class people or about assumed differences in status and the misery they cause.

All this seems a down-to-earth common sense though it is in fact so uncommon as to be a form of high intelligence. The total effect, which is why we use the word 'honesty' so often, is as though we saw the thing, the scene, the incident for the first time.* To be able to write like this was due partly to natural gifts, partly to deliberate professional practice (Orwell always meant to be a writer); and partly it is the product of a moral tension. It is informed by an urgent, nonconforming and humane personality.

To embody this outlook Orwell forged his peculiar style. It is, at first glance, clear and neutral, one of the least literary or involuted or aesthetic (one of Orwell's bad words) styles. "Good prose is like a windowpane", he said, and set about stripping his down. Like Yeats, Orwell thought there was 'more enterprise in walking naked'. His style was a function of his search for truth. He thought of it as a weapon, a political weapon (which is not the same as a party political weapon); "I have been forced into becoming a pamphleteer", he said in 'Why I Write'. He was in no doubt about the importance of language in this respect, as we may easily see from his essay

---

* Two particularly effective short pieces of this kind, both written early in Orwell's career, are 'A Hanging' and 'Killing an Elephant'.

on 'Politics and the English Language' and from his invention of Newspeak in *Nineteen Eighty-Four*. But his sense of the relations between language, thought and imagination was sometimes superficial.

The style Orwell forged was direct, active, cogent and epigrammatic. It rarely qualifies; it has not many 'perhapses' or 'somewhats' or 'rathers' or 'probables' or 'sort ofs' or 'on the wholes'. It uses short and ungenteel words wherever possible, says 'bum' instead of 'behind' and 'belly' instead of 'stomach'. It is directed at a 'you' outside, who has to be convinced; when Orwell is impassioned the 'you's' succeed one another like an indictment. It is demonstrative—'Here is this frightful business of . . .' and 'One of those ready-made steak puddings . . .'. It gives the reader a feeling of relief because it refuses to pussyfoot. It says 'This swindle . . .' and you feel firm ground under your feet. It has a distinctive kick and energy. One critic, Richard Rees, calls it 'debonair'. This is not the word that would come first to mind, but when you think about it you realize that it is true and useful, since it reduces the risk of talking about Orwell's style as though it were only that of a plain honest George.

When Orwell was moved his style lifted to match his feeling and the reader himself feels as though he is confronting experience rawly and nakedly. Look, for instance, at the opening page of *Wigan Pier*. There is the short, direct, placing paragraph* referring to the mill-girls' clogs and factory whistles and then we are straight into the description of the Brookers' lodging house. Notice especially how the epithets and images all work to build up a particularly loathsome impression. They are thrown at the reader, like blows with a wet dish cloth. By the time of *Wigan Pier* Orwell had already gone a long way towards removing the 'civilized' modulations, the literary and 'read' air from his style so as to arrive at an immediate and demotic voice.

At its best this voice of Orwell's is charitable, morally earnest and convincing. At its worst, it can deceive us by the

* Quoted in 'A Question of Tone', p. 188 of this volume.

misuse of just those qualities which elsewhere make its strength. The apparently clear run of the prose can, like that of Matthew Arnold's at times, be deceptive. Orwell can commit, and commits in the second part of *Wigan Pier*, most of the faults he attacks in others. He can write loosely and in cliché. Very soon after the opening of the second part of this book he is writing about the 'dreary wastes of Kensington', of their inhabitants as 'vaguely embittered' and of their 'favourite haunts'. He overuses certain words for quick effects, words such as 'frightful', 'dreadful', 'awful' and 'evil-smelling'. He sometimes overcharges his metaphors and this is usually a sign of emotional looseness. After talking about the evils of imperialism with a man from the Educational Service he had met on the train in Burma, he says, in *Wigan Pier*: "In the haggard morning light when the train crawled into Mandalay we parted as guiltily as any adulterous couple." Some of his larger generalizations only slip by at a quick reading because he has built up a reputation as an honest broker; on a closer reading we find that the invoice has been incorrectly made out. He uses limiting labels as a form of Instant Insult; there are plenty of examples in *Wigan Pier*.

So it is easy to see why some people are suspicious of Orwell, why those of us who are drawn to him need to be on our guard against being seduced by his manner in itself. I use that curious choice of words deliberately because Orwell was one of those writers who gives the reader a particularly strong sense of himself as a man. His personality is inextricably intertwined with his writing; his life and art were mutually complementary political acts, in the larger than usual sense I defined above. As Lionel Trilling says, he belongs to that group of writers who *are* what they write.

He always drove himself hard and no doubt hastened his death, at the age of forty-seven, by forcing himself to finish *Nineteen Eighty-Four* whilst living on the damp and remote island of Jura. For all the apparent straightness of his manner he was a peculiarly complex and ambiguous man. No doubt all of us are complex and ambiguous, but Orwell was exceptional for the strength of his ambiguity and because he expressed it in his life and writing at the same time (and with less than the usual artistic indirection). He was tolerant, generous, brave, charitable and compassionate; he was also irritable, fierce, bitter, and indignant (but not 'righteously indignant' in the self-righteous sense). He was at one and the same time sceptical and sentimental, conservative and radical, unideological or abstract and intensely moralistic (this is a specially English combination), insular and internationally-minded, austere and full of fellow feeling.

Orwell has often been called 'the conscience of his generation'. Alexander Trocchi, whilst agreeing in general, added that the 'conscience' of a generation is not the 'consciousness' of a generation but a less penetrating, because too immediately committed, entity, one too much tied to political action here and now. Similarly, Tom Hopkinson argues that Orwell suffered because he was 'without historical perspective' and adds that this caused the peculiar intensity of his attention to matters of the present day. One can agree so far here—whilst reflecting that Orwell himself might have said that some kinds of 'historical perspective' can make us lose all sense of urgency and intensity in working for reform, so that we more easily accept the inevitability of others' misery.

But there is truth in both these criticisms and they help to define Orwell's limits. To call Orwell the 'conscience' of his generation is just and fair praise. In his actions and writing he is representative. In spite of his frequent wrong-headedness we recognize in him a passionate concern. All of us may not be able to accept all his moral solutions; but we are bound to respect his moral stance. For exiles of Orwell's kind a moral stance rather than a moral programme is probably the way in which they speak to a fellow feeling in other men.

It is therefore a temper of heart and mind that we most respond to in Orwell. In trying to define that temper briefly we find ourselves using (and he would have been unlikely to object) old-fashioned phrases. We say, for example, that he stood for *common decency*; and though that phrase is difficult to define and often woolly, with Orwell it indicated a hope which he tried to embody in action; it indicated his active commitment to the notion of brotherhood and kindly dealing.

It is easy to say that the conditions described in the first part of *Wigan Pier* have almost wholly gone today, and so to feel more comfortable in not taking the book seriously. One might speculate on what Orwell's own reactions would be if he were to come back to Britain more than thirty years after *Wigan Pier* was written and almost twenty years after his own death. He would certainly have been one of the warmest to welcome the clear improvements—beginning with the lines of miners' cars which now stand at the pitheads. He would have enjoyed attacking mordantly those who accuse the working-classes, now that they have TV sets and washing-machines, of becoming materialistic. He would certainly have pointed out that for all the increased prosperity plenty of people—many more than most of us wish to recognize—are still living in miserable conditions on little money. He would have seen that there are still two Britains divided at the Trent, that the Saturday afternoon shopping crowds in Brad-ford and Leicester still *look* different. He would no doubt have pointed out that, when he reported in the middle Thirties, Wigan had over 2,000 houses standing which had been condemned; but that an estimate in the Sixties showed it would cost 45 million pounds to complete the slum clear-ance of Oldham alone.

It would have been particularly instructive to hear him comment on whether the increasing attempt now being made to unify the working-classes and the middle-classes as consum-ers seems near that kind of union between the classes which he urges in the last pages of *Wigan Pier*. At that point he would probably have moved, more directly than he was always tempted to do in the Thirties, into his dominant theme—not so much the physical conditions people endured but the quality of life offered them. And on this George Orwell, today, would have been as disturbing a voice as ever.

1965

THE DANCE OF
THE LONG-LEGGED FLY

On Tom Wolfe's Poise

Tom Wolfe appeals so widely and powerfully not just because he is fascinated by the phenomena he describes; so are many other reporters of 'the contemporary scene'. He appeals not simply because he occasionally jumps outside the massive detail and makes a sharp critical remark about it; others are more effectively critical. Nor does he appeal chiefly because he has considerable verbal talent, though that goes a long way towards explaining the immediacy of his attraction and his great 'readability'. The real cause of his enormous success is his poise.

Almost all the essays in *The Kandy-Kolored Tangerine-Flake Streamline Baby** are in fact about not poise itself but the search for poise today, chiefly among young people. Mr. Wolfe calls it 'style' or more often, 'form'. The kinds of teen-ager he writes about are 'absolutely maniacal about form', 'serious as always about form'. To have realized this is Wolfe's main insight, the thread which holds most of his essays together and gives them their overall energy. It is not, of course, a new insight and others have probed it more.

A paper by Marshall McLuhan, delivered to a conference called *Vision 65* at Southern Illinois University in October 1965, gives a useful pointer. Young people today, says McLuhan, are 'data processors' on a large scale. They have to work hard and constantly at (a) processing all the fluid data (offered attitudes and styles) which their technological, electronic, mass-communication, consumers' society throws at

---

* London: Jonathan Cape; New York: Farrar Straus & Giroux Inc., 1966. Copyright © 1963, 1964, 1965 Thomas K. Wolfe Jr., copyright © 1963, 1964, 1965 New York Herald Tribune Inc. All quotations are by permission of the publishers.

them, and (b) matching that against the more ordered, classi-
fied, scheduled outlook which the classroom, the older, established environment, offers. So they become bewildered,

> baffled because of this extraordinary gap between these two
> worlds. . . . To grow up is to be absurd [McLuhan is ex-
> plicitly echoing Paul Goodman here] because we live in
> two worlds, and neither one of them inclines us to grow up.
> Our youngsters today are mainly confronted with the prob-
> lem of just growing up—that is our new work—and it is
> total. That is why it is not a job; it is a role*

The links in all that are not clear and the meaning of
'growing up' is ambiguous. But McLuhan is certainly saying
that young people settle, not for ends and purposes (which
imply movement out and from), but for balance on the spot,
for overall openness and knowingness, for poise. Towards
the end of his paper McLuhan quotes a young architect
friend speaking about 'his generation': "We are not goal-
oriented, we just want to know what is going on." McLuhan
adds: "The young today reject goals—they want roles—
R-O-L-E-S—that is, involvement."

This situation is neither as new nor as total as McLuhan
implies. He knows this well enough, though I am not sure
that Tom Wolfe does. Still, what McLuhan says there bears
directly on both Wolfe's subject-matter and—a different and
more important question—on his success. On his subject-
matter because, as I have said, he has realized that the search
for poise is the impulse behind much in the behaviour of
young people in commercial mass-societies, the urge to find
a stance before all the free-floating and un-ordered offerings,
a stance which accepts without going under; but which rejects
the calls of the old, goal-oriented world (the 'sclerotic' world
of adults, to use one of Wolfe's favourite words), since to do
that would involve making choices of value, rejections. It
would be inaccurate to call this the wish to stand upright

---

* McLuhan's paper was published in *The American Scholar* XXXV, No. 2
(Spring 1966). Paul Goodman's book is *Growing Up Absurd* (1961).

in Emerson's sense or 'vertical' in Auden's, since both of those speak from the old world, the world which could talk about the need to immerse in the '*destructive* element'—and that adjective summons up a moral order.

Tom Wolfe's success is ensured because in describing the search for poise, he also exhibits one kind of poise. He says, by all the breathy implications of his confident prose, "Look, it can be done." And in doing so he appeals not just to teen-agers, probably few of whom read him, but to a wider range of people who may not be young but who feel a similar difficulty in making sense of mass society. Wolfe's peculiar hold comes from his apparently sure possession of what looks like a possible stance. He has learned a style for the despair, though the style is often self-deluding and the despair not really faced. But that in itself is part of the point, part of the attraction, part of what is being said.

The assurance, the panache, is the most immediately striking quality. Mr. Wolfe has it partly because he knows his material so well, but also because he knows his readers *don't* know it. Like the Fat Boy he is out to make his readers' flesh creep, with conducted tours to 'the teen-age netherworld'. And because his readers don't know that world he can get away with murder. Dwight Macdonald has documented the inaccuracy of Wolfe's reportage. This was apropos a description of *The New Yorker*'s editorial methods. One would have had doubts even without Macdonald's circumstantial analysis. Clearly Mr. Wolfe is a painstaking and tireless leech of a reporter. But he sometimes claims to know so much about what goes on inside that he sounds like an omniscient fictional narrator, the invisible man, the fly on the ceiling. Presumably he feels driven to this because everything has to be hep, to be souped up, lest dullness supervene. Look at this small but typical instance: "One has only to list the male stars of the past 20 years [he lists them] . . . and already the mind is overpowered by an awesome montage of swung fists, bent teeth, curled lips, popping neck veins and gurglings." Well—not quite, though one sees the tiny point. Practically every *aperçu*

131

(and some are shrewd) has to be driven home with a vivid metaphor; and often the vividness of the metaphor seems to have counted for more than its truth. Or it is used to inflate the experience. A youth from Lafayette, Indiana, who was bitten with the bug to 'customize' cars went off to California where that activity is at its most advanced. ("What you have is something like sculpture in the era of Benvenuto Cellini," says Mr. Wolfe.) Then he came home with his own custom-ized car:

> I like to conjecture about his parents. I don't know any-thing about them, really. All I know is, *I* would have had a hell of a lump in my throat if I had seen Ronny coming up to the front door in his tangerine-flake car, bursting so flush and vertical with triumph that no one would ever think of him as a child of the red sulk—Ronny, all the way back from California with his grail.

Sometimes Wolfe's hectic knowingness becomes a parody even of itself:

> O, dear, sweet Harry, with your French gangster-movie bangs, your Ski-Shop turtleneck sweater and your Army-Navy Store blue denim shirt over it, with your Bloomsbury corduroy pants you saw in the *Manchester Guardian* airmail edition and sent away for and your sly intellectual pigeon-toed libido roaming in Greenwich village . . .

We are forced to think that Mr Wolfe is less fussy about accuracy than about making sure that his prose is always swinging. To complain about this is not niggling and can't be brushed aside by the claim that nevertheless the general 'feel' of the descriptions is right. It points to some of the more difficult disciplines in different styles of writing and, since Mr. Wolfe talks a great deal about the strains of 'creating art objects', he ought to think about these disciplines more. Documentary has its limits just as fiction has, and can't pinch from fiction without harming both. Mr. Wolfe, one suspects, gives the glossy finish to his pieces by telling more than he could possibly know from his documentary position—and so does violence to his material and his human subjects. His essay on Harrison, the original publisher of *Confidential* (now in the shade) is full of interesting detail. But by some extraordinarily fortunate chance, on the day Mr. Wolfe is interviewing the anxious Harrison in a restaurant, Walter Winchell comes in, is hailed by Harrison and cuts him:

> Suddenly Harrison's eyes are fixed on the door. There, by God, in the door is Walter Winchell. Winchell has on his snap-brim police reporter's hat, circa 1924, and an overcoat with the collar turned up. He's scanning the room, like Wild Bill Hickock entering the Crazy Legs Saloon. Harrison gives him a big smile and a huge wave. "There's Walter!" he says.
>
> Winchell gives an abrupt wave with his left hand, keeps his lips set like bowstrings and walks off to the opposite end of Lindy's. . . .
>
> By and by Harrison, Reggie and I got up to leave and at the door Harrison says to the maître d':
>
> "Where's Walter?"
>
> "He left a little while ago," the maître d' says.
>
> "He was with his granddaughter," Harrison says.
>
> "Oh, was that who that was," the maître d' says.
>
> "Yeah," says Harrison. "It was his granddaughter. I didn't want to disturb them."

It all comes too pat, like a movie-cliché. It sounds like a betrayal of the relation Tom Wolfe had established with Harrison for the purposes of the interview; it uses him. And for that matter it takes liberties with Winchell.

Still, Mr. Wolfe does know a great deal. He has not only been there; he has looked too. He has noted the curious social rituals of limousine-chauffeurs, waiting for their owners to come out of the opera in New York City; or the ways of New Jersey teen-agers heading for the Manhattan discotheques:

> They headed off up Front Street if it was, say, Plainfield, and caught the Somerset Line bus at the stop across the street from the Public Service building around 7.30 p.m. Their bouffant heads would be bouncing up and down like dande-

lions until the bus hit the Turnpike and those crazy blue
lights out there on the toothpaste factories started streaming
by. They went through the Lincoln Tunnel, up the spiral
ramps into the Port Authority Terminal and disembarked
at some platform with an incredible number like 155. One
hundred and fifty-five bus platforms; this was New York.

He has listened to the jerky, groping-for-contact, gesturing
style of contemporary teen-age talk, the dialogue of "You
know . . . sort of . . . like . . . kind of . . . I mean . . ." He
has thought a little about the inner meanings of teen-age
display. He knows it cannot be explained only in terms of
deliberate commercial manipulation but comes from a more
complicated interplay. To describe it all he has devised a style
which gives his readers the feeling that at last they are really
in the thick of it, immersed in it all and yet still riding. He
is, to repeat, a talented writer; not only a processor—a clever
drawer-upon layers of contemporary curiosities and responses
—but occasionally more than that. He can show talent in
what he would probably call 'the old sclerotic literary sense'
of the word. It is on the whole a single-shot, metaphoric
talent. He can (and this is only one of many instances) speak
about the 'secret needle-toothed fury' of a toy poodle and a
Yorkshire terrier barking at each other. He can make nicely
grotesque juxtapositions, especially about cultural pretensions. The President's wife attends the re-opening of the
Museum of Modern Art: "In a few minutes she will address
them all, in a drawl that sounds like it came by mail order
from Pine Bluff, concerning God, Immortality and Inspiration through Art for the free peoples."

Such gifts being recognized, you still have to separate fairly
obvious devices from more symptomatic elements. Recurrent
devices include the casual, *in medias res* openings ('One thing
that struck my mind, for some reason, was . . .'; 'All right,
Charlotte, you gorgeous . . .'; 'It is a very odd, nice, fey
thing . . .'; 'Please do not get the idea . . .'); and the saturation-
bombing openings ('Pastel cars, aqua green, aqua blue, aqua
beige, aqua buff, aqua dawn, aqua dusk . . .'; 'Hai-ai-ai-ai-ai-ai-

ai-ai-ai-ai- . . .'). Then there are strings of 'in' phrases like 'Whatever became of . . .', and favourite unusual words such as 'infarcted' and 'epopt'. Once he has found a word or verbal device he likes, Mr. Wolfe uses it relentlessly—it becomes a trademark: the sun 'explodes' off windscreens I don't know how many times, and 'sclerotic' is always with us.

His style is to quite a large extent a montage of other men's styles. His great catalogues of proper names recall his namesake, Thomas Wolfe. Hemingway has helped with the use of the continuous present, and with 'and' used as the link between flat successive clauses. Scott Fitzgerald has taught him something about catching the breathless syncopation of scenes from fashionable life:

> Goldie and the Gingerbreads are on a stand at one end of the studio, all electric, electric guitars, electric bass, drums, loudspeakers, and a couple of spotlights exploding off the gold lamé. *Baby baby baby where did our love go.* The music suddenly fills up the room like a giant egg slicer. Sally Kirkland, Jr., a young actress, is out on the studio floor in a leopard print dress with her vast mane flying, doing the frug with Jerry Schatzberg . . .

From Graham Greene he presumably got the three-tier dying fall to end a paragraph ("takes him by the hand and heads for home, the white brick tower, the tacky Louis chaises and the gathering good news"). *Finnegans Wake* makes a small contribution, and there are strong similarities to Aldous Huxley. Huxley likes to penetrate glossy social surfaces by a sudden, brutal anatomical reference. Off with these lendings; back to the poor, bare, forked animal. Wolfe uses this device until it sounds like a trick or tic. The text is scattered with sudden shock references to the ischium and the ilial crest, glutei maximi, trapezii, gemelli, latissimae dorsae. But, to finish with echoes, guess how many you can pick up in this very clever confection. It is Sunday in New York City:

> Anne would make scrambled eggs, plain scrambled eggs, but

it was a feast. It was incredible. She would bring out a couple of those little smoked fish with golden skin and some smoked oysters that always came in a little can with ornate lettering and royal colours and flourishes and some Kissebrot bread and black cherry preserves, and then the coffee. They had about a million cups of coffee apiece, until the warmth seemed to seep through your whole viscera. And then cigarettes. The cigarettes were like some soothing incense. The radiator was always making a hissing sound and then a clunk. The sun was shining in and the fire escapes and effluvia ducts were just silhouettes out there someplace. George would tear off another slice of Kissebrot and pile on some black cherry preserves and drink some more coffee and have another cigarette, and Anne crossed her legs under the terry-cloth bathrobe and crossed her arms and drew on her cigarette, and that was the way it went.

All these echoes have their uses, as short-cuts to the dominant moods. The most revealing is the use of details, of the names of things. Some contemporary English observers like detail too (e.g., Nell Dunn) but it doesn't sound the same. Some English writers have long liked to list particulars and name prices; Virginia Woolf attacked them when she attacked Arnold Bennett. But again it is not the same. I think Virginia Woolf was wrong about Arnold Bennett; for him the poetry was in the particulars. For many Americans—and certainly for Tom Wolfe—the poetry *is* the particulars. The daftest passage in this book is Wolfe's reference to Wordsworth's inventories: 'his glorious delicatessen owner's love of minute inventory would overwhelm him.' Nothing could be farther from the inner meaning of Wordsworth's naming of the names; but it might do for Tom Wolfe himself.

The American love of detail is different from ours, and goes far back and deep into American experience. It has to do with the continuing sense of the need—the imperative, the challenge—to confront the mass and variety and reality of brute experience; it has to do with the need to make sense of the shapeless, amorphous massiveness of democratic existence; it has to do (as David Lodge also pointed out in writing about

Tom Wolfe) with the Redskin/Paleface polarity. For all his cracks about 'an ancient, aristocratic aesthetic', Tom Wolfe is substantially a Paleface pretending to be a Redskin, fascinated and slightly appalled at his own daring but always dragged back to the wild, wild scene. Wolfe's exposure to this situation is not quite the same as that of his nineteenth-century American predecessors. It has a particularly mid-twentieth-century nervous edge. He dives into the mass, rolls in it, shows he isn't afraid of it, comes up with handfuls, arranges it into sharp, sure little structures.

> Murray the K, the D.J. and M.C., O.K.?, comes out from the wings, doing a kind of twist soft shoe, wiggling around, a stocky chap, thirty-eight years old, wearing Italian pants and a Sun Valley snow lodge sweater and a Stingy Brim straw hat. Murray the K! Girls throw balls of paper at him, and as they arc onto the stage, the stage lights explode off them and they look like falling balls of flame.

There is a sort of nervous exhilaration in watching him do it. He is making order out of that 'bafflement'; he's dancing above Niagara on a tightrope. And so he speaks to more than American experience today, though probably especially to that. It is essential to get all the names spinning, not to pin them down but so that the reader can feel 'involved' in 'what's going on', in Marshall McLuhan's phrases. Somehow if you name it you will get a meaning out of it. No: that's the wrong way to put it; somehow, the meaning *is* the thing itself.

Contributing to the total mixture—laced through all the devices, the echoes, the expected big gestures, the naming of the names—is a more personal characteristic which, so far as I know, has not been remarked on before. Wolfe is a very sensual writer, a very sexual writer. Of course, he flogs his inventions to death, here as elsewhere; but you can still tell that a sharp nerve is being stroked. Well may he cry: "Ah, sweet little cigarette-ad blonde!" He is deeply responsive to the nymphets, the 'flaming little buds' as he so often calls them, to the half-exposed globes of their buttocks, their high tight breasts and their 'little cupcake bottoms':

> Elsewhere, Las Vegas' beautiful little high-school buds in their buttocks-décolletage stretch pants are back on the foam-rubber upholstery of luxury broughams peeling off the entire chick ensemble long enough to establish the highest venereal-disease rate among high-school students anywhere north of the yaws-rotting shanty jungles of the Eighth Parallel.

In getting the right poise this is probably the trickiest element. But a good ambiguous adverb can usually hold the scales between an older man's sexuality and the need to be a sympathetic but detached reporter. A group of girls are waiting to get a famous D.J.'s autograph:

> One of them is squeezed into a pair of short shorts that come up to about her ilial crest. Coming down over her left breast she has a row of buttons. The top one says, "We love the Beatles" [and so on down to one button whose motto is only roughly pencilled in]. But so what? The letters are big, and her little mary poppins tremble honestly.

That final adverb just, but only just, preserves the poise. But it does so by being intellectually dishonest, through sentimentality.

Yet the most important ingredient in the whole cocktail—if it is to serve its readers in the way they need—is not the fact that Tom Wolfe loves the material. It's that he also hates it. And that he usually manages to hold these two moods in suspension. It is particularly important to be clear here. I am not pointing to the large, self-conscious, critical gestures, the constant use of OK intellectual names and notions (Weber, alienation, Apollonian v. Dionysian, symbolic logic). Almost all of this is rubbish, as are the frequent historical vistas ('The Emperor Commodus . . . the Earl of Chesterfield . . . Phil Spector'). No more than top dressing; Mr. Wolfe has no real critical distance. His dislike, when it comes out, comes out hard and the boat is only just saved from capsizing. He can, of course, make routine gestures of rejection in the usual form ("It is as if there were a communal fear that someone, somewhere in Las Vegas, was going to be left with a totally vacant minute on his hands"). But he really embodies the rejection when he looks close:

> . . . he was wearing a striped polo shirt with a hip Hollywood solid-color collar, and she had on Capri pants, and hooked across their wrinkly old faces they both had rimless, wrap-around French sun-glasses of the sort young-punk heroes in *Nouvelle vague* movies wear, and it was impossible to give any earnest contemplation to a word they said. They seemed to have the great shiny popeyes of a praying mantis.

He pins Mick Jagger in action with a horrified accuracy:

> . . . this boy has exceptional lips. He has two peculiarly gross and extraordinary red lips. They hang off his face like giblets. Slowly his eyes pour over the flaming bud horde soft as Karo syrup and then close and then the lips start spreading into the most languid, most confidential, the wettest, most labial, most concupiscent grin imaginable. Nirvana! The buds start shrieking, pawing towards the stage.

He has an exact eye for nastiness: vicious whores, brutish cab-drivers. Most of all, he hates and fears the thought of ageing. I gave up counting the number of contemptuous references to the old or unvirile; they include 'bad hair and reedy faces', 'ageing mastoids', 'ratty people with ratty hair and corroded thoracic boxes', 'crusty old arteriosclerotic bastards' . . . all of them 'shuffling their shanks'. He may not fully see the skull beneath the skin but he notes and can't forget that after forty 'the packing under the skin begins to dry up, wither away.' For a thirty-three-year-old this seems a pretty desperate holding-on to youth; there's still a lot of twilight to get through.

Almost predictably, the strongest reactions are roused against women once sexually attractive but now ageing. This is more than setting the young against the old, one generation against its predecessor; it's the old, old elemental retching at the ephemerality of sexual allure, and nausea at its last gestures. The sexual disgust flares again and again:

> Mrs. Janson fades up the street with her rusting gams and her three Welsh corgies.

> Convalescing dowagers taking the rays with lap robes from the old La Salle sedan days over their atrophying shanks.

> So gorgeous Charlotte twists around in the chair with her alabaster legs and lamb-chop shanks still crossed and locked together in hard, slippery, glistening skins of nylon and silk . . .

Mr. Wolfe could be a religious recluse at forty. But he might have to fight harder than he has fought so far to save himself from being the pop-purveyor to the New Manichees.

One could go on, isolating the elements which help to make this elaborate balance. The most effective essays (effective in their own terms) are very cunningly structured, and the best is 'The Last American Hero', which is about stock-car racing in North Carolina and stock-car culture in general. Souped-up, breathless, detailed, it races along and does seem to get close to the feel of the things it describes. Wolfe weaves into it too a sense of its significance as a symbol of traditional tensions between North and South, as an instance of the collapse of lower-middle-class cultural models, as a contemporary form of Southern States' rhetorical-heroic (echoes of Robert Penn Warren here), and so on. It is all smoothly and energetically done. He has a well-developed sense of when to bring in a new theme, when to alter shutter-opening and speed, when to vary pressure—a well-developed sense, that is, of how to do all these things *so that the poise is maintained*.

So I come back for the last time to the question of poise, to the meaning of this apparent grappling with the swirling phenomena of mass society. In intellectual circles the discussion about the larger issues, in the U.S. and elsewhere, often becomes an argument between the defenders of the old 'high culture' and the welcomers of the new. Among contemporary American commentators—though these placings are bound to be too unqualified—you would find, say, Dwight Macdonald and Hannah Arendt on one side and Edward Shils and Patrick Hazard on the other. In Britain you could just as easily and roughly place names on each side.

Where Tom Wolfe and his poise fit in can be made clearer by reference again to the distinction between representative and symptomatic literature. Roughly, symptomatic literature is a symptom of its time, a specimen. Properly regarded, it tells you something about (usually something nasty about) the quality of life in a society. Representative literature examines and explores these conditions and is thus, in a difficult but important sense, outside them. I am not altogether happy with 'representative' as the second term. It could appear to mean 'representing the state of things' and so seem almost synonymous with 'symptomatic'. We need a word which suggests 'exploratory . . . analytic . . . critical'. But probably it is safe to assume that the contrast in meaning between the two terms is sufficiently known.

It would be easy to settle for saying that Tom Wolfe is both representative and symptomatic on the grounds that, though he usually immerses himself in the material, he occasionally floats free. But though his criticisms may sometimes be sharp and brilliant they are, in total effect, local. He never drives them home, never stays with them so long that they hurt. His apparent representativeness is really only an aspect of his symptomatic character. What is at bottom being offered is not a position from without but a poise from within. The most apt epigram—only a little too strong—is in the essay on Harrison of *Confidential*. "Okay, it was bogus . . . But by God the whole thing had style." Such a poise is not juxtaposition; you do not reach it by being enthusiastic in one paragraph and sombrely critical in the next. It's more subtle than that. You have to keep all doors open, yet never fully go through any one. Acceptance must always keep at the back of the mind the idea of—not the acted fact of—rejection. Rejection must not close any doors—never quite close any doors—on the pleasures of acceptance. The delicate, iridescent film must never be quite broken, though it can be made to bend; that film is, verbally, the play of tone within a narrow range; and, intellectually, the play of perceptions, which may be sharp but not so sharp as to break the skin. We are left feeling that we have never realized how glittering, how interesting in itself, the surface is until that long-legged fly danced on it.

This is why Mr. Wolfe is more symptomatic than representative, though very sophisticatedly symptomatic. His style is the symptom of an important characteristic of modern mass communications. When this period's cultural history comes to be written one chapter ought to have the heading: "It ain't what you do; it's the way that you do it." Mr. Wolfe's medium, his stylistic poise, is more important than his message, his manner more than his matter. His spiritual sister is Baby Jane Holzer, the subject of one of his essays: "She does not attempt to come on sexy. Her excitement is something else, it is almost pure excitement. It is the excitement of the New Style." We are back once again with Marshall McLuhan, for whom the medium is the message. The way of doing it is the thing being done. Wolfe's book illustrates both the degree of truth in this dictum and the awful shortcomings of the position it describes (shortcomings McLuhan has so far been reluctant to examine).

In Russia the authorities fear that to expose their people to the open, multitudinous play of messages in a 'free' consumers' society would be to risk making them dissident (in search of other goals). So Russian teen-agers are not required to be 'data processors' on anything approaching the Western scale. You can see this in the different set of their faces (whether they are accepters or rejectors of the status quo) and in their much less fluid style and gestures. But if Marshall McLuhan is right—and Tom Wolfe's success seems to support him—the Russian authorities are mistaken. The best way to keep their people from seeking alternative goals would be to flood them with 'data', to offer them the chance to become anxious only about 'form', so that they came to believe that goals are out and poise in. Then they might keep on playing roles endlessly, and harmlessly—with no political effect. But by God they'd have style!

1966

SAMUEL BUTLER

And The Way of All Flesh

T HE *Way of All Flesh* is one of those books which are
loved as much for their effect on their readers' lives as for
themselves. Since it first appeared over sixty years ago Butler's
novel has seemed to thousands of people peculiarly exciting
and liberating. "Coming at such-and-such a point in my life,"
they are likely to say, "it altered my whole outlook. It helped
me stand up against the tyranny of my family . . . [or] of my
school . . . [or] of the Church. . . . It made me begin to think
for myself." Of course, *The Way of All Flesh* is not likely to
have quite that effect today. It was one of the intellectual
watersheds between the Victorian age and the twentieth
century. Most of its specific causes have been won; its battles
tend to look old-fashioned—interesting, no doubt, but dated.
Yet it still has a peculiar liveliness. It speaks to us, makes us
listen, less for the particular errors it is castigating than for
the way it castigates them: we respond to its temper of mind,
its energy, charity and irony.

We respond to much else too, for this is an unusually diverse book. Although it is sometimes called 'the only proper
novel' of all Samuel Butler's sixteen or so full-length books,
The Way of All Flesh is really a mixture of at least three
forms.

It is partly an autobiography of a kind found in many
literatures—in which a young man rejects his background
and finds his own way. Within that large genre it is among
the more striking of a British sub-group—one of the first
autobiographical attacks on the Victorian and Edwardian
family, and a precursor of many such attacks in several forms;
Edmund Gosse's *Father and Son* is perhaps the best-known
example. Even today, if you write discursively about the
temper of a period and draw upon autobiographical material,
you will, though you are not likely to take Butler as a specific

model, find yourself often remembering him—much as one remembers a gifted but erratic older cousin.

Butler began to write the book early in 1873, just after his mother's death, when he was thirty-seven. He kept at it, intermittently but persistently, throughout that decade, urged on by his friend Miss Savage. He started the revision in 1880 but put it aside in 1884, by which time he had revised only the first part. Miss Savage died the following year. Butler always meant to finish the revision, but somehow never found the heart. He was proud of parts of the book but remained dissatisfied with it as a whole. It was finally published in 1903, thirty years after it had been started, a year after Butler's own death, and when most of the principals—who would have been shocked by their portraits—were also dead.

They would have had good reason to be distressed (as Butler's surviving relatives were), for this is an extremely sharp portrait of a Victorian clerical family. The boyhood of the hero, Ernest Pontifex, is based on Butler's own early life at Langar in Nottinghamshire, where his father had the living. Theobald is clearly drawn from Canon Butler (as he later became) and Christina from Butler's mother. 'Drawn from' can be a misleading phrase and does not mean 'a portrait of'; but I will come back to this question. Much in the characters of Mary and Harriet, Butler's two sisters, has been rolled into the single character of Ernest's sister, Charlotte. Roughborough school is based on Butler's period at Shrewsbury School and Dr. Skinner on Dr. Kennedy, the Head there. Similarly, the Cambridge chapters in the book reflect Butler's time at St. John's College, from 1854 until 1859. The later chapters have much of the atmosphere of Butler's bachelor's routine in his chambers at Clifford's Inn, London, where he lived from 1864 until his death. The only substantial part of Butler's life which is not directly used in the book is his period as a sheep-farmer in New Zealand from 1859 to 1864, which he undertook after a disagreement with his father about the choice of a career. We might say, though, that the fictional equivalent of the New Zealand experience—as a watershed which finally broke the bonds of parental influence—is Ernest's period of imprisonment.

Butler himself certainly regarded the novel as an autobiographical document. His childhood, he used to say, really had been exceptionally unhappy. "I had to steal my own birthright. I stole it, and was bitterly punished. But I saved my soul alive," he wrote in his *Notebooks*. A brief but telling impression of the atmosphere against which Butler felt he was reacting can be gained from his best picture—he was a keen but, usually, unsuccessful painter—'Family Prayers'. It has the stuffiness and rigidity of a group of spiritual waxworks.

The Way of All Flesh is also a bundle of discursive essays and an exemplification, in narrative, of a scientific theory. Desmond MacCarthy, who knew Butler, says he thought of himself primarily as a philosopher. If so, Butler was self-deceived. The middle-aged shambling figure—who spent hours of almost every day in the Reading Room of the British Museum, adding to and brooding over his curious and often off-beat lore, about science, literature, religion, education—belongs rather to the line (a strong English line) of wide-ranging, proselytizing, opinionated, eccentric intelligences. It is a strain which always has something of the engaging amateur in it.

Still, to say only that would be to undervalue the originality of Butler's achievement. He was a virtuoso of the mind, not only a Don Quixote but a powerful guerilla-fighter, waging simultaneously a number of important intellectual campaigns. His book on Shakespeare's sonnets is characteristically idiosyncratic but not inconsiderable. His argument that the *Odyssey* was written by a woman is strong enough to have convinced some well-informed readers, among them Robert Graves. Though he was not a scientist, and scientists did not fail to say so, his scientific ideas were often penetrating and sometimes prescient. His attack on the domestic, sexual and religious hypocrisy and obscurantism of his time was wide-ranging, acute and deeply-felt; he knew these miseries. He fought hard against that obedience to the letter which violated the spirit, against that evasion of moral problems which shows itself in a rigid, unseeing obedience to a formal code. He saw too many people who, like the farmers of Theobald's parish, were "equally horrified at hearing the Christian religion doubted or seeing it practised".

Butler was especially fascinated by the process of change in social and intellectual climates. Much of the convincing warmth of the first part of *The Way of All Flesh* comes from his loving sense of the interpenetration of manners and ideas, as he tries to recreate the temper of late eighteenth-century village England. Later, especially during Ernest's time at Cambridge, he takes his chance to discuss more directly the relation of ideas to society and to an individual's development. One recalls the detail of Cambridge debates in chapters 46 and 47 ("It must be remembered that the year 1858 was the last of a term during which the peace of the Church of England was singularly unbroken. Between 1844, when *Vestiges of Creation* appeared, and 1859, when *Essays and Reviews* marked the commencement of that storm which raged until many years afterwards . . ."), or Butler's pleasure in exploring the intricacies of church dialectic, or his delight in creating the up-to-the-minute 'intellectual' preacher Hawke. ("I put these considerations before you, if so homely a term may be pardoned, as a plain matter of business. There is nothing low or unworthy in this, as some have lately pretended, for all nature shows us that there is nothing more acceptable to God than an enlightened view of our own self-interest . . .").

Most of all, Butler was steeped in theories of heredity and evolution. "Of course he read Darwin's books as fast as they came out and adopted evolution as an article of faith," he says of Ernest. Butler himself had greatly admired Darwin but later had a sustained quarrel with him. That the quarrel was so deeply felt and so protracted was partly due to a misunderstanding. But Butler was critical of the general implications of Darwinism and argued all the time—he wrote four books on his own evolutionary theory—for a kind of purposefulness in evolution, a vitalistic universe rather than one subject to blind chance. In chapter 69 of *The Way of All Flesh* there is a striking celebration of this great movement in life, in the paragraph which begins: "All our lives, every day and every hour, we are engaged in the process of accommodating our changed and unchanged selves to changed and unchanged surroundings. . . ."

Probably the most interesting instance of Butler's insight in scientific matters, which sometimes took him intuitively beyond the established opinions of the day, is his treatment of the unconscious mind (especially in *Life and Habit*). "All the most essential and thinking part of thought is done without words or consciousness," he said. We can see how Ernest's unconsciousness, in spite of the plights which it and other people's unconsciousnesses get him into, steadily pushes him towards his kind of truth and light. With others, the unconscious is more likely to betray them intermittently, to indicate the disparity between the conscious pretensions and the unconscious reality. This, of course, is particularly true of Theobald and Christina. One of the major ironic impulses behind *The Way of All Flesh* is the question: what really goes on behind our public faces and behind our conscious views of ourselves? When Butler says at the end of chapter 5 "I fancy that there is some truth in the view which is being put forward nowadays, that it is our less conscious thoughts and our less conscious actions which mainly mould our lives and the lives of those who spring from us", he is putting with an assumed and amused tentativeness what he firmly believed and was seeking to demonstrate in this novel.

It is especially revealing to read Butler on the operation of memory, for in that—as a reservoir and irrigant—is located more than anywhere else his theory of the evolutionary process. He writes with point about those stores of knowledge which we all have but are not conscious of, about revealing slips and unconscious verbal humour. But *The Way of All Flesh* is informed throughout with this kind of lively and well-observed interest. Occasionally, the evolutionary notions are somewhat dragged in. Chapter 5 has a prosy essay on heredity and environment, prompted by the description of George Pontifex's authoritarianism; later, his sour grumbling at Christina inspires an essay on the inefficiency of nature, in making the generations dependent on one another. Less obtrusively but with some cumulative effect the metaphors repeatedly make similar connexions.

More comprehensively, the actual form of the novel was partly dictated by Butler's theories. The plot illustrates the theory of heredity expounded in *Life and Habit* and the moral philosophy that follows from it. Butler felt himself that the first chapters were a little long, but explained that he was anxious to emphasize the influence of pre-natal experiences. Most readers think their length justified, though not for the reason Butler himself chose. In the book as a whole we are invited to observe the process of evolution from the first kindly old Mr. Pontifex to Ernest's own middle-age. Men *can* learn and improve, was one of Butler's contentions. His hero does gain some enlightenment; courage and intelligence do tell. Yes, but with what sheer good luck, and good friends to help him over the consequences of his crasser errors, we feel like saying. Still, Butler thought luck important, a proper part of the order of things. He admired the Marys of this world—those to whom rewards come by sheer grace—rather than the Marthas, who pay the bills, do the donkey-work in the background, have little luck and are ill-favoured.*

Yet how much does the theory behind the book imaginatively inform its better parts? Very little. And in so far as we do appreciate *The Way of All Flesh* as an intellectual document, we enjoy it not as the projection of a theory but as an illustration of aspects of the temper of late-Victorian England. As we have seen, Butler was one of the more lively and liberating voices against Victorian domestic hypocrisy

* Luke 10.40 is the source, of course; but see also Kipling's poem 'The Sons of Martha'.

(he had little articulate sense of its compensating strengths). In this he had a considerable influence—on H. G. Wells (in *The New Machiavelli*), on Lytton Strachey (in *Eminent Victorians*) and perhaps most directly on G. B. Shaw. He and Shaw have similar strategies for shocking their readers' out of conventional thinking, notably the use of paradox, the inversion of apophthegms, the tail-twisting of expected pieties —such as: "There lives more faith in honest doubt" and "Reasonable people will look with distrust upon too much reason". They share some tones of voice, especially a knowing and cocky tone for laying down the law (though all in all Butler seems rather kindlier than Shaw). Shaw was generous in his acknowledgement:

> The late Samuel Butler, [was] in his own department the greatest English writer of the latter half of the XIXth. century. . . . It drives me to despair of English literature when one sees so extraordinary a study of English life as Butler's posthumous *Way of All Flesh* making so little impression that when, some years later, I produce plays in which Butler's extraordinary fresh, free and future-piercing suggestions have an obvious share, I am met with nothing but vague cacklings about Ibsen and Nietzsche.*

For some time after its publication *The Way of All Flesh* was not greatly regarded by readers of Butler. The allegory *Erewhon* (1872)—and to a lesser extent its successor *Erewhon Revisited* (1901)—was thought to be his best, and in fact only considerable work; *Erewhon* was the only book which enjoyed success during his lifetime. *Erewhon* and *Erewhon Revisited* are still interesting—as are Butler's essays on *Life, Art and Science*, his *Notebooks* and the *Letters* between him and Miss Savage—but today *The Way of All Flesh* holds prior place among Butler's works for most readers. It seems altogether a more interesting book than the others, richer and fuller. It interests us too—and this reveals something of the taste of our own period—for its remarkably 'contemporary' tone. Even more important, it is a fascinating example of

---

* Preface to *Major Barbara* (1907).

tensions between fact and fiction, of shifting and ambiguous points of view. We have seen that *The Way of All Flesh* is part autobiography, part discursive essay. It is also a novel— in many ways a very impressive novel.

Obviously, some of it is mechanical, chiefly because plot is being wrenched to fit Butler's theories. In this pursuit he does not hesitate, when it suits his determination to make his hero follow the desired evolutionary line, to use the chance-and-coincidence machinery of the conventional Victorian novel. Ellen, the servant girl, is most plainly used in this way. Every so often she does spark into life, as when she muses on why she can't endure comfortable married life with Ernest:

> This life don't suit me. Ernest is too good for me; he wants a woman that shall be a bit better than me, and I want a man that shall be a bit worse than him. We should have got on all very well if we had not lived together as married folks, but I've been used to having a little place of my own, however small, for many years, and I don't want Ernest, or any other man, always hanging about it. Besides he is too steady . . .

But most of the time Ellen is a useful small cog, or necessary trip-wire, at various phases in Ernest's development. She pawns the watch Ernest gives her, to help her on her way after she has been dismissed by his parents—and it is found in the shop by Theodore, who thereupon attacks Ernest. Years later, Ernest meets Ellen by chance in the streets of London when he is lonely and depressed, and soon marries her. The marriage becomes a mockery; but again by chance Ernest meets the family's ex-coachman John, who had originally carried Ellen away from the Rectory, and from him learns that his marriage is bigamous, so that he is free again.

Similarly, Towneley comes alive only once or twice—for instance, in that brief and graceless moment when he surprises Ernest in Miss Snow's room and laughs like a bold bounder. Festing Jones* says that Butler wished to present Towneley as a foil to the immature Ernest, an admired instance of successful adaptation. But he creaks like a small-scale character from melodrama, representing, not 'villainy with waxed moustaches', but 'hearty natural ease and good digestion'.

Most striking of all, that whole sequence from the assault on Miss Maitland to Ernest's trial, imprisonment and re-establishment after release uses the roughest sort of plot manipulation. To show that his hero has the wit to learn from experience, Butler has to give him a particularly severe shock. It is handy, though, that Ernest is one of those favoured by luck. Not only is he released, by a word, from his miserable married life with Ellen; he learns also that his inheritance, as a result of delay and Overton's good husbandry, has swollen to £70,000; and he easily finds a kindly, clean, Dickensian-Christmas bargee-family on whom guiltlessly to farm out his two children by Ellen.

We can see Butler's theory showing, too, when he tells us that after a year and a half of comfort Ernest became better-humoured and better-looking. In part, this is good sense; some men do blossom with security and the removal of petty financial worries, as some men thrive and grow on responsibility and admiration. But we would feel this more readily if Butler didn't scamper through this part of the book and assert, briefly and rather bossily, that Ernest has changed now the magic wand has been waved. From being unusually ineffective and immature Ernest suddenly becomes assured and humorous, much like a friendly sketch of the warmer sides of the middle-aged Samuel Butler. And with his other hand he writes controversial books. Butler, as he used to say himself, made many mistakes and messes in his lifetime. But the Ernest who created the peculiarly inept messes of this story, right up to the time of going to prison, was not— in spite of some shrewd qualities—a likely chrysalis either

* Henry Festing Jones, *Samuel Butler, A Memoir*, 2 vols. (1919).

for the middle-aged controversialist Butler or for the middle-aged author Ernest. We simply do not believe in Ernest's tough contentious books.

More important than the rigging of plot to suit theory are those curious elements in the presentation of character which are caused, we are forced to think, by Butler's emotional involvement with the originals of his characters: with his father and mother, with (of course) himself, and—perhaps most poignant of all—with Miss Savage. Alethea is to some extent, Butler said, a portrait of Miss Savage.* She is an engaging woman, dry and warm, charming and direct, attractive in both looks and character. She is a perfect aunt and sensible middle-aged friend. She has a good mind, and her good sense prevents her from making too intimate emotional demands on any of her acquaintance, whatever their age. She dies quietly, cleanly and without fuss. She has a due, distance-keeping, self-control. She is the kind of witty, self-possessed woman a confirmed bachelor feels admiring, tender and gallant towards . . . and quite unthreatened by.

Some of this was true of Miss Savage's character. But as a whole the picture is romanticized. To begin with, Miss Savage was plain, lame and dumpy, physically unattractive to Butler. The portrait of Alethea is a tender tribute, and a sort of substitute; a substitute for what Butler knew Miss Savage might well have hoped for but could not have—love. We need only set the portrait of Alethea against the sonnets Butler wrote about his relationship with Miss Savage to appreciate something of the awful poignancy involved here:

> Hard though I tried to love, I tried in vain,
> For she was plain and lame and fat and short,
> Forty and over-kind . . .
> . . . .

* In his edition of *The Way of All Flesh* (*Ernest Pontifex*, 1965), Professor Daniel F. Howard argues that Alethea, in spite of Butler's own claim that she was based on Miss Savage, is much more an idealized projection of Butler's mother. I do not find this argument convincing.

A man will yield for pity if he can,
But if the flesh rebels what can he do?
I could not; hence I grieve my whole life long
The wrong I did in that I did no wrong.

But a greater irony in the situation was pointed out by John Middleton Murry. From the evidence of the letters between them, Miss Savage had a far more lively and complex mind than Butler managed to present in the portrait of Alethea. She may have been less elegantly attractive but she was a much more interesting person than her fictional tribute.

The most difficult questions concern the treatment of the Pontifex family, and here one has to be exceptionally careful. To some extent one is making deductions drawn from a knowledge of Butler's life; yet one is dealing with a work of art which is not just 'a picture of life', and has its own rules. It is difficult but important not to confuse the two. Certain incidents, certain kinds of treatment, are extreme; but they are justifiable as art and should not be attacked because they 'distort' life: for instance, the scene where Christina and her sisters play cards to decide who shall set her cap at Theobald. Chapter 11 begins briskly: "The next morning saw Theobald in his rooms coaching a pupil, and the Miss Allabys in the eldest Miss Allaby's bedroom playing at cards with Theobald for the stakes." This is farce and should be read as farce, for fun and as caricature, revealing a kind of truth through comic excess. To read it otherwise is to miss its serious undertone. Young ladies did not actually play cards for husbands, it is true. But husband-getting, behind the genteel forms, could be a dreadfully calculating business. Card-playing for a husband no more exaggerates one aspect of the truth than the conventional romantic pieties about courtship exaggerate it in the other direction. By redressing the balance Butler was, in a phrase he would probably have enjoyed, blowing the gaff.

Other scenes and treatments—for example, Theobald's

repetition of 'We can't wish it prolonged' at Christina's deathbed—are disturbing, because they seem to be cruelly distorting, as though some debt is being paid off. Butler was involved, perhaps more deeply involved than he knew. *The Way of All Flesh* has been described as a gust of fresh air directed against the stuffiness of Victorian family life; but it was also, as J. B. Fort has said, 'a cruel book'.

Butler is often both unfair and untender. He manipulates his situations so as to highlight natural incapacity and weakness as well as stupidity and folly. He drives his nails in very hard indeed. George Pontifex, pleased that young Theobald is working hard for a college fellowship, offers as a reward the works of any standard author he might select. Theobald chooses the works of Bacon and duly receives them. The paragraph ends with a brief sentence: "A little inspection, however, showed that the copy was a second-hand one." Chapter 20 has a similar ending, relating to Christina: ". . . it was long before she could destroy all affection for herself in the mind of her first-born. But she persevered." Years later, immediately after Christina's death, a paragraph about Theobald's response ends: "And he buried his face in his handkerchief to conceal his want of emotion." Those, or any three or four similar touches, might pass unnoticed. But touches like them come so often, and are so well placed to make their full deflating effect, that they give the impression of cruelly gratuitous flicks. The reader enjoys them because they are, after all, funny. But it is a slightly guilty pleasure. This is true of the treatment of virtually all members of the family, but most of all of Theobald. Christina is often hardly treated, but occasionally there is a hint of tender exasperation, almost of awe at her capacity for self-deception.

Butler's unhappy relationship with his father seems to have been founded in a natural antipathy. We know, because even Mrs. Garnett* tells us, that Canon Butler did beat Samuel. And Ernest said he remembered from his childhood relationship with his father no feeling but fear and shrinking.

* R. S. Garnett, *Samuel Butler and His Family Relations* (1926).

So Theobald is not given much quarter. He can hardly get off his knees after one bout before Butler hits him again. He is even mocked because he cannot whistle properly, which may be excruciating to a musical expert like Butler but is hardly a sin. Most striking of all, in throwing the full weight of odium upon Theobald, is the scene at the end of Chapter 22 in which the little Ernest tries to say 'come' but can only manage 'tum'. It is a powerful, effective and—in some respects—liberating scene. But it is hard; especially (and typically) in its last sentence, with the appalling final adjective:

> "I have sent him up to bed," said Theobald, as he returned to the drawing-room, "and now, Christina, I think we will have the servants in to prayers," and he rang the bell for them, red-handed as he was.

And yet, even as one accuses Butler of hardness, one recognizes his rage, his generous rage, at cruelty. He felt this always, and meant his readers to feel it too. One remembers also, on the other hand, that Butler did show some sympathy and pity for Theobald; for his sick realization on marriage that he had been trapped, and for the dogged way in which he tried to follow such lights as he saw. Both he and Christina did wrong to Ernest; but their environment had treated them hardly too, and neither grace nor luck favoured *their* escape. To some extent Butler recognized this.

By contrast, Ernest himself is not clearly focused. He is not only the younger Butler but the younger Butler seen through the special vision of the narrator, Overton; and this gives a different effect from what would have been given if Butler had narrated the story impersonally or in his own person. Overton has a bachelor-uncle's-eye view of the family, slightly indulging the child, amused by his immaturities and siding with him against the parents. This particular kind of distancing eases certain problems; by using Overton, Butler is able to be kinder towards Ernest than would have been possible in an impersonal or first-person narration. In the

later chapters of the book all these three characters—
Ernest, Overton and Butler—merge; but into an unsatis-
factory blur. Miss Savage, as so often, put her finger on the
trouble: "Is the narrator of the story to be an impartial
historian or a special pleader?"*

It is therefore interesting to set these portraits against
what we are told about the family by others. Canon Butler's
letters to Samuel were often firm. They were never, of course,
as hilariously will-wagging as those from Theobald to Ernest.
But neither were they as cruel. Mrs. R. S. Garnett, in *Samuel
Butler and His Family Relations*, is too ingenuously out to
justify the family in the face of their portraits in *The Way
of All Flesh*. Still, the details she gives about family life at
Canon Butler's rectory often create, convincingly, an atmosphere of decency and pleasant good sense.

Or we can go direct to Butler's own remarks elsewhere,
and compare the description of the visit home by the grown-
up Ernest in Chapter 82—in which he now confidently sees
through them all—with this from the *Letters*:

> Three times over I said I had enjoyed my visit very much
> and it had done me good, but not one of the three times did
> they say 'Well you know we are always glad to see you,
> come down as often as you can etc.' But then they are honest,
> and I am not. They received my compliments in silence each
> time.

How strong and teasing that tiny scene is: it suggests
regions of relationships deeper than those broached in the
novel.

Most of all, in trying to establish the relation of the fiction
to life, one has to go to the heavily autobiographical Memoir
at the front of *The Fair Haven*. Butler describes there his
mother's foolish religiosity, and at this point we recall
Christina. Then he adds:

> I have given the above in its more amusing aspect, and am

* *Letters between Samuel Butler and Miss E. M. A. Savage*, ed. Geoffrey
Keynes and Brian Hill (1935).

half afraid that I may appear to be making a jest of weakness on the part of one of the most devotedly unselfish mothers who have ever existed. But one can love while smiling . . .

That admission may partly be inspired by a familiar Victorian family piety. But it sounds as though it means more than that; it seems to express the strong ambiguous hold of a genuine emotional relationship. In *The Way of All Flesh* we do not often feel quite that strength, or hear quite that moving double note.* Instead, we have a safer distancing and a masterly caricaturing. In facing these close personal problems fiction was, for Butler, less a means to truth than a way of loading the dice. Behind *The Way of All Flesh* is a bigger book than Samuel Butler could bring himself to write. As a result, the novel provides a fascinating example of involvement and separation, of shifting points of view, of double focus and selective perception.

Butler thought the book tails off, and most modern readers agree with him. The early narrative chapters on the older generation are unaffected, full of interesting historical detail and well-observed (though occasionally slightly sentimentalized, as when old Pontifex says 'Good-bye, sun' just before his death). The manner is quiet but the movement fast. Then the mood and attack change as we move on to the married life of Theobald and Christina and the childhood of Ernest. Again, but in a different way, this part is powerful. Roughly at the fifty-first chapter, when Ernest leaves Cambridge and goes to London, the decline sets in.

One possible reason for this decline was suggested earlier, in the discussion of Butler's tricky relationship to the material from real life on which he drew. At this point in the record

---

* See, for one instance, chapter 71 when Ellen, of all people, voices it. Butler always liked an unexpected reversal. " 'Oh, your pore, pore ma!' said Ellen. 'She was always fond of you, Master Ernest: you was always her favourite; I can't abear to think of anything between you and her.' " And we are surprised, both at Ellen's sudden coming to life and at the new dimension in Christina she opens with one remark.

of his hero's career he apparently found the relationship between himself and Ernest more difficult to control. He solved some of his problems by becoming melodramatic. Miss Savage was the first to point out the unreality of the Miss Maitland catastrophe; she could have extended the criticism to all those chapters in which Ernest lives in Mrs. Jupp's lodging-house, with a blindness to what goes on around him that invites ribald comment.

When one stands back from the book as a whole it shows a shape, after the first dozen panoramic narrative chapters, like that of a range of peaks separated by flatter ground. The peaks are large dramatic scenes; the intervening parts are connecting narrative or discursive commentary. The first such set-piece is in chapter 13, in the coach after the wedding, when Theobald insists that Christina order the dinner. Suddenly the narrative movement stops and we go close in for a scene with full dialogue, which takes almost as long to read as it would have taken to live through. Scenes of this size are supported by smaller scenes, each precisely observed: Gelstrap's dismissal after the dropping of the Jordan water, or old George Pontifex's dinner-stopping fury at being served with lobster sauce made with a cock-lobster. Of them all the grimmest is that whiplash scene over Ernest's inability to say 'come'; and the finest, in the economy, tone and timing of its comedy, is Dr. Skinner's supper. At their best these dramatic pieces are releasingly funny or grim, cunningly controlled, and only very occasionally obtruded upon by Butler's own comments.

Many less obvious elements contribute to the book's peculiar temper; for example, Butler's fond habitual use of brief, impressively consummatory or 'cliff-hanging', chapter endings. Or one thinks of his variety and fullness of invention —a quality he shares with many earlier Victorian novelists. He produces complete speeches, a full sermon by Mr. Hawke, and a dozen different kinds of letters in full*—the most subtly

---

* But some of these materials were not wholly Butler's invention; they were adapted from originals he found in family documents.

in character being Charlotte's invitation to Ernest to stay at her house:

> Could you like the thoughts of a little sea change here? The top of the cliffs will soon be bright with heather: the gorse must be out already, and the heather I should think begun, to judge by the state of the hill at Ewell . . .

That appalling letter is a reminder that Butler has a good ear for the nuances of voice and their relation to character. It echoes, from seventy-five chapters earlier, Mrs. Allaby's speech to Theobald after he has finally nerved himself to ask for Christina's hand ("She is heart-whole yet, dear Mr. Pontifex . . ."). Heredity certainly tells here; awful gentility of this kind runs strongly in most of the women in the book. Mrs. Jupp is naturally an exception; of her speech Butler is especially fond. He used to take notes of racy speech heard in London; Mrs. Jupp enshrined the best and inspired some new inventions. She is a little too evidently being offered as a latter-day Wife of Bath, but still her language is vivid and energetic.

In general, the most successful scenes in the book are those in which Christina and Theobald appear. But in what way do these two 'live'? What does it mean to call them 'caricatures'? That, as compared with Maggie Verver and Prince Amerigo or Bloom and Molly, they are 'two-dimensional'? But such comparisons in themselves say little more than that *The Way of All Flesh* is neither *The Golden Bowl* nor *Ulysses*. One has to try to define the nature of the caricature in *The Way of All Flesh*, its peculiar life.

Christina and Theobald are rather more complexly presented than I have suggested, since I have concentrated on possible reasons for a hard presentation. Still, they are overwhelmingly—and brilliantly—creatures of deflationary farce. Butler had a fine eye for ludicrously revealing, slightly dotty behaviour; for example, Christina's determined visits to the Royal Academy—to look at types of female beauty—just before the birth of Charlotte. He likes to have Christina and

Theobald together, so that their individual follies can be heightened from the tension between them. He loves, too, the freedom—the almost surrealist freedom—which interior monologue (not so common a device then as it has been for the last fifty years) gives him. He enjoys himself hugely when he has Christina and Theobald together, in a coach say, but each wrapped in a private myth.* His greatest single pleasure is in Christina's unrivalled capacity for fantastic day-dreaming, which first appears at the beginning of chapter 21 ("Strange! for she believed she doted upon him") and after that is woven throughout the story. When the two day-dreams meet in the open the result is triple-layered ironic farce:

> "We, dearest Theobald," she exclaimed, "will be ever faithful . . . O Lord" (and she turned her eyes prayerfully to Heaven), "spare my Theobald, or grant that he may be beheaded."
> "My dearest," said Theobald gravely, "do not let us agitate ourselves unduly . . . Such a life let us pray God that it may please Him to enable us to pray that we may lead."

Set against his father and mother Ernest can easily seem a slight character, since he hasn't their vividness. But he is not presented in caricature, and so really belongs to a different kind of novel. Even if he had been wholly successful in his own way, as a 'three-dimensional' character, there would still have been this contradiction between his kind of characterization and that of his parents. Since he is blurred even in his own terms—part the product of personally involved reminiscence, part that of theory—he cannot often stand up to his parents' simpler but bolder personalities.

Still, he does have a life of his own—as a child and young man. As a child he conveys something of the character of a little lost dog seeking love, a touch of Oliver Twist's frail appeal. He is by nature shy, amiable and hence easily put upon. Both as a boy and as a young man he 'holds himself too cheap'. But he has reserves of strength. Slow to size up a

* See Chapter 29.

situation, especially when he is being duped or duping himself through his diffuse goodwill, he nevertheless acts directly
and honestly once he does see. It only requires Towneley
to show contempt for sentimentality towards the poor for
Ernest to recognize how much he has been humbugging himself, and to face that insight. He is free of cant. All the more
pity that his assurance in the final chapters of the book is
so imposed and theoretic. Miss Savage rightly called him
'priggish' then; he is passionless and smug.

Without being fanciful, we can probe further into the
appeal of the younger Ernest. He belongs to an old allegorical
stock. He is partly what I called earlier a 'Martha' figure,
clumsily and painfully learning by hard experience, 'under
law' (to use Butler's terminology). But also in part he is,
again as Butler might have said, a 'Mary', 'under grace'.
He has the natural good sense, when it comes to a crisis, to
act according to instinct, unselfconsciously, as one favoured
of the gods (much like a young and deeply-loved Swiss friend
of Butler's, Hans Faesch). Seen in this way Ernest is the folk-
lore figure of the lucky fool, the fallible and inept 'younger
son' who nevertheless, through niceness, lack of calculation
or malice or self-conceit—and with some sheer luck and help
from the gods—comes out on top in the end.

Butler's irony operates in several ways, most of which
have been suggested already in this essay. *The Way of All
Flesh* is ironic in structure; it turns inside out, takes a rise
out of, the conventional novel about a family's life through
several generations. The irony towards individual characters
has, usually though not always, several layers; even the secure
Ernest at the end of the book is partly being laughed at. But
the irony through inventive verbal energy, more than anything else, gives the book its peculiar pace and sparkle.

Butler's use of bold scenes and characterization are echoed
by his dramatic use of metaphors. His comparisons tend to
be larger than life and sometimes outrageously unexpected,
to drive home moral issues by the play of unusual comparison.
Incidentally, and rather surprisingly, in this he is like George

Eliot. He can quietly place a verb so that its metaphorical charge stings sharply: "Theobald," he says, "rummaged up a conclusion from some odd corner of his soul"—though there the whole metaphor is working with the verb to be wittily contemptuous. With characteristic largeness in image he remarks that Dr. Skinner one day "had fallen upon [Ernest] in hall like a moral landslip". Later, Towneley catches Ernest 'morally speaking, by the scruff of the neck'. When Butler likes a metaphor he will repeat it, with variations. 'Religious wild oats' early in the book is varied many pages further on, in 'we must all sow our spiritual wild oats'. The best known of these images is also the neatest: "The clergyman is expected to be a kind of human Sunday". The most sustained is that in which Ernest realizes that he must no longer trust his mother with his boyish confidences:

> The mangled bones of too many murdered confessions were lying whitening round the skirts of his mother's dress, to allow him by any possibility to trust her further.

Butler's tone, though it sometimes seems old-fashioned, more often sounds contemporary. When it is old-fashioned, it has a touch of Victorian pawkiness. Or occasionally there is a prim donnishness about his humour and it is then heavily obvious, in-groupy, wordy and not very funny: "I never yet knew a man whose sense of his own importance did not become adequately developed after he had held a resident fellowship for five or six years": or there is a pedantic play of rhetorical questions: "Who so *integer vitae scelerisque purus*, it was asked, as Mr. Pontifex of Battersby? Who so fit to be consulted if any difficulty . . . ?"

But this is rare. "It reads as smooth as cream," Miss Savage said of the book, and in general she was right. It has the quick run of lively speech, of a man talking. We say Butler has a 'plain' style but this shouldn't suggest only the lack of certain qualities. It *is* an economical style, and well stripped down. It is also offbeat, quirky, slangy, vigorous, dry and mordant—all suggesting an undeluded commonsense.

It has the relaxed air of some modern novelists who do not want to seem 'literary' or Olympian:

> Some poets always begin to get groggy at the knees after running for seven or eight lines . . .

> . . . he had devoured Stanley's *Life of Arnold*, Dickens's novels, and whatever other literary garbage of the day was most likely to do him harm . . .

> I don't like being too hard on even the Mer de Glace . . .

> [To parents on the firm handling of children] You carry so many more guns than they do that they cannot fight you. This is called moral influence and it will enable you to bounce them as much as you please . . .

> How these babes and sucklings do give us the go-by surely . . .

> With his usual presence of mind Mr. Pontifex gasped out a month's warning to Gelstrap . . .

> It was all the same old will-shaking game . . .

> If it was not such an awful thing to say of anyone, I should say that she meant well.

The crusty, mischievous, attractive note of that last quotation is frequent in Butler. How far does it represent his own personality? The answer can't be simple. It seems right, finally, to turn from the book to look more directly at the man who wrote it.

That character was more complex—the gaps between appearance and reality wider—even than appears from reading *The Way of All Flesh*. The deeper tracks were well covered. We saw earlier that in one sense Butler was a progressive, looking forward to the twentieth-century world of men like Shaw and Wells. In another sense he was an eighteenth-century figure. He could mock the myth of a rural golden age, insist that mid-nineteenth-century peasants were 'stolid, dull, vacant, ungainly, uncomely, lifeless, apathetic', and give a cheer for their smarter and more hopeful descendants. But he did admire the comelier aspects of eighteenth-century life, as is plain from his portrait of old Pontifex; and only a page after the description of peasants quoted above he was writing nostalgically about the disappearance from churches of the old musical instruments. V. S. Pritchett is surely right in linking Butler, too, with eighteenth-century figures such as Swift and Fielding . . . for, respectively, his dry iconoclasm and his curiously-learned plain-man's air.

Butler was also a Victorian bourgeois gentleman, who reacted against his family but had a strong sense of family ties and could not bear to loosen them altogether; a solid bourgeois; not a radical, but an admirer of bourgeois habits and pieties, on the side of the powers-that-be. He admired easily-confident gentlemen, like Towneley. He had a keen sense of the importance of money, so that he resolved *The Way of All Flesh* into a well-heeled middle-aged bachelor's dream. He was a worldly man, in both good and bad senses. There is an interesting contrast (since neither their backgrounds nor their times of writing are greatly different) between his attitude to inherited money and that of E. M. Forster in *Howards End*.*

> Money pads the edges of things. God help those who have none . . . You and I and the Wilcoxes stand upon money as upon islands . . . we ought to remember, when we are tempted to criticise others, that we are standing on these islands, and that most of the others are down below the surface of the sea. The poor cannot always reach those they want to love . . .

Butler's world is fairly sharply divided into 'nice' and 'nasty' people; but the nice are often and too easily the fortunate 'Marys' whom luck favours, who have comfortable investments and ride without much questioning on the backs of the 'Marthas'.

But Butler also seems modern in some of his attitudes, against the pressure of Victorian earnestness, full of relaxed commonsense, capable of saying:

> Nothing is worth doing or well done which is not done fairly easily.

* Though Forster admires Butler and has been influenced by him in other respects.

Pleasure, after all, is a safer guide than either right or duty.
It is the function of vice to keep virtue within reasonable
bounds.

[One has] the duty of seeking all reasonable pleasure and
avoiding all pain that can be honourably avoided.

Heaven is the work of the best and kindest men and women,
Hell is the work of prigs, pedants and professional truth
tellers. The world is an attempt to make the best of both.

He was against pomp and cant and the merely fashionable,
and for ease and natural growth. Here he sometimes fore-
shadows elements in D. H. Lawrence's work, especially in
Lawrence's poetry.* He had a rough, grainy sense of the
attractions of Victorian city life but, probably more than he
hated anything else in his age, he hated its gracelessness and
rebelled against its lack of 'style'. But, like a good Victorian,
he also suspected 'style'.

So the air of the iconoclast which Butler wears is always
ambiguous. His complex character was more withdrawn and
insecure than his confident prose-manner suggests. One may
understand this better by reading about his relations with his
manservant Alfred.† To the end of his life he was uncertain
within himself and this, as is often the case, made him sharper
in controversy. He was lonely and badly needed affection;
he was tender and vulnerable. He sought friendships shyly
and in one instance was for years cruelly deceived (by the
New Zealander Pauli). He was harsh to the ugly Simeonite
Badcock in *The Way of All Flesh* (even the name is a blow)
as though to be poor and plain were a sin, or at least culp-
able carelessness. He listed among his seven deadly sins 'want
of money and bad health'. His idea of good luck was to be
born with good health, an assured income and good looks.
All this was fed by a feeling that he was himself an ugly
duckling. He felt drab, shabby, baggy and clumsy, a 'Martha'
—there is a photograph of him in his rooms at Clifford's

* Butler's poem 'A Psalm of Montreal' even sounds like Lawrence.
† There is an admirable short essay on this by Betty Miller, published
in *Horizon*, No. 107.

Inn which has just this air—and in compensation he was attracted to the 'Marys', idolized Pauli, created Towneley, felt lost when Hans Faesch sailed for Singapore, clung closer to Alfred and—alternating with his remaining close friend Festing Jones—paid regular visits to the woman he called 'Madame', for sexual relief. All Butler's friendships were paid for in one way or another.

He called himself an Ishmael and felt like an outsider looking in at the successful, the confident, the ebullient. So he built his defences, each day for years and years following the same pattern, with Alfred as the guardian of order. He made this pattern—the routine in his chambers, the daily trip to the Reading Room of the British Museum, regular foreign holidays—a ring-fence within which, secure, he could comfortably sit. He did not want to expose himself to any man's patronage or contempt or pity, to be beholden to any man. He helped to secure himself by limiting his perspectives, by not asking too much from life, by giving it no more hostages than he could avoid. He created a style of life based on cutting his losses, on so far as possible controlling his situations, being emotionally economical. All this being done, he could live reasonably happily with his chosen pleasures. He could, on the basis of his mild stoicism, enjoy his mild hedonism: the weekly visits to Madame, the regular trips abroad.

It was a moderate and unexpectant view of life and at bottom slightly fearful and bloodless. Mrs. Garnett made a shrewd hit back when she accused Butler of being 'a little lacking in moral robustness'. Yet, at the very moment one agrees, one remembers that he had remarkably dogged powers of moral self-preservation. After all, he did fight his family —and win.

When all is said, Butler is, as a creative writer, a minor figure. His vision was too limited, too much affected by his time and temperament, for greatness. It would be silly to use others as sticks to beat him with, but perspective is always useful; and one need only compare some other novels about childhood, family relations, the pains of adolescence and the pressures of society—say, Turgenev's *Fathers and Sons*, or Stendhal's *The Red and the Black*—to recognize the limits of Butler. *The Way of All Flesh* then seems parochial, slightly stuffy, insular. In Turgenev we breathe a larger air of the spirit, and in Stendhal recognize a tougher and more complex sense of the life of the mind and its relations to society. In Butler there are none of the 'high and destroying moments'. In his way of life he was a Victorian townee. *The Way of All Flesh*—in both its limits and its considerable powers—is the book of a spiritual townee.

But it would be too limiting to end on such a note. *The Way of All Flesh* is full of acute perceptions and virtuosity of expression; it vividly recreates the feel of a period; it blows a wind of ironic laughter, farce and caricature through some rooms of the mind that had become very musty; it shows a fascinating interplay between art and the raw material of a man's life; at its best, it speaks out for unpretentiousness, honesty and a charitable, pragmatic openness to life.

1966

THE NEED FOR LOVE:
KILVERT'S DIARY

Wednesday 29 March

Went down the meadows to Mrs Tudor's. Handsome Tudor was working in his garden. By the door lay a salmon rod on the ground, so I knew the Squire was having luncheon in the cottage. I went round and there he was with old Harry Pritchard. He brought out his telescope and we had a look at Crichton and Mrs Nicholl both wading in the river and fishing under the red cliff.

A BEAUTIFULLY attentive cameo, faithful and particular as a Bewick engraving. Coming to Kilvert* for the first time I expected such scenes, of course, and much else of a similar kind. And it is all there—what someone has called 'the placid afternoon of the Seventies': the daily minutiae of a curate's life, relations good and bad with respective squires, villagers' recollections which Kilvert seemed able to charm from them (of the mother who walked briskly across the fields to see the execution of her own son, of the soldiers leaving Chippenham for Waterloo—"they looked very much down, for they knew where they were going", of mad parsons, riots between villages, the Indian Mutiny), croquet games with girls of suitable class while the long light falls across the lawn, enormous meals. Through it all this obscure curate weaves his pattern of visits—of the young and old, rich and poor, sick and well. It creates, first, a sense of firm identity and continuity, of known generations and place, of 'a dignified and commodious culture'.

This is to idealize the picture, by failing to touch in its rougher lines—the widespread poverty (so many often cold and hungry), the harder impacts of status. Seen from this softening distance it attracts us a little like parts of Beatrix Potter—that small ordered warm world where mother hedge-

---

* *Kilvert's Diary*: a one-volume selection edited by William Plomer (1944).

hog will always sit rocking in the little armchair, smiling with
endless forgiveness over her wire spectacles. But it can't all
be dismissed in this way. A lot remains to set us thinking yet
again about both our social relationships and our personal
routines. Let me take one such instance of each kind. We
have had these thoughts many times before; they are
twentieth-century intellectual clichés. But each is given fresh
force after a reading of Kilvert.

First, the social. It seems wrong as well as futile to regret
the end of this old rural order. Yet we might take better
measure of how much it embodied social responsibilities.
Some kinds of charity—for instance, towards the old—were
assumed within that order, even if the assumptions were
not always lived up to. This struck me more sharply because
I was reading at the time Professor Titmuss's Fabian pamphlet *The Irresponsible Society*, which is at bottom a call
to put back this kind of charity, by acts of will and conscious
decision, into an increasingly centralized and prosperous
society.

And then the private reflection, which is just as trite until
it is recreated. In Kilvert the world slows down and we
realize how fast we have been running for years. Here, everything is more sharply defined and we can hear again how
people speak and see the detail of their movements and those
of nature, sharp and clear. Kilvert's natural descriptions are
rightly admired, though they are occasionally overwritten.
But he can note quite simply and briefly: "The women of
Clyro walk like storks—" and you feel how the insight
struck through his eyes. Or he looks, absorbedly, at a sleeping pig:

> I went round the premises late at night to see if the out-
> houses were locked up. All was still and the white pig lying
> in the moonlight at the door of his house, fast asleep, with
> the moon shining on his white face and round cheek.

All this is a long way from the 1870's as we usually think
of them. Kilvert was, certainly, politically unaware, out of
this world. But he was out of this world in another sense.

He was one of the 'once-born': he had little intellectual curiosity or interest in theological inquiry. He seems simply to have seen the world as always under the shadow, embracing, loving and firm, of God. He had in his bones a sense of an order outside our societies which both diminished them and sheltered them. The world was for him peopled with creatures—from cows to men—foolish but by instinct gentle. This may seem itself a foolish view but it is a high folly. For Kilvert the world was, as he says, 'a curious and wonderful thing'; not a thing to be made over or pushed around—after all, it wasn't going anywhere—but to be ruminated over and loved. At times, as he celebrates this world, he recalls Hopkins, and at times, Vaughan; just once, on the road to Lanhill at night, he had a mystical experience much like those of Vaughan. For such a man nothing is done by way of show and the voice is never raised. A sort of love flowed from Kilvert's finger-ends. He was the most charismatic of curates and when he left Clyro his parishioners literally wept and he wept too.

Yet I suppose all this does make Kilvert sound soft. He wasn't; he could be shrewd and dry, though he was never worldly or sardonic. He watches tenant farmers waiting for a free dinner:

> No viands had yet appeared but a savoury reek pervaded the place and the tantalised tenants walked about *lashing their tails*, growling and snuffing up the scent of food hungrily like Welsh wolves.

The italics are mine, though they are hardly necessary; the image vibrates from the sentence.

But such instances do not occur often. What does prevent the diary from having the placidity suggested by all I have said so far is another quality which runs throughout. This is the weft to the warp of Kilvert's natural and social observation. In the language of the old emotional cliché: Kilvert was a love-starved curate. His diary roughly spanned his thirties and ended just before he married. And the most important recurring item is—girls. It's not simply that he falls in love successively with well-nurtured young ladies, but that he is immediately excited by all sorts and aspects of girls: girls at school, the daughters of parishioners from two to twenty, girls in paintings at the National Gallery, Irish tinker-girls met on a train journey, girls glimpsed rolling on hillsides or heard laughing from haystacks, girls being bathed on the hearth in their drawers, girls' feet peeping from under their dresses, girls showing a curve of soft white breast or a rounded bottom or thigh:

> The girl suddenly slipped off the swing seat. . . . Unfortunately her clothes had got hitched up on the seat of the swing and were all pulled up round her waist and it instantly became apparent that she wore no drawers . . . I suppose I had set her down with her clothes rumpled up and her bare flesh (poor child) upon the board and as her flesh was plump and smooth and in excellent whipping condition and the board slippery, they managed to part company with this result.

There are a score of similar items. Simply to mention them is to recall all the old sniggers about lovesick or peeping curates or to invite an exercise—which would certainly have point—in the analysis of sexual frustration. But whilst we were laughing, or analysing, the richness of Kilvert's responses would escape us.

Kilvert had an enormous capacity for love in all sorts of aspects—for sensuality, for tenderness, for regard and affection. He wanted so badly to marry; he wanted a daughter to care for; he wanted to look after all his parishioners; he wanted a wife to love physically. And it all became one, a part of that whole world which he saw as 'curious and wonderful'. So he was incapable of looking at anyone as a 'type' or as a 'subject' for ministration, but saw them only as individuals; fresh, sharp, drawing love.

This is not one of the great diaries: I have put into relief its two strengths and said nothing about its weaknesses. But through all the unprofessional clumsinesses, here is a real human being, exposed in the round. We want to sit down and think, slowly, about the strangeness and beauty of human life after watching this little curate—wandering on his careful round over the fields and hills of Clyro and Langley Burrell, starting with desire as he catches sight of a girl's bare shoulder near a stream, dreaming of a possible wife, comforting the old and strengthening the sick—gentle and tender and vulnerable.

1960

A QUESTION OF TONE

Problems in Autobiographical Writing

Almost all autobiographical writing today is strikingly attuned to readers in a particular mood, a mood which has literary, social and cultural elements. No doubt genius will always find its own way. Just as certainly the general workmanlike level of any literary form in any period is largely decided by a number of common factors: the accepted status of that form in relation to other forms, the present condition of the form 'in itself' and the expectations of the audience from it, and assumptions about individual and social life shared by writers and audiences.

The audience for autobiography today is particularly undiscriminating and gives little support to a writer. A novelist can expect at least some critics, and some readers, to attempt a considered judgment of his work; almost no one is interested in the formal problems of autobiography. The audience will accept almost any tone, especially if it is a pastiche, and is particularly ready to enjoy certain kinds of relaxed tone: for instance, the aristocratically-elaborate, the naïve and wide-eyed observer, the engagingly unbuttoned, the wryly winning, the ripely humane, the casual 'I suppose we all recall . . . '. This audience will accept a great many literary and social tricks ranging from those which draw on well-loved literary styles to those which draw on well-accepted social styles—and these in turn may range from airy upper class to down-to-earth working class. I am not suggesting that such tones are always false, wherever we find them. I do suggest that they are often used out of habit and convenience and are not sufficiently considered by the writers; and that therefore a serious modern autobiographer will have to get this matter of tone straight first.

It is only too easy to illustrate the tones most used today

174

and most easily accepted by the audience—and so most tempting to a writer. Autobiography is difficult at any time, and I am not suggesting commercial calculation on the part of most writers. So I've chosen examples from a number of autobiographies, by writers with widely different reputations. And I won't identify the quotations, since they are more representative of their generic type than of their separate authors. I admire other work by most of these authors, and I admire parts of their autobiographies. But I think they have not realized that it is as difficult to write a good autobiography as to write a good poem or novel.

The most popular style today, then, is the 'poeticised-shimmer', or the style of rampant sensibility. It is a style about which reviewers use phrases such as these: 'gifted and imaginative', 'delicately perceptive', 'extreme sensitivity', 'beautifully observed', 'enchantingly affectionate remembrance of things past', 'must go at the side of our bed with Kilvert'. It is the style which tempts publishers to seek the services of, say, Mr. Ardizzone or some similar if less-talented illustrator—hoping that he will draw large nostalgic children's hoops or make even sooty privet look as though it has been seen through a veil, lightly. Then the reviewers are likely to say that the illustrations are 'the perfect complement' to the text. At a much easier level it is the style of those short, reminiscent radio essays in the afternoon—in the 'old gaffer amid the flowers' or 'my father was a drunkard, but I loved his tobacco-stained waistcoat' mood. Above that level one finds more and more elaborate, more and more refined, instances. If a poet is writing, the sensitive observation is likely to obtrude like large raisins in a sweet rice pudding:

My earliest memory is a smell of bacon. It has become the memory of a memory, for I can never recall it now with the direct, almost sensual assurance which, vague and dreamy though this memory was, used to distinguish it when it recurred in the long, white forenoon of childhood, as I lay ill or convalescent, wafting up through the muted sounds of traffic, footsteps, voices, or as it came to me, more legendary now but still authentic, at moments between sleeping and waking in adolescence. From very far back too, and with the same sensual magic, there reached me another smell—a stale, sweetish smell, which I dimly associated with breadcrumbs on a sideboard in a room that has not yet been aired after the night. The smell of bacon and the smell of breadcrumbs have always been closed memories for me, leading nowhere, bringing nothing but themselves.

My only visual recollection, which seemed to possess the same archetypal quality—but it may have had its source in a dream or a picture book—is the recurring image of a white china cup in a green wood: the leaves and grass are a sullen, emerald green; the whiteness of the cup, standing alone on the grass, is dazzling: the whole picture, clear yet elusive, is bathed in a brooding, sub-aqueous light.

Here is another author:

On those high summer Saturday afternoons in Poplar the light, in memory, lies always level across the grey-green roofs. All sounds were low, too,—horizontal: a muted murmur just below the level of real awareness. I could go on reading whatever book had then caught my burgeoning imagination (it might be Percy F. Westerman; it might be Tolstoy; it might be anyone between these two poles).

But I was happier simply because the noise was there, this low susurrus of family and neighbourhood sounds—a front door banging down the street, my mother turning on the back kitchen tap to fill the kettle for tea, the tragic-plover's cry of a footballing boy two streets off, the steady warm hum from the shops and traffic of the main road three or four hundred yards away. All this established the ground within which only and from which my spirit could begin to soar. It spoke a subtle, comforting, establishing language of love and interest and belonging and respecting. That being given, like some first magnetic mark, my heart was freed to explore, with a freedom I have never since known. I would find it hard to over-estimate the value of such rooted assurances at that time in my life.

So as the light sank lower and the air grew chillier I began slowly—very much like someone in the last hour of a night's sleep—to come to the surface, ready to reassume my other life (but they were really all one, and happily so).

I would then, as like as not, hear my father's solid charge-hand's tread and decent low voice as he rounded the corner with his workmate, John Armitage. The football match was over; Rangers had lost or won for another week. I heard the unmistakeable, sensuous plop of tinned salmon as it left its tin to land on the largest tea plate; and I could smell the newly baked oven-cakes.

I went in. . . .

And a third author:

The milkman would ride down the street with his great brass-labelled churn swinging between the sparkling, prettily-painted wheels of the milk float; he would ring a hand-bell, shouting 'Mi-ilk! Milko!' and I would go out with a flowered jug and wait, holding it out carefully, while he plunged his half-pint measure into the churn and brought it up dripping and foaming, and frothed it into the jug. He was a devil-may-care young fellow, with a straw boater always on the back of his brilliantined head and a village rose in his horse's headband. He would give a flick of his longwhip, leap whistling on to the back step of the float, and off he would clatter down the cobbled street—his rosy cheeks a memory of seaside fields and farms on the edge of cliffs.

Then there was the tea man—Lipton's Tea. I remember his smartly-painted, black and green, high, elegant horse-drawn vehicle that looked almost like a gipsy's caravan. When he opened the big doors at the back, there were piles of plump, different-coloured packets of tea inside—pink, blue, white, yellow and green packets, all at different prices.

I'm not sure, but I believe I remember an old muffin-man calling his wares in the twilight of a winter evening in the foggy front street—

And finally, in this style:

The June grass, amongst which I stood, was taller than I was, and I wept. I had never been so close to grass before. It towered above me and all around me, each blade tattooed with tiger-skins of sunlight. It was knife-edged, dark and a wicked green, thick as a forest and alive with grasshoppers that chirped and chattered and leapt through the air like monkeys.

I was lost and didn't know where to move. A tropic heat oozed up from the ground, rank with sharp odours of roots and nettles. Snow-clouds of elder-blossom banked in the sky, showering upon me the fumes and flakes of their sweet and giddy suffocation. High overhead ran frenzied larks, screaming, as though the sky were tearing apart.

For the first time in my life I was out of the sight of humans. For the first time in my life I was alone in a world whose behaviour I could neither predict nor fathom: a world of birds that squealed, of plants that stank, of insects that sprang about without warning. I was lost and I did not expect to be found again. I put back my head and howled, and the sun hit me smartly in the face, like a bully.

All these are from autobiographies with some good parts—except the second. That was concocted by me in twenty minutes or so. The objection to such a manner is, first, that life is not like that and never was quite like that, even for the autobiographers. Life is being seen through a retrospective haze, in a romantic winter evening's gaslight, in 'a brooding, sub-aqueous light' or as 'a perpetual summer's day'. We have come a long way from what might well be the source:

The corn was orient and immortal wheat, which never should be reaped, nor was ever sown. I thought it had stood from everlasting to everlasting. The dust and the stones of the street were as precious as gold: the gates were the end of the world. The green trees when I saw them first through one of the gates transported and ravished me, their sweetness and unusual beauty made my heart to leap, and almost mad with ecstasy, they were such strange and wonderful things. . . . Boys and girls tumbling in the street, and playing, were moving jewels. I knew not that they were born or should die; but all things abided eternally as they were in their proper places. Eternity was manifest in the Light of the Day and something infinite behind everything, appeared; which talked with my expectation and moved my desire. The city seemed to stand in Eden, or to be built in Heaven. The streets were mine, the temple was mine, the people were mine, their clothes and gold and silver were mine, as much as their sparkling eyes, fair skins and ruddy

faces. The skies were mine, and so were the sun and moon
and stars, and all the world was mine. . . .

Occasionally, one meets a harsh reaction away from the
brooding manner. But it is not usually an improvement; not
in British writers. It sounds like childish bad manners, as
though they are using a semi-American style so as to shock
the bourgeoisie:

> I think private life stinks; more think that public life
> stinks; life however, does not—which is the point worth
> making against our philosophies of despair and our
> romances of chaos. As for personal salvation—it would be
> disgusting if it were possible. . . .
> It has been my misfortune to lack, not only identity with
> all of us, but a sufficient number of those passports of
> acknowledged attributes that are the rewards of sufficient
> residence in one place, class and profession, or with one
> group of people. I have always been on the move; and the
> lack of identity that caused the first move was increased
> by all other moves. . . .

To be able to write in the raw and direct manner for
which this writer is striving may be possible for an Englishman; but it would require an unusual combination of ability
and circumstances. In the above passage the author is trying
to will such a style into existence. Here, as contrast, is an
American. There are one or two uneasy touches, but the
staccato attack, the timbre, the lack of social lubrication,
come more easily to him than to most British writers:

> I am an American, Chicago born—Chicago, that somber
> city—and go at things as I have taught myself, free style,
> and will make the record in my own way: first to knock,
> first admitted; sometimes an innocent knock, sometimes a
> not so innocent. But a man's character is his fate, says
> Heraclitus, and in the end there isn't any way to disguise
> the nature of the knocks by acoustical work on the door or
> gloving the knuckles. . . .
> My own parents were not much to me, though I cared for

my mother. She was simple-minded, and what I learned from her was not what she taught, but on the order of object lessons. She didn't have much to teach, poor woman. My brothers and I loved her. I speak for them both; for the elder it is safe enough; for the younger one, Georgie, I have to answer—he was born an idiot—but I'm in no need to guess, for he had a song he sang as he ran drag-footed with his stiff idiot's trot, up and down the curled wire fence in the backyard:

> Georgie Mahchy, Augie, Simey
> Winnie Mahchy, evwy, evwy love Mama.*

I am not attacking others for doing badly what I wouldn't myself dare to try. I have committed (though in an incompetent way) most of the faults I am describing in others. As a result I am more than ever convinced that there is no easy solution; that if we are to write good autobiography we must have a more careful and firm eye on the way our language works than most autobiographies today. I know from my own experience how easy it is to slip into indulgent, throat-catching rhythms—and how willingly one's audience will accept them. There are hundreds of different deceptions. Here is a very small one, a simple instance of many. At an early stage in writing my book *The Uses of Literacy* I was trying to describe the impression made on a twelve-year-old by the corner shop in his working-class district. I wanted to recall the sense of confusion and richness and much else, and at first I opened the detailed description by saying something like this: "It is all a glorious tangle of odds-and-bobs." 'Glorious' is the tell-tale word in that passage; it shows it for what it is—an 'eye-on-the-reader' passage. The word was a substitute for the word or words one can only find by working harder and more disinterestedly, the words which don't ask the reader to join in in the wrong way and be mildly amused. 'Glorious' was an epithet from another attitude and another social world; it was coy. You can see a similar quality in

---

* Saul Bellow, *The Adventures of Augie March* (1953). 7.

those passages I first quoted—this audience-struck quality,
this tone of sharing a secret with the reader, this easy nudging
rhetoric.

I said the world 'glorious', as I had used it, came from
another social world. The danger of keeping one's eye too
much on the audience is increased when there is a social
gap between the readers and the writer or, more accurately,
between the readers and the writer's material. In this
connexion we could think of the tones of 'silver-spoon'
autobiographies; but I shall stick, because this is my own
experience, to those which a working-class writer often uses
to describe his early life. Again, it is difficult—far more
difficult than most of us want to recognize—to describe a
poor childhood, to avoid dropping into either harshness or
sentimentality. It is particularly easy to create an urban form
of those bucolic, pigs-and-flowers, autobiographies. I learned
to know the danger-points because at those times I could feel
myself going soft whilst writing. If I was tempted, for
instance, to dwell too long on the beauty of the grass growing
between the flagstones, or found myself making too much
of the horses dropping their steaming manure on the cobble-
stones, I took such moments as signals to be tough with
myself again. A working-class writer is tempted—writers from
other classes will have their own kinds of temptation—to be
saying implicitly all the time: "Really, the people I grew
up among were after all wiser and nicer than yours, in spite
of . . ." As I write this, I wonder whether the point is so
obvious as not to need saying. Yet when one hears people discussing this kind of thing, or opens yet another such autobiography, one knows that few people are really aware of
the problem. There is no simple remedy. But at least a
serious autobiographer should try to acquire a better idea
than most have at present of the interrelations between class
and tone of voice. I do not know a contemporary autobiography which sets out to describe, in the sort of depth the
subject warrants (by 'depth' I do not mean solemnity), that
movement between classes which so many of us have made.

Some time ago I had the opportunity to read a number of autobiographical essays written by sixth-form girls in a York-shire L.E.A. grammar school. The essays had been handed in unsigned and were not read by any of their own teachers; so the girls felt freer than in writing a normal school essay. The most striking impression was of authenticity, of experience described in convincing and significant detail; it was an authenticity one does not often find in contemporary autobiographies, however skilful they may otherwise be.

Once again, the reader will not help us. He may, though he wishes to help, actually hinder. Let me again give an instance from my own experience. In trying to write as full and 'open' an account of northern working-class life as I could, I had obviously to say something about sexual habits. With a good deal of effort and as neutrally—plainly, dispassionately —as possible (though making use of what seemed relevant and proper images) I described the sex life of the streets in which I had been brought up. At a certain stage I sent my manuscript to several readers, readers with different backgrounds and different casts of mind. Their reactions were surprising and surprisingly varied.

A literary person of the upper-middle classes (I do not, incidentally, assume that the combination of social background and subsequent training determines each person's reactions . . . but it is relevant) was delighted with the descriptions and asked for more. He mentioned Chaucer and Rabelais and used words like 'earthy' and 'gusto'. I was naturally pleased that he liked the passage, but on reflection decided that this was one pat on the back I could not afford to accept. For I think he was, quite unconsciously, seeking to remove (and so reduce) this description of working-class life to a realm where it was not real, where it became an instance of the archaic-urban-bucolic. And that was not what I meant at all.

A historian had much the same reaction, though he responded with too much enthusiasm to almost any instance of 'fine descriptive writing'. Other reactions were harder to meet. A Marxist objected on the grounds that, whatever my intentions, the effect—since many people want to keep the working classes at arm's-length—would be to allow them even more to discount working-class people since they would now be regarded as sexually 'dirty'. He had a point, though I believe he carried it too far.

Most difficult of all, a generous-minded social historian (who had a considerable knowledge of and interest in working-class organizations), was upset by the passage. He respected working-class people too much to wish to have them put in a glamorous light; he did wish to see them straight. He was a characteristic member of the public-spirited, conscientious but rather prim sector of the middle classes. I imagine he was not much used to reading novels, for if he had read any one of a number of working-class novels, he would have known that what I had written about working-class sexual habits was true. Or perhaps he had read the novels but put them in another part of his mind, marked 'fiction'. Yet this was discursive writing, not so easily to be put away. After he had read this part of the typescript he said: "You know I am interested in working-class history and, in particular, that I try to help working-class people who get into difficulties. But if such people really do act in the way you describe, then I lose a lot of my sympathy. I think this is shocking behaviour, and all your explanations do not help." Here was a peculiar situation. If I had been writing fiction—or even a 'straight' autobiography—I suppose I would have printed the passage as it stood. But this section was part of a discursive book, a book which tried to sustain and carry through a fairly extensive argument. To me, of course, the section in question was not shocking; nor was it intended to shock others. I had long ago removed the bits whose writing I had too much enjoyed. If I had written: "The sexual experience of many working-class people is more direct, nearer the surface, more varied, and begins earlier than that of most middle-class people"—if I had used some such general or abstract terms, I would have caused no alarm.

But here as throughout the book I wanted concrete detail, the closeness which comes from the exact naming of events.

I worried about this problem for some time and finally toned down the passage so as not to distort its place in the whole book. I am still not sure whether I did right. Perhaps, even in a discursive work, one should not so much bother with all this questioning and cross-questioning. Perhaps a good writer will impose his vision, his integrity, his compassion on his readers. But most of us—and this is the point of the story—can gain from being more aware of the risks we run; not so as to amend out of fear, but the better to control our own literary situations.

So far I have talked about problems in autobiography which are connected with the writer's sense of an audience. Now for more direct formal problems: problems of the genie and the bottle. Autobiography is, by definition, self-conscious. It has few, if any, formal rules. It is therefore always in danger of disintegrating, of sinking under its own weight. It needs controls.

This is particularly true of autobiography as we approach it today. We come to autobiography with more intimate and self-conscious intentions than our grandfathers. And we are less sure of assumptions shared with our readers. The major nineteenth-century autobiographies often have an impressive assurance: but these tones are unavailable to us. Here is yet another reason why so many autobiographers are tempted to adopt the tone of a man talking to himself, with extreme sensitivity. The self-awareness of modern autobiography makes it important for an author to find something to take the place of the formal disciplines imposed by the various types of 'creative' literature. He needs controls, against himself and to save himself. A seriously approached autobiography is taxing in a peculiar way. It is a form of mirror-gazing or, to change the metaphor, root-digging. Even if we avoid the obvious coynesses I spoke about in the beginning we feel ourselves, a while after, like that mythological creature which ate its own bowels, endlessly. We begin to feel deeply sick at the parade of our own self—the self so unfinished and ragged, and yet so persistently wanting to present itself as interesting. We have to fight this as much as possible; and it is bound to be a hard fight. Little of value will come if we do not take these risks; honest autobiography exacts a considerable psychic cost.

It would be ludicrous to try to weigh against each other the costs to the author in writing, respectively, a novel or an autobiography. Almost everything will depend on which novel or autobiography and which authors. I am inclined to assume, as would most teachers of literature, that the novel is the harder job—in spite of all I have said so far. Still, I think we can say that in one respect the novelist has an easier time. The novel usually works dramatically, by staging or presenting outside the self. In this sense the novelist is, at least for a start, in a more obviously manageable relationship to his subject and to his readers. Admittedly, this does not take him far. 'Never trust the teller; trust the tale'; the novelist is both there and not there. But he can have—and make good use of, if he has a mind to—a sort of distancing. The autobiographer, unless he finds formal controls (and they easily look contrived or mannered), is always *there*. More: since he is there, he is tempted to engage in special pleading on his own behalf with his readers. It is difficult, too, to get away from the sound of the one insistent voice. It may be the voice of an interesting personality, but it is only one voice. Not only the reader, but the writer, too, would like to alter angles—to stand outside himself like an Olympian narrator, to see himself as others see him, to be—most relieving of all— ironic towards himself from the outside. All these changes are possible in autobiography, but they are harder to manage than we usually realize. Again, I think of the variety of achievement within what we simply call 'the novel', and wish autobiography would stretch itself more. Think, for instance, of the way a good novelist can make you see a scene, a moment in relationships, from several angles at once (all of them 'true')—as comic and sad and ironic. Tolstoy was a master of such scenes. But Tolstoy writing as himself, the autobiographical Tolstoy, could not reach that dispassionate, many sided, objectivity. Fiction has its problems, and I do not want to make artificial contrasts. My point is that there are almost no immediate, ready-to-hand, formal aids in autobiography today; it is hard to switch angles, to use a saving irony towards the self, to alter the texture of the writing. In trying to write an autobiography which seeks to be more than a mild rumination you first and quite soon become heartily tired of yourself, of yourself in the same position.

Still, before we need worry greatly about these larger structural questions we have a great deal to do in trying to find a usable plain tone—not an imitation of an established 'literary' voice, nor one which slides unconsciously across a lot of social assumptions. I say 'unconsciously' because the richness of available social tones is one possible source of strength for a British autobiographer; it makes a stronger texture, and especially an ironic texture, more possible. I would like to find for my own use a voice which could carry a wide range of attitudes and emotions without being socially self-conscious or derivatively literary. Among modern autobiographers I know hardly anyone who has found such a tone, this clarity which seems almost like talking to yourself, since no one is being wooed. Edwin Muir's autobiography has this quality, and about it one can properly use phrases like 'sensitive integrity'. He used his poetic skills here in a disciplined way, not like a man taking time off to doodle; perhaps also he knew more about himself—after facing his psychological disturbances—than most of us; and perhaps his Orcadian upbringing—unliterary and free of the class overtones of most places in Britain—helped. At any rate, his autobiography is both austere and painfully naked in a way that more obviously 'sensitive and intimate' autobiographies are not.

Most of us have not had Muir's striking breaks in experience; nor have we his creative talent. Where, then, do we

186

start? Again, I can speak only for myself. I find myself—at
least with every present beginning—led more and more into
a sort of neutral tone, one washed as free as I can make it of
accidental literary or social overtones. In the end one hopes
to find the real, right tone for one's own personality; until
then, better what may look like no personality at all than any
of the artificial ones. And by a 'neutral' tone I do not mean
that informed, intelligent, decent voice which is so useful a
medium for certain kinds of writing (e.g. critical discussion).
In autobiography it would muffle the mind. The right tone,
for any one writer, will always be difficult to find and probably
always distinctive. Until it is found, one may be forced to
paddle in the shallows of a 'neutral' reporting. As an illustration of the difficulty, listen to this. I would call this unin-
hibitedly honest writing; the writer is anxious not to take
any emotional tricks in describing a scene which must have
tempted him to a great number of tricks. On the other hand
the writing is without character; I doubt if this is how he
feels and thinks about it all, in recollection. There is no
pressure, no sense of a personality meeting its experience,
within the writing:

> Bradshawgate in the town centre was the most popular
> parade of all: on Saturday nights, Sunday afternoons and
> Sunday nights. ('Let's see if we can pick owt up on't Gate.')
> There were two sides, a 'bob' and a 'tanner' side. These
> parades served a very useful purpose in that you had a good
> chance of meeting a girl again, perhaps one you had quar-
> relled with. When you wanted to stop a couple of girls you
> arranged with your pal to watch for the next time they came
> and then blocked their path. This needed some nerve and
> skill and very often you'd miss them altogether. On Satur-
> day nights there were parades round the side and back
> aisles of two cinemas. The Olympia (the 'Lymp') and the
> Runworth ('Rummy'). These were for the 'younger end'
> between the ages of 14 and 17. They were boisterous affairs,
> especially the one at the 'Lymp', and you never got a chance
> of taking home the kind of girl you wanted. It seemed that
> all the noisy lads had all the fun but they got the girls in
> such a mood that they wouldn't go home with anybody.

Harry Crow and I had gone through all this in search of a girl. And we each went home on Saturday and Sunday nights full of misery and frustration.*

This is meant to be a kind of sociological 'reportage'. But I do not think its character is wholly explained on that ground. Had there been a more responsive style available for personal documentary it would have served the author's purposes better than this, which is baffled and held back.

I imagine that George Orwell's discursive style was hammered out in the course of struggles such as I have been describing: that he very much wanted not to use echoes of old literary styles and also wanted to shake off anything suggesting class assumptions (since he was so often writing about working-class people, and was himself middle-class, he had to steer away from a great number of ways of sounding *de haut en bas*). He wanted to sound like a man being hit by experience and putting it down, directly. This may explain the unfashioned or unstructured movement of his paragraphs, the cumulative piling-up of flatly named objects—and also his habit of dropping a word just where it will sound like a slap across the face. These words are usually starkly colloquial, sharply idiomatic; they co-operate with the other qualities of Orwell's style to stop you from reading him in any mutedly 'literary' or intellectually removed way:

> The first sound in the mornings was the clumping of the mill-girls' clogs down the cobbled street. Earlier than that, I suppose, there were factory whistles which I was never awake to hear.
>
> There were generally four of us in the bedroom, and a beastly place it was, with that defiled impermanent look of rooms that are not serving their rightful purpose. Years earlier, the house had been an ordinary dwellinghouse, and when the Brookers had taken it and fitted it out as a tripe-shop and lodging-house, they had inherited some of the more useless pieces of furniture and had never had the energy to remove them. We were therefore sleeping in what was still recognisably a drawing-room. Hanging from the

* *Britain Revisited* by Tom Harrisson. Gollancz.

ceiling there was a heavy glass chandelier on which the
dust was so thick that it was like fur. And covering one wall
there was a huge hideous piece of junk, something between a
sideboard and a hallstand, with lots of carving and little
drawers and strips of looking-glass, and there was a once-
gaudy carpet ringed by the slop-pails of years, and two gilt
chairs with burst seats, and one of those old-fashioned
horsehair armchairs which you slide off when you try to
sit on them. The room had been turned into a bedroom by
thrusting four squalid beds in among this wreckage.*

It is obvious that, except as a first protection against some
of the simpler forms of stylistic self-deception, we do not
want to be 'neutral'. We usually want, as I've already said,
to find a style that bodies out our personality (and, yes, our
background too). So I do, in principle, sympathize with those
writers of the autobiography of sensibility whom I criticized
earlier. They are right to try to express the fullness of personal
feeling. I criticized them because they do not recognize that
to convey these feelings properly requires discipline. I think
I can now reach further into my doubts about such writing.
Listen to this passage, which is typical of many:

Here, too, was the scrubbing of floors and boots, of arms
and necks, of red and white vegetables. Walk in to the morning disorder of this room and all the garden was laid out
dripping on the table. Chopped carrots like copper pennies,
radishes and chives, potatoes dipped and stripped clean from
their coats of mud, the snapping of tight pea pods, long
shells of green pearls, and the tearing of glutinous beans
from their nests of wool.

Grown stealthy, marauding among these preparations,
one nibbled one's way like a rat through roots and leaves.
Peas rolled under the tongue, fresh cold, like solid water;
teeth chewed green peel of apples, acid sharp, and the sweet
white starch of swedes. Beaten away by wet hands gloved
with flour, one returned in a morose and speechless lust.
Slivers of raw pastry, moulded, warm, went down in the
shapes of men and women—heads and arms of unsalted
flesh seasoned with nothing but a dream of cannibalism.

* See also p. 125 of 'George Orwell and *The Road to Wigan Pier*' in this
volume.

Large meals were prepared in this room, cauldrons of
stew for the insatiate hunger of eight.

There is talent in this writing, of course. But it is indulgent, a saturation bombing of the senses, a rhetorical spray
of highlighted images. At bottom it suggests a kind of sentimental excess, like (to use a suitable image) someone who
thrusts heaped plates of uncooked food at a hungry child.

And yet one can see several reasons why a writer is tempted
to use this manner today. If he is not sure of shared background and assumptions he knows at least that we share the
immediate impact of sensuous experience. Here, to contrast
with that last quotation, is Richard Steele:

The first sense of sorrow I ever knew was upon the death
of my father, at which time I was not quite five years of age;
but was rather amazed at what all the house meant, than
possessed with a real understanding why nobody was willing to play with me. I remember I went into the room
where his body lay, and my mother sat weeping alone by
it. I had my battledore in my hand, and fell a-beating the
coffin, and calling Papa; for, I know not how, I had some
slight idea he was locked up there. My mother catched me
in her arms, and, transported beyond all patience of the
silent grief she was before in, she almost smothered me in
her embraces; and told me in a flood of tears, 'Papa could
not hear me, and would play with me no more, for they
were going to put him underground, whence he would never
come to us again.' She was a very beautiful woman, of a noble
spirit, and there was a dignity in her grief amidst all the
wildness of her transport; which, methought, struck me with
an instinct of sorrow, that, before I was sensible of what it
was to grieve, seized my very soul, and made pity the weakness of my heart ever since.

I quote that as an interesting and illuminating contrast,
not nostalgically. Steele is manipulating an available eighteenth-century mood and manner; we must find our own, with
less to lean on than Steele.

I have only rarely found a manner of writing that would
carry the particular way I meet my own experiences. But I

have discovered one or two things about my weaknesses—
and possible strengths. I have found, for instance, that if I
work through the disguising layers—the attractive, cliché dis-
guises—of my own memories I every so often arrive at a perception which seems true. I was once trying to describe the
way my grandmother would tell a story. She had a stark,
monumental, biblical, grand quality, one would have said
at the start—in that froth of adjective and metaphor which
comes first to the surface of the mind. On this occasion I
teased further. I realized after a time that what, more than
any other element in her speech, sounded for me the note
characteristic of her way of speaking and of her life was her
easy use of certain words. They were words so elemental, so
dramatic that I have only rarely heard them used thus since
my grandmother died. In the normal course of the life I and
my colleagues lead one does not speak of 'sorrow' or 'hardship'
or of 'taking the bread from my mouth' in the direct way my
grandmother did. To use these words with her unassuming
seriousness you needed something like her background—the
product of generations of rural and then urban working-
class life, always on the edge of poverty, with few social
services, with ten children born but several dying in childhood of the usual diseases. It was part of your experience as
a mother to walk, with a black shawl round your head,
behind a little coffin by the time you were thirty-five—
probably not once, but several times; or to hear a knock at
the door in the middle of the working day and to open it
and hear one of your husband's mates say 'Thee mester's
bin 'urt'. In these circumstances you used certain words as
though they had been carved out of stone. And then I remembered where I had heard them so used before— in the
Anglo-Saxon poets:

> I can utter a true song about myself . . . how in
> toilsome days I often suffered a time of hardship,
> how I have borne bitter sorrow in my breast.

At this point I knew that I had got near—nearer than ever before—to understanding the central quality of my grandmother's speech.

At another point, I wished to describe the appearance of my mother's face after several years of looking after three young children, on her own with very little money and in a bronchitic condition. Again, many words came into my mind . . . grey, bloodless, matt, lined, and so on. They were unexceptionable but vague and distant; and I had again the irritable feeling that I needed to push through. Then I remembered something particular. I did not invent it; I remembered it: but I only remembered it after working through other possibilities. I remembered that, if I saw my mother's face in a certain light, I saw not only the lines scored into it—but saw that the lines were embedded with fine dirt. It is the kind of thing a child photographs in close-up—unsentimentally, perhaps a little put-off, but with no desire to tone it down. I saw now that those dirt-lines went with a whole way of living, with years of snatching quick washes in cold water, using coarse yellow soap or no soap at all, under the one tap in the back kitchen. This was the face of a woman only just over forty. As I remembered and understood all this I knew it was the detail I wanted—but that I would have to be careful not to over-emphasize it, not to exploit it.

Let me give one other instance—there are only a few of them—again from my grandmother. All these examples are from women; I felt the pressure of remembered emotion most strongly there. At one point there came into my mind a picture of my grandmother, sitting in her rocking-chair at the side of the kitchen fire. She was rocking to and fro; this was a characteristic movement on the few occasions when she had a little time to sit doing nothing except—as she always did on these occasions—stare into the fire. Then I remembered that, if she was really in repose, one hand would gently but quite steadily work from back to front along the arm of her chair, stroking it. It was a rhythmic movement and quite firm; it didn't seem a nervy gesture. It seemed to body out a good deal in her life—a steady going-on-going-on, an even hand and measure such as were needed if you were to make do on little, a firm acceptance of these conditions day after day after day. Some time afterwards I found a similar movement described by Lawrence in *Sons and Lovers*; he no doubt saw it in his mother. He didn't, of course, try to analyse it; he looked at it with that exact attention we give to something we know means more than it seems. It is possible that I had remembered this gesture from an earlier reading of *Sons and Lovers* and transferred it to my own grandmother. But I do not think so; in any event the two movements are not exactly alike.

I learned, in my own efforts, that the first objective was a combination of honesty and patience: honesty, to work through as many as possible of the deceptions; patience, because you can't force anything. In one sense you have to sit down before your experience: it might come up and offer itself to you; it might not. But you can't will it to come up. You can best use your conscious skills in keeping out, in controlling, the phoney qualities.

You are all the time trying to tap the sources where your imagination is strongest. Oddly enough—because I had no idea that this was so before—I found that my strongest gate to experience was the sense of smell. My ears and eyes are undistinguished in their powers; taste and touch are much the same. But I can smell my way down a street so that it comes alive in memory—people, habits, and events with their associations and overtones. Perhaps smell is the easiest, the crudest, of the senses. Or it may be for many of us the sharpest of the senses in childhood. Offhand, I do not think it is given much scope in novels though there are some striking exceptions, such as Proust. Apart from fairly obvious moments—the smell of a meal, the perfume of a woman who is loved and so on—one doesn't often notice the characters reacting by their sense of smell. But if we turn to autobiography we usually find that the sense of smell is predominant, especially in childhood. This passage is typical:

> Inside there was a good smell of spicy cooking, jam-making, chintz, minced meat, musty books, coal fires, flowers—generally chrysanthemums—and mint imperials, which my Granny used to suck 'for her chest'. It was an utterly different smell to the one in our little flat in ——— Street, which was a compound of strong tobacco, wood shavings, boiled onions, floor polish and soot. I loved the sweet, old-maid smell of Granny's house, though I always felt that our own was the only right smell for a house to have. I was peculiarly sensitive to the smell of other people's houses. My Granny Johnson's smelt of snuff and shaving soap and boot polish and Woodbines. Mrs. Battey's smelt of washing and hot girdle scones. But most of the houses in our street had the unmistakeable unforgettable smell of poverty—an airless, stuffy, rancid smell, as if the very air like the tea leaves, had been used over and over again. It was a stale and sour smell of cold, unwashed sheets and bodies, the greasy aroma of pans of vegetable broth, the mustiness of dry crusts, the breath children exhale when they chew dry bread—the very essence of misery.

That is well observed and has some acute touches. It is also one form of that saturation bombing of the senses which I described earlier. The author is luxuriating, wallowing. But, properly controlled, the sense of smell can be one of the major imaginative gateways for autobiographers of childhood.

I have described so far—on this question of 'finding a style'—chiefly problems we meet in our own personalities, in particular temptations towards various kinds of excess. 'Social' problems in finding a style haven't had much attention. When I pick up, say, *A Passage to India* and read the first page, I feel an odd mixture of reactions—admiration for the author's skill; a sense of loss (since even people of Forster's social group could hardly speak to one another with so assured a tone today); and a sense that this kind of tone is not one I could ever have properly acquired:

> Except for the Marabar Caves—and they are twenty miles off—the city of Chandrapore presents nothing extraordinary.

Edged rather than washed by the river Ganges, it trails for
a couple of miles along the bank, scarcely distinguishable
from the rubbish it deposits so freely. There are no bathing-
steps on the river-front, as the Ganges happens not to be
holy here; indeed there is no river-front, and bazaars shut
out the wide and shifting panorama of the stream. The
streets are mean, the temples ineffective, and though a few
fine houses exist they are hidden away in gardens or down
alleys whose filth deters all but the invited guest. Chandrapore was never large or beautiful, but two hundred years
ago it lay on the road between Upper India, then imperial,
and the sea, and the fine houses date from that period. The
zest for decoration stopped in the eighteenth century, nor was
it ever democratic. There is no painting and scarcely any
carving in the bazaars. The very wood seems made of mud,
the inhabitants of mud moving. So abased, so monotonous
is everything that meets the eye, that when the Ganges comes
down it might be expected to wash the excrescence back into
the soil. Houses do fall, people are drowned and left rotting,
but the general outline of the town persists, swelling here,
shrinking there, like some low but indestructible form of
life.

That is plainly an establishing paragraph; it establishes the
setting of the novel. It also begins to establish the tones
within which the novel will be conducted. It has the voice
of a civilized, literate, English middle-class observer of the
early twentieth century. Look, for example, at that refusal
to say flat out that the city of Chandrapore is dull. It says
instead that the city 'presents nothing extraordinary'—a nice
example of the understatement typical of a particular English
social group at a particular time. Or there is what I think of
as a characteristic Cambridge precision in the next sentence,
which begins not with the main clause but with the subordin-
ate clause about the river—it is 'Edged rather than washed by
the river Ganges . . .'—and goes on with quiet irony to describe the river as 'scarcely distinguishable from the rubbish'.
There is a more overt irony immediately after, when we
are told that the river '*happens* not to be holy here'. The
author is having a gentle, outsider's laugh at the fact that so
many natural objects in India have been given religious

meanings. Then Forster gets into his full stride, placing each adjective with the sureness of a man who knows exactly the overtones which his milieu can allow. "The streets are mean," he says, "the temples ineffective." That 'mean' is a well-bred visitor's judgment; the proportions of the streets are skimped, and so they are not aesthetically satisfying. But to call the temples 'ineffective' is even more aesthetic. In what sense are they 'ineffective'? Not as temples, surely, not for their religious purposes. But 'ineffective' to the European visitor who sees them from outside (since their religion is not his religion) but nevertheless is ready to recognize beauty when he sees it; to him they *present themselves* inadequately.

Best of all is the latter half of this same sentence, where Forster tells us that "though a few fine houses exist they are hidden away", and only the 'invited guest' is likely to penetrate so far as to see them. To call them 'fine houses' doesn't mean simply that they are handsome. 'A fine house' also suggests a house in which 'fine living' may be presumed to take place; it carries the style of a class, a class of people who would be likely to have 'invited guests'. One recalls the 'civilized' English middle-classes at the turn of the century, living in their fine country houses or town houses and having at weekends, for good conversation and agreeable pastimes, 'invited guests'. "The zest for decoration," Forster goes on, "stopped in the eighteenth century, nor was it ever democratic." There is a world of meaning in the slightly amused irony of 'zest', and a dry intelligence about the relations between Indian society and its art in that 'democratic'. So one comes to the final sentence with its repetitive ruminative clauses, its quiet rhetoric, its air of being meant to be read, to be savoured reflectively, rather than spoken; "Houses do fall, people are drowned and left rotting, but the general outline of the town persists, swelling here, shrinking there, like some low but indestructible form of life."

It is an extremely assured passage, sure of its own stance before its material, sure of the responses it will draw from its audience. It's undramatic; the movement of its feelings, the way it approaches the experiences with which it is dealing, its obliqueness and quietness, all this is like subtle piano-playing rather than large orchestration.

It is an admirable passage. But, as I've said, I could never write like that. At the most I might manage a pastiche. But it would be dead, miles away from a style which expressed me personally or socially (I do not think the two can be altogether separated). I am not showing an inverted snobbery. Much as I admire the passage above, I know that its movement, the graph of its feelings, the way it approaches its narrative, its timbre, are different from mine. Not better nor worse—different. I would like to learn to score as well as that for my own imaginative instruments. The peculiar pressure of my approach to experience is partly personal to me (as to any of us); but is also in part an inheritance from my background. The movement, the rhythm, of our kind of life does not often get into prose—not in the way that Forster's tone may be said to embody the approach to experience of a whole group. In this sense, it is more difficult to find your style if you are from the working-classes. Almost any ex-working-class writer can produce reasonably lifelike dialogue or remember striking individual words. But you get nowhere by sprinkling 'daft' and 'mucky' in odd places. I have only once or twice and then in very brief passages felt that I was getting into my prose the particular run or rhythm of my own make-up. This is partly, as I have admitted, a problem for any writer at any time, whatever his background. But still the social aspects count—it is easier for certain socially-conditioned manners and tones to express themselves, because so much of our writing has traditionally been expressed in those tones of voice. I remember a peculiar excitement when one day I read the opening of *Sons and Lovers*. I had read it many times before; but this time saw something (or heard something) more in it. At first glance it is not a particularly impressive passage. But I realized on this reading that its movement, its 'kick', its voice, were those of a working-class man who had become articulate and—instead of acquiring

rhythms foreign to his deep-rooted ways of feeling—had kept
the rhetoric of his kind and so (this is the point) could better
say what *he* had to say:

> 'The Bottoms' succeeded to 'Hell Row'. Hell Row was a
> block of thatched, bulging cottages that stood by the brook-
> side on Greenhill Lane. There lived the colliers who worked
> in the little gin-pits two fields away. The brook ran under
> the alder-trees, scarcely soiled by these small mines, whose
> coal was drawn to the surface by donkeys that plodded
> wearily in a circle round a gin. And all over the country-
> side were these same pits, some of which had been worked
> in the time of Charles II, the few colliers and the donkeys
> burrowing down like ants into the earth, making queer
> mounds and little black places among the cornfields and
> the meadows. And the cottages of these coalminers, in blocks
> and in pairs here and there, together with odd farms and
> homes of the stockingers, straying over the parish, formed
> the village of Bestwood.

The moment you hear it, it sounds quite different from the
Forster passage. The words are used differently; sentences
are put together differently; the emotional keyboard is different. To begin with, it is more direct. Look at the brevity of
that first sentence—'The Bottoms' succeeded to 'Hell Row'.
The writing hits you more, has more attack—'Hell Row was
a *block of thatched, bulging cottages*'. It's more dramatic and
demonstrative: '*There* lived the colliers who worked in the
little gin-pits . . .' Emotions seem more plain and exposed,
more in front of you—'whose coal was drawn to the surface by
donkeys that plodded wearily in a circle round a gin'. And
there's the urgency of those 'Ands' used successively to start
sentences—'*And* all over the countryside were these same
pits'; 'And the cottages of these coalminers, in blocks and in
pairs . . .' It doesn't suggest, as Forster's passage does, that
several centuries of civilized intercourse have given a texture, a variety of weight, an obliquity and irony, to the prose.
It sounds less as though it's meant to be read than as though
a man is speaking. It reminds me of the talk I heard as a boy
in an English working-class home. This is how you shape

up to tell a story, it says to my memory. It dives straight into its subject as though it's about to *tell a tale*, with the almost jerky directness of a narrator who lets the shape of his paragraph be decided by the immediacy and urgency of the details as they come to him. For me it recreates something of the peculiar feel of experience as working-class people live it, just as E. M. Forster's prose suggests that of the intelligent middle-class.

I know that this is not a full account of the differences in tone between these two openings. One has to be careful not to ascribe to social causes contrasts which are due to differences in the authors' personalities, or to differences in what they are trying to do within particular novels. Nor am I setting one against the other. I am saying that one would like one's prose to carry one's own rhythms, and that to find them has interesting complications for a writer from the working classes, since most of his models, his often attractive models, come from and come with the tones of other social groups.

Obviously, such an effort is worth making, whatever the kind of writing and whatever one's social origins. In writing autobiography it is particularly worth while. In the degree to which we find our own voice we are less likely to fall into the various traps I have talked about—into false gentility or 'ham' writing, into second-hand 'give-away' rhythms and sentiments, or equally second-hand vicarious toughness. Or even into the deadpan laconic, which is an inhibiting insurance policy against most of the other errors. And that is not good enough; it ignores the graph of feeling, it inhibits the movement of the emotions. I remember being swept off my feet as an adolescent by the portrait of the father in *How Green Was My Valley*, by Richard Llewellyn's readiness to open the organ-stops of Welsh rhetoric to carry that portrait. I seem to remember that it rises to a final invocation which starts like this: 'Men like my father never die . . .'; and this used to move me more than anything else. It was, of course, an easy rhetoric, and like many others I could today resolve it into fairly obvious parts. But I am not ashamed of being moved and I should be sorry if some writing didn't move us as powerfully as that, on occasions. The trouble is that, where we wish to speak of something which moves us deeply, we are now almost always without a style. In the life I knew as a boy—others must speak for themselves—there *was* a dramatic, a melodramatic quality. I wish I could write so that the timbre of that life was carried in my prose.

1961

TEACHING WITH STYLE

(On Bonamy Dobrée)

I SUPPOSE Bonamy Dobrée came to Leeds University in
about 1935. I remember that those of us who were then
sixth-formers in the city's grammar schools and hoping to read
English heard about the rather strange new professor the
University had acquired. I went up in 1936, on a local
scholarship. He must then have been about forty-five.

On the opening days of session, the registration days, the
University ran what used to be called the 'Freshers' Bazaar'.
The Great Hall did look as much as anything like a parish
festival or church bazaar; it is a Victorian Gothic building
and resembles many a big chapel interior in the North. There
were great numbers of society stalls and club stalls; and there
were tables for each department, manned by members of the
academic staff, where you signed on for your Honours or
Subsidiary courses and in your confusion sought whatever
advice was available.

Bonamy Dobrée was presiding at the English table when
I reached it. I remember being struck straight away by his
'style', though I wouldn't have then described it like that.
He was unusually upright and brought to mind all sorts of
words and phrases which were still just in currency then but
now seem dated, such as: 'a military-looking man' who 'bears
himself well'. He had a heavy well-clipped moustache, rather
like those worn by decent majors in films about the 1914 war.
He was slightly tweedy, and smelt of pipe-tobacco.

So far I have made him sound a little too heavy. He also
had a sort of brightness. His hair was quite thick and long
and brushed well back, but already was almost completely
silver. He had a bright, bird-like eye and a quick smile which

he used freely, partly to put you at your ease but also because he did enjoy being with students. To a Leeds youth his voice was the most remarkable thing about him. It was light and high-pitched; and when it rose with enthusiasm took on what one can best call a feminine ring. It was a mannered voice, and in drab Virginia Road—the English department was in a Victorian terrace house there—as exotic as a flamingo. I suppose it was compounded of southern upper-class, Hailey-bury, the regular Army—and then laced with the slightly nasal sing-song characteristic of Cambridge.

I felt he was rather grand, of course, as undergraduates used to feel about professors; for a long time I was immensely impressed by the number of books he owned and had read, by the range of his other affairs and by the brisk speed with which he handled them. So I was fascinated by the whole person or by as much of it as I saw. I do not remember then seeking to imitate him or to be like him, except in some professional particulars; there was a lot in his 'image' which seemed a little dubious to a Yorkshire adolescent. But he was always interesting: he had a sort of style, as I've said. And those qualities were very rarely seen in so elegant a form in Leeds.

I imagine he began to notice me, as a 'promising' student, towards the end of my first year. Somewhere about that time he stopped me and said he wanted a word. By now I have forgotten what it was about, though I seem to remember, and this would be entirely in character, that he wanted to give me advice based on a knowledge of some particular need I was in. I do clearly remember a small circumstance in that meeting because it was the first example of the contrasts in social habits which were to be brought out in our friendship. We had run into each other on the half-landing and after stopping me he said: "Hang on a minute. I must go in here for a pee." I remember a double reaction. First, my respect-able-working-class mind was slightly shocked; then my 'wide' teenager's mind took over and asked: "What's up? Is he trying to show that he's unconventional?"

After the second year had started he began rather more deliberately to pay attention to me, to include me in the cluster who were loosely under his wing. Inevitably, since I was at that point the junior, the other Dobrée protégés seemed grand and suave. There was I. F. Porter who sounded organ-voiced, magisterial and assured. He was said to have London literary and intellectual connections. He left to lecture in a central or eastern European university, and Dobrée kept in touch. I think he eventually came back to join the Foreign Office. There was Kenneth Young, who went into journalism. He seemed both a literary man of affairs and an intellectual maverick. My own favourite was Tom Hodgson, a beautiful and intelligent young man with a sharp and dry but charitable wit. He went to St. John's, Cambridge, to work for a Ph.D., which was never finished. He was killed in the war. I still have some of his Cambridge letters and a small Routledge volume of poems, *This Life, This Death*.

Each year Bonamy Dobrée seemed to pick one or perhaps two students to keep an eye on. We were probably the brightest, in both the good and bad senses of that word. We were intelligent but also likely to be quirky and offbeat, rather than steady and reliable. At our weakest we were bright rather than deep. I think some other members of staff gave an eye to other students according to their interests. Dobrée always had more time for the creatively untidy than for the steadily reliable. Though I must add that I was on the whole a reliably hard worker and not particularly creative; but in general the distinction is true.

This is not to say that he encouraged a sloppy bohemianism, as some members of staff in other departments were said to think. He was almost always something of a disciplinarian. It wasn't only in his carriage that you could still see the marks of the regular officer. He never withheld saying what he thought was the right thing for fear of hurting your feelings. I suppose his principle was that feelings soon recover, but bad advice can affect a lifetime.

It was in this way that he corrected me at the second-year

bazaar day. Standing at the trestle table, I asked to be allowed to read psychology as a new supplementary subject. He may have thought me a promising student but he had a fairly clear sense of my weaknesses. Quite shortly, he refused permission: I needed all my spare time, he said, to develop my English studies. I suppose this implied that I would have spent too much time on an exciting new subject like psychology. The rebuff stung badly and I still feel eighteen when I remember it. I think now that it was good for me to be checked sharply at that point. I was a hubristic hurdler— always halving my hurdles in advance—and he had realized that. "Don't make Aunt Sallies of your enemies," he said later, after listening to one of my tutorial essays. "It's bad intellectually and tactically."

These personal notes seem the best way to bring out the particular nature of Bonamy Dobrée's interest in his group of undergraduates. I do not know if I was a more than usually raw and uncertain character. (I had been an orphan for ten years, living with my grandmother. She died at Christmas in my first year.) I certainly was raw and uncertain—and proud thin-skinned and callow. The combination made for some silly but painful difficulties and seemed to attract Dobrée's charismatic nature. Obviously he had to make most of the going, and he was patient and relaxed enough to be willing to do so.

So I began to see more of him, outside the University. I can best recall the variety of attention he gave, and some of what seem interesting elements in the relationship, by recounting a few incidents: they differ a good deal but all are typical.

One morning at about 8.15 there was a knock on my door. I was then living in a university hostel because of my grandmother's death, and was very hard up. I was still in pyjamas, unshaved and dreary from a late night's reading. Dobrée came in, smelling freshly as usual. He had driven up there, off the road that took him to the University, to tell me that there were hopes of some extra grant, and would I go to see the Registrar's department as soon as possible. I hadn't known that he was doing anything on my behalf.

On another occasion I was being taken by him to the beautiful house he and Valentine, his wife, had built on the Wharfe at Collingham. It was mid-afternoon and we were in his cheap, boxy Ford—an early Anglia, perhaps it was. He stopped before a confectioner's in a narrow street and said he ought to get some cakes, since there would be other visitors at home. "Come in and help me choose," he said. I knew at a glance that this wasn't 'a good shop'. I do not mean that it wasn't a Fortnum & Mason among confectioners; obviously it wasn't. But there are good cheap shops and bad cheap shops, and this was a bad cheap shop. In fact it was a now defunct chain-confectioners, and a member of the respectable poor could tell at a glance that its stuff was 'all show and no body'. Bonamy Dobrée, with a cheerful politeness which dazzled the assistants, bought a garish cake. He carried it out with panache; I tagged along feeling altogether older and unillusioned. Ironically, he liked sometimes to show that he had both feet on the ground, that he knew a hawk from a hand-saw. He used to say, with a touch of pride in his practicality, that he would always buy only the cheapest serviceable car; it was simply a means of getting quickly from here to there. Early in the war he proudly explained how he had learned to save petrol by switching off and disengaging the engine at various points on his way home.

On the afternoon he bought the cake the house seemed full of visitors, though indeed there were often some people there—especially writers and painters. It was all heady and —in small-minded self-defence—one was sometimes tempted to join those who made fun of it as self-conscious salon-making in the North, with a few selected undergraduates being allowed to mix. But he—they—did not *have* to take that kind of trouble with students; the conversation among the people there was intellectually quite tough and honest. I was not used, any more than are most youths with my background, to much intellectual directness or toughness. In my world you tended to sheer away from arguments and especially from abstract argument: partly because you were not used to handling general ideas, but also because such arguments as you did have might end in blows or 'bad blood'.

On Bonamy Dobrée's upper-class intellectual's directness was superimposed a touch of the professional army officer, with a no-nonsense approach and a quick mind. Sometimes a little too quick. Once, just after the war, we were walking down the corridors of the old university building at Leeds. For me it was the first visit since 1940 and by then that seemed a whole generation ago. My nose caught the smell of institutional polish, a smell which would always be associated with walking along those corridors to lectures. I remarked that the smell brought everything back—perhaps a little too nostalgically, for he said smartly: "Mustn't look back, Richard—soon become sentimental." He was right in one sense, of course; but I think he rather too quickly dismissed a bit of experience.

On another occasion I was out at Collingham for dinner, on my own. We had a gin-and-something before the meal. It was probably the first gin I had ever had. Then he said: "Drink up, Richard. Dinner's ready." I drank and put down my glass, leaving—without thought—about half a teaspoonful in the bottom. That is to say, I did not tip back the glass to drain it. Why? I suppose it was a habit. In my district you did not, for instance, drain your tea to the dregs. It was considered more polite to leave a little in the cup bottom. You also reduced the risk of getting tea-leaves in your mouth. More, I suppose this attitude was inspired both by fear of seeming vulgar (we didn't want to look like rough workmen who put their heads back and drain a pint) and by defensive pride (to show that we were not so hard up as to need to drink the *last* drops of anything).

Bonamy Dobrée was not attuned to all this, of course. His proprieties were different. He said at once: "Come, Richard, drink up. Gin costs a lot and is a good drink anyway. Why should we leave any in the bottom of the glass?" It was all said quite directly and with a laugh. But I was a bit disconcerted. I was more disconcerted on another evening. Again, we had just had a before-dinner drink. (This makes it sound like a habit, but in fact the total number of such occasions was not large. He had many other demands on him.) We were standing in the drawing-room, I think. As we rose to go I thoughtlessly put my glass on a shining mahogany table. "Ah, Richard," said Dobrée, "you'll mark the surface." He picked up the glass. There was indeed a rim of gin on the table. He drew out a large clean white handkerchief and carefully wiped it dry.

At this point I suspect that I am overemphasizing the slightly directorial air. But I have almost done with such aspects by now. I've mentioned them because they show best that tension between different notions of conduct and manners which seems so interesting.

To come back to that glass of gin. Of course, Dobrée's attitude—and mine—are not wholly to be explained by our environments. But still they have a social point. In my world the equivalent to the error with the gin would have been, say, putting a cup of hot tea on the polished sideboard. We would no more have drawn a visitor's attention to such a mistake, as we would say, 'than fly'. We would have been too anxious not to embarrass him, as I was embarrassed then (though my embarrassment was increased because I also felt grubby-finger-nail'd again). Even today I could not bring myself to point out such an error to a guest. I would be worried about the table; and I would probably be irritated that he had put down his glass so thoughtlessly as to leave a mark—and even more irritated because I was inhibited from doing anything about it. I might have clumsily run back once he had left the room and wiped the table. But whatever the urgency I would not have spoken to him.

It may be that behind the hesitancy of our kind of working-class people in such a situation there is a gentleness and a quiet delicate anxiety not to hurt another's feelings. On the other hand one can be too nesh and let relationships bog

down in gentle evasions. If a table or sideboard really is likely
to be marked unless something is done quickly it seems a pity
that we can't be direct enough to say so and take the saying.
Obviously each social group respects and stresses certain
attitudes more than others, and I certainly do not want to
set up a pecking order of attitudes by classes. But one thing
I have come to admire, in some upper- or upper-middle-class
training, is this particular kind of directness. I admire it, that
is to say, if it is reasonably tied in with other decencies and
disciplines. I still hate it smboulderingly where it is only
a vestigial, socially acquired habit in people who are otherwise
evasive and inefficient. Then it tends only to be used down-
wards and is boss-classy and enough to make any workman or
clerk feel thoroughly bloody-minded. But I still can't act in
that way myself except in some limited and well-defined situations, such as academic discussions.

A last word on Bonamy Dobrée as a firm teacher of young
people. One day he swept in (the over-used verb fits here)
for one of his weekly lectures, looking very angry indeed.
He then upbraided us because we did not go to the public
lectures which the University occasionally arranged. The
previous evening Sir Ronald Storrs had been talking about
Lawrence's Arabian campaigns. The hall must have been
half empty and Dobrée, looking round, had seen few of his
own undergraduates there. This had really riled him. He
admired men of action; for himself, he tried not to be a
sedentary bookworm; he respected a man of affairs who was
also an intellectual and a soldier. At that stage in the term
his teacher's charity was probably becoming worn, as it does
with all of us. So perhaps he saw us that day as another kind
of man might have seen us for much of the time—as a bunch
of rather pasty, cautious, calculators, as derisive about the celebration of courage as about that of patriotism; main-chancers,
insurers, play-safers. We might laugh at the public schools and
the professional army, but with what justification? Like the
traders in Conrad's *Heart of Darkness* we would not recognize the heights to which men might be called or, for that

matter, the depths to which they might fall. We were Dante's middle range of people, fit neither to be saved nor damned. Not that he said anything like all this, and I do not believe that much of it went through his mind. But I think that something like this was driving him at that moment, and he made no bones about saying how little he thought of us for refusing to put out our imaginative necks so as to feel a more challenging air.

But it was Bonamy Dobrée who—alone or almost alone among the professors—would regularly push into the noisy Union coffee bar to talk with undergraduates. His attitude towards his northern students was obviously a complex one and no doubt it changed a good deal in the twenty odd years he was at Leeds. I knew it intensively only in the earlier years. I think he did recognize some of the peculiar strengths these students can show—a sort of awkward pawky pushing at the truth, a refusal, as he would say in testimonials for people of whom he approved, 'to take anything at second-hand', and especially a refusal to join the 'posh club' of the knowing intelligentsia, a stubborn and unstylish search for the light that would really serve their condition. He saw that kind of thing. But I have the impression that much else in the deeper grain of northern life—good and bad—passed him by. It would probably have needed altogether too much of an effort at that age and across that gap, and in any case he had other preoccupations. But he could sometimes walk across the deep water of those differences simply by pretending that they did not exist—and in one sense, though not in others, they then did not exist.

He did not romanticize the North in the usual cliché-ridden way. He was not one of those southern-trained, ruminatively pipe-smoking professors whose fortune has placed them in northern universities for a quarter of a century, and who have become hammy experts on the wit of the Lancashire man or the dry salty humour of the Geordie. Grey, dirty and damp—physically Leeds is, or used to be, like a large, tough old mongrel whom only the family could love. The contrast with Dobrée's native Channel Islands or with London or Cairo (where he had taught) must have been acute. Yet I don't remember hearing him grumble about being in the North, as one can hear assistant lecturers grumble at length; nor did he speak with nostalgia about Cambridge. He seemed to enjoy being in Leeds, to feel challenged and determined to put his best into it.

One side of him, slightly romantically, saw himself bringing a little more sweetness and light to the benighted North. And he did have, as I have said more than once, a certain style; he was more colourful than most Leeds professors, and more cosmopolitan. He was particularly fluent in French and belonged to that intensely Francophile generation which came to maturity just before the First World War. My own generation is not, as older people sometimes say, Francophobe and resentfully insular. But we think some British provincial strengths have been underestimated; in our day France has not given the best of democratic examples; and when we look outward we tend to be especially interested in the United States, as a country whose virtues we discovered for ourselves when most of our teachers were still ritualistically talking about 'Coca Cola civilization'.

If Leeds seemed drab to Dobrée, he naturally seemed strange to Leeds. The *Yorkshire Post* knew it could usually get a quotable reaction from him on North v. South issues, and he in his turn enjoyed giving them a good run for their money. I remember one minor newspaper storm when he refused to pay his dues to one of the great Yorkshire gods. We talked too much about the splendours of roast beef and Yorkshire pudding, he said; there *were* other good dishes but Yorkshire seemed hardly to have heard of them.

He liked (again, one is inclined to use rather Edwardian phrases) to cut a bit of a dash, to shock the bourgeoisie. Among his many ancestors one of the most obvious was Lytton Strachey. He liked to be a little odd and uncustomary. I came in to his room one day and found him smoking as usual over his work. The smell was strange, though, like something

wafted over damp meadows in autumn. "Get out your pipe,"
he said, "have a fill." It was herbal mixture—'bucketful for
half a crown, you know'—mixed with his Dobie's Four
Square. He was pleased at both the discovery and the economy. I do not know how long he smoked the mixture, but I
used it for years afterwards.

Or he could be frivolous and boyish, especially when he
was anxious to shake someone out of 'stuffiness'. 'Stuffy' was
one of the most potent words in his dictionary of dislikes.
Our students' English Society 'socials' usually brought this
side out. We had at those times no visiting speaker. We tended to sit or bump around, uneasy because we were out of
the context within which we had grown used to one another
—that of a competitive Honours group or 'year'. At such a
party Dobrée once, sitting between two particularly phleg-
matic girls, ate a high tea backwards (from 'sweet' to 'savoury')
because it was 'less dull, more interesting you know'. On
another occasion he came in, in evening dress, when the
social had reached the party-game stage. He had been to an
official dinner at the University. We were then playing—at
this stage we always seemed to be playing them—literary
games. He didn't at all like that kind of shop talk. Within
minutes he was introducing us to some particularly complicated party game. Two or three of us brooded irritably; who
did he think he was anyway, jollying people along; we would
work our own way through our own awkwardness; this wasn't
a Duke of York's camp for clean-nosed apprentices.

He enjoyed a fight, and could be mischievous at times. I
have seen him running downstairs on his way to Senate smiling broadly in the expectation of a battle. I knew little except from hearsay about his part in the inevitable larger
struggles within the University. I knew about more marginal
matters, such as his support for the famous but controversial
Eric Gill relief, or his continuous barrage about the badness
of university food, or his fights to get some decent contemporary pictures for the University or to save as many trees as
possible in the massive rebuilding. But I have heard that

he was regarded as a nuisance by some on Senate, and probably they had some justification for feeling like that. I expect that some felt—again not altogether without grounds—that he could be dashingly unwise; and that he made them feel like stolid, inhibited, stiff-necked provincials. But the fair-minded would also recognize that he was never contentious in a mean way and never a calculator.

The same vivacity informed his lectures. They were exciting and stimulating rather than comprehensive or exhaustive. He deliberately moved across the formal boundaries of specialisms. He laced his lectures with side-comments, odd *aperçus* from other disciplines, sudden changes of level, irruptions into contemporary affairs. I can trace the origins of some of my own less formal literary-and-social interests to incidental comments he threw out—on Faulkner and violence in literature, for instance.

He was, and still is, an immensely hard worker. But he would have regarded it as a weakness to complain or even to show the effects markedly. You should carry your load lightly; after all, you have made your own choices. But to get through all he got through—and pay dues to the personal values and teacher's values he respected—he must have imposed a hard discipline on himself, in distinguishing the light-hearted which deserves time from the trivial which wastes it, and in distinguishing solid work which demands steady application from the merely drudging.

When I was a student he was in what could be called his early prime, and at that time was producing—heaven knows how—about two books a year They varied in depth, and in subject ranged 'dangerously' widely. But they all bore witness to his dream of literature. I need to stress this because, inevitably, some people called him a butterfly. He had some butterfly qualities, it is true; but butterflies are bright so we ought to be glad to see them more often in universities. Yet at bottom his manner and his range were fed from deeper sources than that tag implies.

We all have our images of what we admire and would like

to aspire to. Bonamy Dobrée had a dream of 'the man of letters'—a widely read man, a good scholar who yet wore his scholarship easily (but anyone who has seen him at work on a thesis or a manuscript will think twice before they talk lightly of butterflies; he is a stickler for detail, very well informed, pertinacious and severe). But still his ideal man of letters will carry his scholarship well, will not be borne down by it. He won't be musty or dusty, not one of the "bald heads forgetful of their sins/Old, learned, respectable bald heads". He will have one foot always in the foul rag-and-bone shop of the heart, or at least in the untidy garrets where literature is often written. In his school of English he stressed less the steady grind of historical or textual scholarship (though these had their due) than the sense that literature came out of living men who put their hopes and pain into the making and the meaning of it. So, among those he presented for Honorary Degrees were: T. S. Eliot, Edwin Muir, Wyndham Lewis, Edith Sitwell, Storm Jameson and Henry Moore. This attitude too, I suspect, decided which students he took special care of, why he would prop up an unstable poet before patting a steady worker's back, seek out the surprising impressionist before the reliable or predictable. As a result he occasionally enlisted very odd characters for his department—whether staff or students—as well as for his friends. But the special quality of the Leeds school was that you never lost the feeling that the study of literature was different in kind from the study of most other academic subjects. Literature had its history and its scholarship, yes; but its raw material was alive, was made out of the stresses of individual lives . . . lives not necessarily ordered or respectable or earnest.

I have stressed throughout that my undergraduate relations with Bonamy Dobrée had a number of subterranean cross-currents (he told me later that he had been, and is, much less aware of them than I am). So this is a peculiarly subjective essay and may tell more about its author than its subject, though I have tried not to let that happen. But, partly as a result of these cross-currents, I was always a little inhibited with him. He may have felt this underneath. Or perhaps he decided that I had more the caution of a critical than the dash of a creative mind. At any rate he unbuttoned himself more, dropped the stance of the teacher more, with those who had more of a flair or who approached him more uncomplicatedly. I remember a much younger protégé telling me that Dobrée, when they were washing-up in the kitchen at Collingham one night, had run over his life and achievement very frankly and ended by saying: "But, you see, I have to recognize that my mind isn't absolutely of the first class." I was touched to hear again the voice of the old straight teacher, but also slightly hurt (and ashamed) that he had never in my own early acquaintance with him been so frank, been able so to relax his role.

This is a crablike movement to a conclusion. Before I try to sum it all up I want to mention two qualities which were more quietly exercised than others but were important parts of the whole texture. He was extremely courteous, and careful not to give offence where he felt someone needed special care or wasn't strong enough to take direct contradiction. In his courtesy towards women he was slightly old-fashioned, even slightly gallant. I suppose he had lived for most of the years up to his early manhood in a predominantly male society (as I had lived in the woman-centred living-room of a working-class home). So I was particularly struck by the formality and attentiveness of his courtesy towards women. I remember once that my wife (as she is now) and I were walking with him in his garden. I grew very interested in the conversation and Mary fell back for a moment, perhaps to look at some flowers. I knew she had fallen back but kept on walking—partly because I was very interested and partly because I simply expected her to catch up. Dobrée cut straight across my talk and, slightly quirky, said: "Shall we wait for Mary?"

Second, there were the simple kindnesses; kindnesses which had no show about them, which went well beyond the line

of duty or normal acquaintanceship, and implied a good deal
of steady and precise thought. They were—and I hardly expected ever to apply these lines in earnest—"little, nameless,
unremembered acts/Of kindness and of love". Many young
writers waiting for a commission knew he was always good for
five pounds. I do not suppose anyone could trace the ramifications of all this help. I can mention some of his particular
kindnesses towards me, from quite small to large ones. On
our degree day, when T. S. Eliot was given an honorary
degree, he took care to tell Eliot a little about me and steer
him across to meet me since I was more than usually interested in Eliot's work. After we had both joined the Army he
sent me some good khaki socks, saying he had more than he
needed and knew that recruits in basic training were never
flush.

Earlier, in fact in my third year, he said suddenly one day:
"Richard, I want you to go down to the *Yorkshire Post* offices
at eleven tomorrow morning. I've arranged for you to have an
interview with Arthur Mann." Mann was the formidable
editor of the *Post* at that time. Dobrée had, of course, acted
autocratically in deciding that I might make a good journalist,
and in arranging the interview without asking me. I reacted
true to type, by being a little put out but not saying so. But
I was put out less because he had acted without speaking to
me than because he had decided that I would make a journalist (even though on a good paper). Starry-eyed about the
academic life, I was hurt that he had not thought of me as—
and only as—a fit candidate for its ranks.

Last of these instances: just before the Easter of my Finals
year he happened to be sitting next to the Director of Education for Leeds at a public dinner. He knew that the Director,
an idiosyncratic man, had given me an impromptu £30 nearly
two years before so that I could go abroad for the first time.
They spoke of me and Dobrée said that I had a good chance
of getting a First a couple of months later. But I was over-
strained and needed a break. There was no money for a
holiday. Wouldn't this be a good opportunity for the Director

to repeat his earlier inspired kindness? Dobrée called me in a day or so later and told me with a typical mixture of warmth, briskness and perkiness—he really loved to bring rabbits out of a hat—that the money would be there if I would go straight away to the Education Offices near the Town Hall. I spent Easter in Venice.

He was, it is plain, in many respects a substitute father for me, at a difficult time. But he kept the relationship taut, well-brushed and not indulgent. And this I liked too: here working-class nonconformist attitudes chimed in with those of an upper-middle-class professional and military man. But I am, again, too quickly making the social point to the neglect of the personal. Others with his background would not necessarily have acted as he did. In spite of all I have said, the basis of our friendship was affection for each other as individuals; and in my case a great respect for him, a respect which overrode considerations of social class. He showed me in action (though I don't claim to have learned them all) qualities such as these: hard work and thoroughness, a detailed attention to whatever job was in hand; a complex teacher's care; a touch of the happy warrior, an attack and gaiety; a disinclination to calculate and a refusal to sentimentalize, a kind of stiff dignity, courtesy and magnanimity.

All these have been brought out in the long and severe illness of his wife, Valentine, which has overshadowed the years of their retirement (and which she has borne with a similar courage and grace). The last time I saw them at Blackheath was in an interval between two of her painful operations. She had insisted that they get a leg of lamb, and stayed up for a while. We talked over the meal, very straight and relaxed, and later he took me to the nearest tube and—now with an openness not snagged by little unknown eddies—we talked of his work and his life in retirement. As the train moved off, he gave his familiar radiant smile, and I remembered with sudden force Yeats's line about 'gaiety transfiguring all that dread'. So I salute him more strongly than ever now, understanding much better the puzzling interactions which used to go on in our relationship, still full of respect for him as a great teacher; but, overwhelmingly, feeling love for the man.

1964

TEACHING LITERATURE
TO ADULTS

English Studies in Extra-Mural Education

THE long courses in English arranged by university extra-mural departments may vary in length from one session of twenty-four weekly meetings, each of two hours, to the tutorial class of three such sessions; they may be taken by full or part-time tutors; and they require guided reading and regular written work from their students. The tutor has an unusual degree of freedom in planning: he must have regard for his students' interests, but has to meet no examination requirements, and the regulations on minimum numbers need cause little anxiety. Many courses are carried out in conjunction with the Workers' Educational Association, whose traditions importantly affect their character.

Speaking roughly, we may say that in the late nineteenth century the impulse to attend adult education classes was, for many students, that kind of moral purposefulness which had established Nonconformity and the Labour Movement. The demand was predominantly for 'education for social pur-pose', by which was meant something simple and recogniz-able . . . education which equipped a man to take his place as a citizen of a democratic community, and, usually, to work for the good of his social class. The students came because they saw the problems before them and wanted equipment to tackle those problems. Today it would be truer to say that many come because they feel morally and politi-cally confused.

Of course, individuals join such a group for a variety of reasons. Some may come for further professional training, some because they think that the sign of a 'cultured person' is the ability to talk about books, some because they suspect they can gain from reading a pleasure they are at present denied. But probably the most important reason, common to almost all who stay after the first month (however hidden this may be from the student himself), is that each of them is in some way dissatisfied with the terms of his life, and seeks a basis for criticism and perhaps for action. He feels that literature will speak to his condition. Further, the good class can become a community of a kind rare today and of great importance to its members. It is for these reasons that the student is prepared to submit to the considerable demands of attendance.

All this throws a heavy initial burden on the tutor. He can assume nothing, but must examine the ground on which he stands in relation to his subject and his class. Why does he think the teaching of literature to adults valuable? Has it, indeed, anything to say to their condition? What dangers does he invite if he becomes too conscious of that aspect of his work? What duties does he shirk if he ignores it?

The dangers are numerous. He is tempted to present his subject in a manner decided by the students' unspoken demands. In working for voluntary bodies conscious of social purpose, the literature tutor can suffer from a feeling of guilt about his subject. He may find it easy to counter the students' inclination to study only the social reformers of literature; he will find it less easy to avoid constantly searching himself for some grim purpose to serve as a certificate of study-worthiness for an activity sometimes labelled—and the implications are heavily pejorative—'dilettante'.

Again, he has the difficult task of trying to establish the right relationship with his group, and with each individual in it; and those relationships will be peculiarly intimate. He has to accept this as a characteristic of the work, whilst resisting the temptation to set up as a lay priest or psycho-therapist. There are many bad kinds of intimate relationship; to find a good one demands tact and humility. The best safeguard is the disciplined study of the subject, with the shared assumption that that discipline is salutary and has to be obeyed.

With all these considerations in mind what may we reasonably hope to achieve? Clearly, methods of presentation need thought, though one can become clumsy through thinking too much about them; the best 'technical equipment' is a well-grounded scholarship in and an enthusiasm for the subject. But adult students are so easily over-impressed, so much readier to be humble before the tutor than before the work, that we may slip into thinking that all is going well when little of importance is being achieved. We may begin, for example, by giving bright and informative lectures about lots of books . . . lectures which are enjoyed but form a barrier between the books and the students.

We soon learn that the adult class is really a seminar, and that the lecture figures in it only rarely. We have not so much to give something as to make certain things happen; we have to learn not so much what information to provide as what questions to ask, questions which will set off thought and stir sensibility in the students. The answers are usually there, inside the individual members of the group, if we find the best way of eliciting them. We have to connect with the students' experience, to translate into terms they can recognize. We need always to seek parallels, analogies, helpful correlations. If we do, we discover that many of our students are in some ways better equipped by nature than we are.

The more particular aim is to help the students to read better, to increase their 'comprehension', to give them the elements of that 'discipline of intelligence and sensibility' which literature offers. Most adult students, like most other people, read too much, too bittily and too quickly; they have no gears in their reading. Many of them make a thin response because they give little body—in terms of tone, manner, emotion, and so on—to their eye-reading; their inner ear is almost dead. They need to hear literature read well, and to practise reading it aloud. They have a narrow range of response . . . they like Romantic poetry but dismiss Cowper as 'artificial'; they find irony unserious and 'wit' unpoetic.

Since they are anxious to reach moral judgments, those judgments are often based on inadequate evidence; they tend to reach conclusions about a book before they have understood what the author is trying to say.

Still, we cannot ignore the students' assumption that literature is concerned with the moral life, simply because they have a narrow view of the nature of that concern, and perhaps associate it with the writing of novels exposing social evils. Their predilections may affect literary study in the wrong way, so that meetings on Hopkins' poetry are wasted in discussing the nature of the Jesuit order or the validity of conversions to Roman Catholicism. Yet we would be wrong if we implied, when we are keeping our eyes closely on the text, that the text is an end in itself, and that the discussion of moral and metaphysical questions is, not simply out of place in a literature seminar and beyond our professional competence, but irrelevant altogether; that the search for significance and order which lies behind great writing does not matter. It is sometimes useful to raise such issues through planned exercises. I have used parallel passages from William Faulkner's *Sanctuary* and James Hadley Chase's *No Orchids for Miss Blandish* to lead to an examination, through the texture of the writing, of the difference in scope of the imaginations behind them.

The actual procedure used in classes has in recent years been much influenced by the principles of the 'practical criticism' and 'Scrutiny' schools, as they have been expressed in a teaching method by a number of writers. This is not surprising. In part we are grateful for something resembling rigorous method in a subject so amorphous and so often attacked as a 'soft option'. More importantly, we now see how, in detailed class work, we may move towards our main object of teaching the students to read; we know better how to keep literary matters central and how to establish connections between literature and 'the consciousness of the age', and literature and 'values'.

The limitations of the method call for care by the tutor, as

SPEAKING TO EACH OTHER

I. A. Richards demonstrates in a chapter of *Interpretation in Teaching* (where he examines an analysis by E. G. Biaggini), and as Roy Meldrum stresses in the introductory chapter to *An English Technique*, where he says: "In the effort to get a really scientific response, free from sentimental prejudices, from stock responses and so on, the result may quite easily be that there will be no genuine emotional response at all, or that the mood for the appreciation of one poem may be much more difficult to feel under (certain) selected conditions than the mood for the other. If that is so, the judgment given will come most conveniently from an intellectual response, a conscious gymnastic, a solemn exercise in an unreal balance-room." On the tutor's side there can easily be a self-righteous sense of speaking for 'the minority', which is an unsuitable frame of mind to approach the special problems of adult students. It is fairly easy to assume that someone else has 'thoroughly dulled responses'. But our students' response to experience is usually richer and more courageous than we suspect. We should base our work on this, should aim more at encouraging and developing what is already there, instead of behaving like an anti-tetanus team in a primitive community.

In what is sometimes called 'pre-literary analysis' especially (the analysis of advertisements, newspaper leaders, public speeches, and so on), we run the risk of not giving the students a fair chance, of unnecessarily hurting or embarrassing them, and of encouraging the 'debunking spirit', the 'spirit that denies'. In proscribing sentimentality we may inhibit sincere emotion; one would prefer some spilling over of emotion to the sour 'knowingness' which can be induced.

The dangers arise from the temptations this approach offers to the uncertain and conscientious to use it as a system for the training of taste. The same half-dozen or so novels are named again and again in syllabuses. Young tutors can obtain double satisfaction—pride in being among the elect, and a sense of security in not going outside the established canon. We have both to 'awaken sensibility' and 'train discrimination', and those are two aspects of one problem. If we rely too much on the kind of comparative exercise I have criticized we will emphasize the latter at the expense of the former, and the discrimination created may be narrow and mean.

In any one session our main aim should be to persuade each student to read a number of whole works, to guide him to as full and legitimate an understanding of them as he can reach. The greater part of each year's course should be spent on the study of these few carefully-chosen texts. One of the signs of an improving class is the slowing of its pace from year to year. Not all works are suitable for intensive study of this kind but there are enough for our purposes. The students read the set work several times at home, probably following lines suggested by the tutor after the first reading. Then we move through the text in class, altering speed for different sections, spending most time over crucial passages, passages which reveal important points about the way words work for this author, and making sure that the students acquire some understanding of the organization of the whole work. General critical issues are only discussed as they arise from an actual problem in reading. Similarly, various forms of critical exercise (comparisons, variants and so on) are introduced only as the need for them appears in the reading. To be able to produce a relevant illustration at almost any time requires a large stock of examples, but that is not difficult to build up.

One proceeds, so far as possible, by question and answer; one has to envisage beforehand the main lines on which the discussion is likely to run, and yet be flexible enough to alter the plan if more urgent issues arise; and one hasn't to be afraid of an occasional vacuum and so speak too quickly or often. The speed of reading varies with each class, but in general four to six tests are sufficient for a year's work (counting several representative poems by one author as a text). One expects to spend four to six weeks over a novel, much longer over a tragedy by Shakespeare. For wider reading a subsidiary list of recommended books is added to the syllabus.

I find the process easiest with poems, hardest with plays. The reasons for this are probably partly personal, but clearly a poem is more easily treated in this way than a novel or play. But again, the most rewarding material, my present experience suggests, is a group of Shakespeare's plays, which raise most of the important literary questions, and can form a good base from which to consider some of the central points about the relation of literature to society and to belief.

If a group of miscellaneous texts from one period is chosen for a year's syllabus the detailed study can be interspersed with discursive and correlative lectures relating the texts to their literary and intellectual background. This is neither to give an 'outline' nor to present 'literature as social history', but to go as far as a single tutor usually can in that work of synthesis among the humane studies for which literature is particularly well fitted. Correlative lectures need to be prepared with special care, if they are to be seminal and intelligible, as well as sound.

Supporting all this is the students' written work, in which the production of formal essays plays a part, though not necessarily the primary one. These may be 'creative exercises', designed to encourage the student's response by setting him some of the problems every writer has to meet: reviewing, or criticizing reviews of a book they have read; and the presentation of papers to the group after some research, however small. Written exercises have to be graded in accordance with differences in intellectual ability or educational background; they have to be marked with unusual care (since a student places great importance on what he has produced, often under difficulties), discussed in class, and followed by private suggestions for practice and further reading.

To sum up—we have to be thinking all the time of ways to encourage in our students a more active and discriminating sympathy. The procedure need not be grim or falsely emotional. It should have the excitement which arises naturally from the study of an exciting subject. The same points will have to be made again and again in different ways. There are many students on whom we will have, after years, no apparent effect; there are some for whom we will be a guide and stimulus. But this is true of internal university students too. On the external side we are lucky, since there are no examinations and prescribed syllabuses, to have towards our students no official duties other than those of teaching our subject in the way which seems best suited to it, and to their needs.

1951

Poetry and Adult Classes

The most interesting and important influence on our work, as extra-mural tutors of literature, is our students' expectations. In so far as they have a common aim our students join classes because they are in some way questioning their lives and the lives around them. Maybe they choose literature rather than philosophy or psychology because literature embodies this questioning concretely and in particulars, rather than abstractly and in generalizations. Perhaps the literature class draws those who have become suspicious of the larger abstractions, who feel that literature will speak to them better than more generalizing disciplines, because it is still dealing manifestly with the life they live as individuals, the life in which they make love, quarrel, eat and sleep.

Whatever its origins, this direct moral interest in literature is probably the most important cause of bad reading. New students tend to look for statements in literature, for a kind of discourse, a manner of approach to experience, which is not peculiarly nor most importantly that of a creative writer. They often prefer fiction to poetry, and of fiction the more discursive kinds, such as Wells and Huxley. This suggests that they are unlikely to be able really to read fiction. How much less can they read poetry, since it demands a 'vertical' reading that is more difficult than the 'horizontal' reading which sometimes appears adequate for fiction?

A common error is therefore that of confusing what a poem may be taken to state with what it really 'is'. Agreement with the apparent statement leads to the judgment 'This is a good poem', and vice versa. 'I like this poem; I like the sentiment,' has its counterpart in, 'I think this is a bad poem; the writer has a depressing view of life.'

There are many wrong ways of meeting this situation, and we may be tempted to try them all in turn. The questions themselves are often badly phrased. But to ask . . . What does this mean to me? What does it say about life? is to ask important questions. We have to ensure that, whilst insisting on the study of literature rather than the discussion of ideas, we are not led to suggest that there is no relation between our students' moral preoccupations and the experience of literature. Our duty as specialists in a single subject is to meet these questions only as they arise from the discipline of the subject. What does it *properly* mean to *them*? This involves trying to know the students well enough to be able to go back to their points of departure; it involves also learning to teach our subject as literature, that is, learning to satisfy in the right way our students' sense of literature's concern with the quality of living. There will always be a tension, but it should be fruitful.

We may do our best never to say more than is relevant, but we know that before long we are probing into moral assumptions, that the judgment of language is a judgment of attitudes, that the words cannot be separated from the outlook of the personality using the words. To appreciate a certain poem requires our students, we find, to examine attitudes they have hitherto taken for granted, have acquired from the atmosphere of time. We do not ask directly, "Do *you* approve of this," or "Isn't it surprising that you assume this today?" But simply trying to appreciate the poem, trying to look at experience in the way the poet has done, involves a temporary withdrawal from the climate in which

226

they have so far unself-consciously drawn their breath. The experience will be important; it may be the students' first experience of looking from outside at the conventional background of their age.

If we study, for example, some poems on death from different centuries up to the present we are soon deeply engaged. In an age in which we 'lay to rest' rather than 'bury', in which we 'go to sleep in a garden' instead of being 'cold in the earth', in which the worms are hidden—at least for the brief public ceremony—by artificial grass mats . . . in such an age Christina Rossetti may still be approved but Shakespeare, who talks about worms and being 'compounded with clay', is likely to be thought 'morbid', 'unhealthy' and 'unnatural'.

So the case for a predominantly intensive approach is strong. Add that our students are with us for only two hours a week for twenty-four weeks in a year, and probably for no more than three years in all, and that as readers most of them are too extensive when they join a class—and the case for intensive work becomes overwhelming. To have only one reading-speed, and that a fast one, is to be ill-equipped. In our short courses it is essential that we try to develop other speeds. The primary need is for slow reading that is thoughtful and sensitive.

Our aims are to increase range and depth in reading, though the two cannot be separated in reality. I say 'increase' because I assume that the capacity to respond to language is possessed by practically everybody, no matter in what degree. There may very well be a small proportion of people who are to poetry what the tone-deaf are to music. I remember one student saying of the phrase 'the surly sullen bell' that he could not 'see' it at all; you just could not call a bell either 'surly' or 'sullen'. Another had never, so far as I could discover, responded to rhythm or sound or the less obvious kinds of suggestion; a line like 'Cover her face; mine eyes dazzle; she died young' was to him—he said—simply three staccato injunctions. But such people are rare, and for practical purposes we can assume that they do not come to literature classes.

In trying to increase our students' range we are more often than not trying to persuade them to entertain types of poetry other than the overtly moralizing or romantic. Many of them are unconscious romantics; they think they know just what attitudes and subjects are proper to poetry, and what not. They expect the direct expression of emotion, the cry from the heart—'my heart leaps up' or 'And then my heart with pleasure fills'; they expect to find joy about the accepted joyous things and sorrow about the accepted unhappy things. Hence the frequent use in early exercises of the epithet 'sincere'; 'I like this poem; the poet seems to me sincere' often means that the poet has not roused mistrust by being oblique, that is, witty, satiric, or ironic. Pope therefore is difficult; there are parts of him we can introduce with little trouble, but 'The Rape of the Lock' would have to be very carefully led into.

Conventions are often suspect. Elizabethan sonnets, because they obey firm conventions of form and manner, are likely to be thought insincere. Even more, the conventions of a whole age may be mistrusted. The quiet, public deployment of moral abstractions by an eighteenth-century poet seems hypocritical. Cowper's easy traffic in such phrases as 'dear eyes', 'filial grief', 'the perishing pleasures of man', 'a frail memorial, but sincere', 'constant flow of love', sounds artificial. Any man who uses words of that sort so easily must be phoney—as he probably would be today.

Comparisons such as these are not best used at the beginning of a course. Better to begin with several good poems on a common theme from the same period. In teasing out the individual qualities of each, with the emphasis scarcely at all on comparative value, the students should soon see behind similarity of subject to differences in tone, purpose and way of using language.

By increasing depth in reading I mean what I called trying to help students to read 'vertically' instead of simply 'horizontally'. There is, we have seen, a direct relationship between their emphasis on what the poem seems to state and their almost entirely 'horizontal' reading, their reading for the 'straight' prose meaning. Subsumed in this attitude is the view that the things done with language in poetry are decorative, not constitutive. Poetry is prose dressed up. Students find it hard to realize that what the poem is, is not something which can be abstracted from the whole, from these words in this order, or to appreciate that form and language, used in this way, embody a greater intensity and immediacy of experience than prose can achieve without itself tending to become poetry.

The various drafts of a poem may be compared so that the students come to see that the poem is what it is because in the end a certain form of words was used. Or words can be omitted from a passage of poetry and the students asked to replace them, and then to compare their results with the original: or there are 'creative exercises', by which students find images, and other kinds of phrase, to express some experience they have all had, and then compare their results in class, probably with the tutor holding a good example in hand, in case no one has much success. I find that usually at least one excellent image is produced on each occasion— 'a mouse's ear' to describe a dried lupin pod, by a student who was otherwise almost entirely silent, is only one of many. Or there are many ways of illustrating the relationships between form and subject. And as the class progresses we may compare, say, Ben Jonson's and Shakespeare's blank verse (though this would be likely to take place only in the course of a study of their drama), and arrive at some sense of the way different imaginations make use of the same line. Or we may study for a number of weeks the development of one of those poets who shows with special clarity the constant interaction between a changing response to experience and a changing manner of expressing it. Yeats is particularly valuable here. General points (e.g. the symbol; ambiguity, etc.) can be broached as they arise from particular problems in reading. Once they do arise it hardly matters how much time discussion of them takes, so long as it remains pointed.

The following notes on the actual conduct of the class are rough generalizations drawn from one tutor's experience. If they sound mandatory that is because they are injunctions to myself. They are not a statement of what I always manage to do, or of what I think others should do, but are what have occurred to me as useful rules-of-thumb.

Choosing the Right Time

We should not raise questions for which the group is not ready; if the students have not 'come to where the words are valid' they will not understand and may be hurt. We must go as far as we can on the capital of goodwill, sympathy and understanding already accumulated; if we go too far we will frighten and inhibit. This applies particularly to the temptation to 'debunk'. 'Debunking' may brace at the right time; at the wrong time it will make the students think they are being 'got at'. I remember enjoying too much a discussion on Eliza Cook's 'The Old Arm Chair'; the students were not able at that stage to separate agreement with the apparent statement from judgement on the poem itself, and were sure I was laughing at 'simple but sincere love of mother'.

Condemning for the Right Reasons, and Basing Condemnation on Literary Judgments

Our generation seems to reserve its 'debunking' for the 'debunking' of sentimentality, of overdone emotion. It might be better—it is just as useful an exercise, and one less likely to trouble the students in the wrong way—to examine clever and cynical writing instead.

'Base condemnation on literary judgments'—on the way the words work, on the flatness of the images, the second-hand quality of the phrasing, the lingering over rhythms for their own sake, and so on.

Whilst bearing in mind the warning about gentleness and caution we should be ready, if really necessary, to give the hard word. But nearly always it will be best just to leave the matter. We may appear to have proved our point rationally, but will not have touched the emotional barriers underneath; no one will be moved until he is ready. The process is finally one of agreement on values: "This has been looked at as thoroughly as we are able; it is now clear that it tends towards this or this (which is good/bad). You agree?" They may or may not; they may want to go away and think. There is a point at which we can't do any more.

Starting with the Best

It is important to begin with fine single poems, in which many good qualities are to be discovered, and to leave until later comparison with the bad. It gives the students something to fall back on when we come to the point at which a cherished poem or attitude is likely to be undermined.

Comparisons of all kinds are invaluable. The good-versus-bad kind I use with a lot of caution today, usually only introducing one where it seems likely to be useful during the sustained study of a major writer.

Having a Working Group Rather Than a Class Meeting

We should aim at the atmosphere of a seminar; wherever possible the students should be grouped round a table with their notebooks and texts.

They should have known for some time what poem is to be studied, and the week before it should have been specifically introduced . . . some pointers given (not to 'fix' an interpretation but to prompt useful personal enquiry), and incidental hindrances to their private reading removed, e.g. some of the background to 'Easter 1916' would be given so that students did not worry unduly about, say, who it was that 'rode his wingèd horse'.

Some further introductory remarks will probably be needed at the beginning of the evening, so as to establish

the right atmosphere for reading the poem aloud. In the
early stages of a course this will usually be done by the tutor,
and the most common remark is likely to be, 'It sounds quite
different when you *hear* it'. Most new students are unable
to recreate a poem in their heads, to give body to their silent
reading. Throughout the course they should be hearing
poems read aloud, and should take turns at reading themselves, after preparation. That preparation will be towards
an intelligent and sensitive rendering, not a dramatization.

There may then be a short clearing away of difficulties.
Thereafter the work should be essentially that of discovering
co-operatively what is in the poem, although at the end
everyone will not share the same interpretation. Each one
will take from the evening only what he can handle.

'Only Connect'

We have to accommodate ourselves to the life of the group,
be prepared to follow unexpected openings as far as they lead,
and suggest more possibilities when the discussion is slacken-
ing, or being overforced on one side, or becoming distorted
through lack of background in the students. We must try
to work almost entirely through questions, and through
questions which do not, cumulatively, impose a pattern—
and this is an extraordinarily difficult and tiring process.
But the answers must as far as possible be drawn from the
students, for a number of reasons—we are not there to give
them something so much as to bring their own latent powers
into play; if we tell them what to think they are not likely
to learn how to read themselves; if we give them everything,
and even make them feel the truth of all we've pointed out,
they are likely to be so surprised at the complexity a poem
can have that they will be discouraged from reading themselves. They think *they* will never see all that in a poem.
Even when the meanings have been drawn from the group
something of this feeling may remain, but we can point out
that many of those meanings were hidden from all of us until
the evening's discussion revealed them, and also bring in

T. S. Eliot's point about a poem of any complexity and depth having meanings in it concealed from the author. We must draw answers from the students because probably each of them is in some respects better equipped than anyone present. Differences of background, of age, of ability, count for relatively little after a few weeks. Indeed an apparent advantage—for example, the educational background of a teacher—may be a hindrance. Someone used to the customary technique of literary study may be harder than others to bring to the point where a personal appreciation is being made. Such students have sometimes to make a greater adjustment than others if they are to stay with the group.

Learning to Wait

We have to learn to wait; to wait during some evenings through a complete silence of some minutes; to wait until a number of entire meetings have passed before some individuals speak. Though everyone else is contributing, their silence may indicate shyness or that their speed is different from that of the majority, and that they recognize this (their written work will be a guide). We have to know when to move on, even though there may be much in a poem which several have not understood, and though we realize that there have been faults of emphasis in the discussion. We will rarely have the feeling of having 'done right' completely by any one work. But what we have difficulty with in the first poem will be more easily grasped in the second; and the second may well readjust something neglected in the first . . . and so on throughout the whole three years. We have to know when to prune discussion and be firm, and when it's necessary to relax; when it may be valuable to move outwards from the text; when the text has to be firmly followed. The same things will have to be said again and again and on some students there will be no apparent effect. Many of our own mistakes will be committed again and again, but the occasional signs of success should be sufficient encouragement.

1952

Notes on Extra-Mural Teaching

These notes about five aspects of extra-mural teaching—
the syllabus, the class-meeting, students' reading, discussion
and written work—are not comprehensive, and exceptions
can be made to them all. But by and large these are the lines
on which, after my first few years, I found myself working.
I suppose I have had in mind usually the manner of work
of a second-year tutorial, or a sessional with moderately
experienced students. But practically all I describe has been
done with new and inexperienced groups by the second term
of the first year, so long as I have kept my main aims in
mind and have tried to work towards them from the beginning.

The Syllabus

I make the syllabus a sort of map or guide to the shape
of the course. It sets out the general aims of the year's work
(and in a tutorial its place in the three-year scheme) and
is laid out so as to give the students a sense of the way the
work will move and vary in pressure, of its form and
emphases. I try to make it above all clear and helpful, a
tool for the course which the students can keep in their
class folders and refer to from time to time. I suppose our
most common faults are at opposite poles: either we produce
a thin syllabus which indicates what we have so far only
roughly thought out; or we prepare one so full of detail that,
though it may impress the students, it also confuses them.
I believe a syllabus is most effective when it distils a lot of
prior thinking about the nature and probable conduct of
the course; it then helps not only the students but us, because
courses run more effectively when this kind of preliminary
work has gone into them.

I usually plan my literature courses around a fairly small
core of detailed reading; say, four novels in the session, and
perhaps the work of two poets or dramatists; or variations

on this rough total. This is the centre of the course and shows as that in the syllabus. I also indicate some material which will be treated in a less detailed way. But the closer reading occupies about two-thirds of the course. Each of the major texts stands out in the syllabus, and there is a preliminary indication of the order of reading them and the point we are likely to reach by Christmas. For each text (and to a less extent for the less detailed work) I suggest critical and background reading, though not too much at this stage. Some students use these supporting lists when we reach a text which particularly interests or puzzles them. The supporting reading for each text, here and in class, is shown by specific chapters or page numbers wherever suitable. Before I get the syllabus into final shape I check that the adult education department has sets of the texts for special study; if they haven't, I ask whether they can be bought. And I check which critical and background works the department has in its library. I find also that a look through the critical and biographical (and historical) sections of the library catalogue usually unearths a few useful supporting texts I hadn't thought of or didn't know we owned. When any of these books are available in cheap editions I note this on the syllabus also.

The next point can be debated more than the others and has to be taken carefully. I usually put at the end of the syllabus a short section about what the course will require from a good student: in attendance, reading, discussion and written work. I have tried over the years to find a form of words which will warn off anyone who isn't likely to find the time and effort, but will prepare others without frightening them away. Some tutors prefer to do this during the first few weeks, before the register is made up. I reserve for this later time the advice that they should be ready to give up one evening a week (or its equivalent), in addition to the class-night itself, for preparation and reading.

The Class-Meeting

Most of my class-meetings are seminars, not lectures with discussion. I don't know whether anyone today regularly uses the one-hour lecture/one-hour discussion form, but I hope not. I do give lectures occasionally—or longish talks—for necessary background or to introduce a group of writers who are not to be studied in detail, and so on; and these, apart from their other uses, help to vary the course. And though I spend most time in most meetings on fairly close group work I take time off, wherever I feel suitably prompted, to sketch in background or develop a general point. None of these points can be thoroughly treated off the cuff, but they can be usefully aired just where they come up; and they will almost certainly recur later in the course.

I usually allow two, three, or four weeks to each novel for detailed study, and the order of approach to each is roughly planned in advance, according to the novel itself and the nature of the group. On some of these evenings I begin with about half-an-hour's introduction to the night's theme; at other times, especially in the middle of work on a text and fairly well on in the course, we may begin with close work—previously prepared by them and me—on the text itself.

In any event, I think it important to break the evening into a series of interesting chunks (not a number of scrappy parts). I usually talk to one or two students, probably about a point in their written work or about their reading, as the class is assembling; and perhaps the first quarter of an hour will then be spent in hearing prepared notes on the first main subject of the evening. Some tutors use a log-book and I know they give useful training in organization and reflection; and they help to knit the course together and bring last week's absentees up to date. After their first worries students become proud of them. But I have stopped using them and now emphasize prepared notes, because I found the log snowballed on me. Students tried to live up to one another so much (the best were excellent) that for a week before, and in the class itself, the log-keeper was aware chiefly of the need to get down practically every word—and then had a relapse of attention for a week or so.

To come back to the breaking-up of the class-period: generally I think of two main chunks of talk-from-me with discussion, broken by coffee if that is available. I think the middle-break a good institution, well worth the time it takes because of the fillip it gives to work in the second half of the evening. I usually reserve for it the odd announcements of public lectures and items of class administration. I always try, without damaging a good discussion, to bring things to a close about ten minutes before the class ends. I spend this time preparing for the next week's work (and outlining the shape of things for the next few weeks) and drawing attention to some books in the box.

One small final point. I began with a disinclination, which may affect other university teachers, to using the blackboard. I still don't use it in the way I remember it was generally used at school. But I find it invaluable for some things at some points—showing what I mean by the shape or development of a novel, reminding the students of the way we may think of a poet's work as moving through phases, and so on.

Reading

My general rule here is again a double one: not to smother the students by presenting a list of books so long that hardly anyone is likely to have time to read them: and yet to remember that, if they are carefully and individually guided, they can read a lot more than I or they may think at the outset.

I think of students' reading in two groups. First, the basic minimum which they must do on most occasions if they are to benefit from the course. I try not to outface them but to keep them steadily going from week to week and over the Christmas holiday (and especially over the summer break, in continuing classes). A variety in the type of reading— novels interspersed with poetry would be an obvious instance

—helps a lot. Naturally they are abashed if two long and difficult novels follow one another without a break. Much of this planning is shown on the syllabus; but I try to keep it current from week to week, especially in the last ten minutes, e.g. 'By now you should be well into your preliminary reading of . . . (a novel to be begun in about a month). For next week we will, of course, be going on with . . . I want you (they know this novel in general and parts of it pretty well) to pay special attention to the scene where (pp. . . to . . .) and the scene where . . .'. And so on to the detailed guidance which I will later talk about. The crucial point about this minimum reading is that so far as possible all students have to be encouraged to keep up with it.

Second: critical reading, background reading and general wider reading. The amount will vary from student to student but again more can be done by more people than seems likely at first, if it is kept constantly in view and if individual attention is given. A good supply of books for the class helps enormously, of course. So does frequent reference to those books, and especially to interesting books on-the-side which the students might avoid if I didn't say something about five or six of them each night. Sometimes I simply riffle through a book and say I think the author is illuminating on so-and-so but a bit one-sided on so-and-so. For each special text, just as it is being approached in class, I enlarge on the side-reading I have already noted in the syllabus; and I pull the relevant books from the box and indicate the chapters they should look at. To each of them, and especially in conjunction with their written work, I try to recommend books which should be right for each of them at each point. Sometimes I find myself more or less running a student's spare-time reading of all kinds for the year or so he is in the class. It is surprising how much can be done by this unobtrusive individual encouragement. I know it is beginning to work when I find—and try to sort out the muddle—that they are running a private swopping of background books, short-cutting the class librarian.

As to guided close reading it may be best to take a typical example. The class is spending, say, three or four weeks on *The Portrait of a Lady*. They may have read it during the summer and should certainly have read it shortly before the class work on it begins. I've decided how I think (subject to better developments during the meetings) I might divide the weeks with this particular group, aiming to look at one, two or three major aspects each night. I've thought about how best to cope, bearing in mind the larger unity of the year's work, with general background and period. We've reached, say, a meeting (this will be fairly late) at which I want them to appreciate as well as they can the focussed concentration of James's writing, when he is using his re-sources to create an intensely evocative scene full of subtle but detailed insights. I've decided to let the evening pivot on chapter 42, where Isobel sits alone in the drawing-room until the small hours, and reviews her life with Osmond (this may easily take up the whole two hours; but I usually have some supporting scenes in reserve). I ask them to read this scene several times during the coming week (and supporting scenes less intensively). I suggest specific features which might help them to see how James's art works. I try (this is harder) to ask questions which will prompt them to find for themselves particularly illuminating items. I ask them to look at the text with these questions in mind, and to think; and then to make notes. The aim, here and in the subsequent discussion, is to help them reach, largely by working them-selves, as large an appreciation as possible of the scene's rich-ness and power. We can only treat a few selected sections in this way, even in four weeks. But if we try to 'do' the whole novel we will end by doing it thinly; and this procedure helps them to read the rest—and other novels—better. Of course, I take all occasions (sometimes by preliminary talks, sometimes by summary talks, sometimes at a suitable point in the middle of an evening) to relate the chapter and the whole novel to James's other works and indeed, if this seems relevant, to novels of other authors and times.

All the students won't do all this preliminary work for each meeting. But some will do all of it each time; and all will do some at some times.

Discussion

I think discussion is much the hardest part of a class-meeting, though it looks easy. We are often tempted to have a rambling general conversation and decide that, anyway, it was all 'stimulating'. Or we are tempted to act as a sub-Socratic god, in a way Socrates himself never did. Or we can give a long and maybe clever lecture on Symbolism in Virginia Woolf (with some classes at some point this may certainly be all right) or on 'The Meretricious World of Sinclair Lewis', instead of taking thought in advance, and meeting challenges on the spot, so as to give the students a more helpful evening. They aren't likely to urge us to take this greater trouble. They are usually unduly humble before a tutor and in any case will probably enjoy the lecture, as a *tour de force*. They will say, and if we overhear we know it is we and not they who have failed, "Mr. A. is awfully clever. He talked very well last week about myth in *Ulysses*. I think it all came down to a journey in the end, but I wasn't quite clear. I suppose I'm not up to him. But he really is clever and an awfully nice young man." I had a different experience early on. I was sent, on appointment, to Middlesbrough where the Adult Education Department then had connections. The first class-meeting I ever took was on Auden and I gave, I think, a reasonably good lecture which subsequently formed the basis of a chapter in my book on Auden. But most of them were experienced Tutorial students and one, who later became a friend and took a scholarship, stood up when I announced that discussion would now begin, and told me that I'd left them with nothing to get hold of to discuss; I'd assumed too much; I'd said too much all at one go; I'd talked over their heads.

We can easily be tempted, in many not very obvious ways and especially if we are tired, to take tricks intellectually, to be evasive and cut short a challenging line by a smart turn. I think it's true to say, though, that most of our points can be grasped by most of our students in most of our classes if we take enough trouble in presenting them. I believe the essential need is to find the right questions, the right way to put them, and the right way to pursue them. What students lack is not, usually, brains or sensibility, but familiarity with our way of looking at and talking about literature. How can they take our points if we don't first act as mediators? And we for our part often don't see how good their answers are (or may be, if they are encouraged to develop them) because we don't always try, not to find a gold nugget in every proffered item, but to see what they are in fact saying. I believe we should think of ourselves as providing handholds, for them to do the stretching from one point to another. If we do this we will often be surprised at the goodness of their equipment. And they will develop a respect for each other's particular kinds of insight, a respect which is probably the most genuine foundation for that sense of community which a good group acquires. You know this is emerging when they pause and look at someone—not necessarily one of those with a university degree—at a certain stage in a discussion, because they all know he is usually 'very good' on this sort of point. I used to leave the shy ones alone much more than I do now. I still don't approach them very much during class until I have come to know them through private talks and through marking their written work. Then I find that they will come on well—and be grateful I prompted them—if I keep an eye open for questions on which I feel I can ask them to speak, because I know they have some strength there.

In one sense no discussion is ever finished. We can give, and they take, only so much at a time (perhaps if circumstances are good on both sides three or four points can be taken, with supporting material, on any one night). The important thing is not to cover an area but to try to make something happen—some new illumination or challenge—to as many of them as possible on each evening. And circumstances are rarely good for all of us at once. We have our off days and so do they. They are working all day and they have a family life and relatives and problems. Sometimes the best, those we expected to help us a lot on a particular night, disappoint us (but someone we expected little of may come up and force us to readjust our opinion of him). Getting to know their personal circumstances can be taxing and certainly should not be overconscious. But we will find that we do get to know them, sooner or later, and will then have a better idea of what good class attendance can cost.

I don't think a discussion should have a firm plan leading to a 'conclusion' we expect to reach. But it should have a shape, roughly worked out beforehand so that we take first things first as far as possible and gain from a development which hangs together. We need to be ready to scrap even this, if approaches more interesting or important than we had foreseen appear. But on the whole I try to have a fair idea of the three or four points I want to explore and their likely ramifications. I think of it as an exploration by them, an active participation under guidance; and I try to draw it together at the end (not to 'sum it up' like the minutes of a meeting, but to lay it out sensibly so that they can see the area worked in. It is, anyway, useful for them to see how a mind with more professional training sets about such a job).

Written Work

Written work is the best single guide we have to the ability and needs of each student. I aim to have it done consistently but in various forms—varied according to the type of class, the individual students, and the stage reached. But of course it is generally regarded as the bugbear of adult teaching, by tutors and students alike. In some ways it is, at first, since many students are frightened of it. But practically all students can be writing by Christmas of the first year, even if their first piece is a private essay, done over the

Christmas break, about their difficulties with the course and what they have found most interesting. Until I begin to get written work from each one I feel as though a whole wing of my work with the missing students is out of action. The shy ones need this private contact so that we can see where their strengths and weaknesses are; the more talkative ones may reveal weaknesses we would hardly have guessed from the discussions in which they played so big a part. So I am sure they have all to be persuaded to sit down, think, plan and express. Prepared notes for next week's discussion are not the most important form of written work, but they are a steady and continuous foundation. I tend to let two or three do them each week, sometimes from different angles. If only one does them, they can become—like the log—too much of a set-piece. To have several preparing them, sometimes in conjunction, lessens shyness and gives more students practice early. I try to avoid the danger of their simply waiting till their turn comes round by ensuring that they realize they are all to think on the topics (and to make notes, though not for delivery to the class except in the run of discussion), and by keeping them involved during the actual presentation of the notes—asking if they had seen that themselves, or agree with this and so on. These notes set off the discussion and so are related to my own notes on its probable shape for that night. I offer to take their notes afterwards and write comments on them; and some do ask for this. In the first three or four weeks I let volunteers do the prepared notes. But I find it's important to switch from this approach before I have run right through the volunteers and am left with half a dozen students looking at each other in a frightened way. But by the end of these three or four weeks I am beginning to know them pretty well and can begin to suggest that the coming week's topic might well suit Mr. B. and that I'll be glad if he'll take it on, and will talk to him about it after the class if he wishes. They will almost always accept this, if I have chosen carefully.

There are many other kinds of written work, from a brief

appreciation of a poem or a scene in a play right up to a formal essay. At the right point for each student I believe the formal essay is irreplaceable. But again it should be tailored to their individual needs. I usually suggest two or three topics in class, ask them to propose alternatives and discuss them, or to come up and find a theme from scratch with me. When a tutorial is well-established I like to get about three of these (apart from the less formal written work) in a session. I often get more, from some students. I'm certain that the most important part of written work is the marking. A word of thanks, an odd hieroglyphic at the side, a sentence of commendation and advice—no one (nor all) of these is sufficient. Extra-mural marking should be very carefully directed, to each student's needs. This takes time, but if the alternatives are to have more written pieces and quicker marking, or less written pieces and more thorough marking, the second course has to be chosen. This is the closest personal contact we have with the mind of each student. Whether we correct every item of their grammar and phrasing will depend a little on them (I usually offer to do this at the start and most accept but some can be embarrassed). The rest is common to good marking anywhere, I suppose, but here it has really to be shown, so that the students have something to get hold of—where their planning was weak; where their logic was at sea; where their insight failed them or they got into a groove. We need to try to spot weaknesses, and suggest what they may do about them; spot strengths, and suggest how they may be developed; scatter in relevant questions so as to set them thinking afresh or further; suggest new reading, inspired by their special needs as shown in this piece of writing; ask them to see us before the class, to go into a point or tendency which needs time (I give them my address and ask them to write to me at any time).

Last, it is useful to keep an eye on those who consistently fail to hand in their written work. If we don't, some, largely through fear, will hardly ever do it. I keep a pencilled record in the register and either send a postcard reminding them or, better, speak to them privately and try to sort out the difficulty. I often find surprising and unlikely blockages; but these can usually be removed without jollying.

1959

SCHOOLS OF ENGLISH AND
CONTEMPORARY SOCIETY

CAN one really say anything worthwhile about Schools of English and contemporary society? Doesn't such a title suggest a failure to recognize the 'timeless' nature of the work that should be central to a School of English? Isn't it only another indication that one more teacher has succumbed to the cult of contemporaneity? Won't such an interest distract us from our central, our manifestly proper work?

I know the importance of all these questions. Much of the work of an English School should have little direct relation to the particular forms and fashions of contemporary society. There must be historical, textual, editorial, bibliographical and literary critical research into a thousand years of linguistic and literary change. Here the Schools are repositories of knowledge, and contributors to knowledge about their past. Young scholars have to be trained to take up this advanced work and others trained so that they may go out to teach our language and literature. Here the Schools of English are active transmitters.

One can easily appreciate certain other arguments: That, even if Schools of English may be more relevant to modern society than has been suggested in the preceding paragraph, they will do best not to bother directly about the contemporary world whilst they are at work. That if their students come to grips with *The Canterbury Tales* or *Paradise Lost* or even *Love's Labours Lost*, or with medieval England or Renaissance England as literature reveals them, this will in the long run do more for their understanding of modern society than will a constant reaching after modern instances. That the steps toward a loss of depth, toward the point at which you are satisfied with the glitter of the new and fashionable, are gradual and painless steps, since apologetics are provided—by modern society itself—all along the way. That the real profit of a training in English is a tempering of mind and imagination.

Although I am going to argue that time should be given —more than most Schools give at present—to the study of certain aspects of modern society, I am sure that even this will not be done well unless English Schools keep central to their work those elements I have called fundamental. And those of us who choose to work in this contemporary area will not work well unless we regularly refresh ourselves with traditional work, and remind ourselves that a special occupational risk is loss of balance.

The essential aims of a training in English ought obviously to include the encouraging of a love and respect for language, for its complex relationship with individual and social experience. Most people do not paint or compose music each day or indeed any day, but virtually everybody uses words every day, and uses them not only functionally but emotionally, not just as tools but as ways of expressing his personality. He uses them and misuses them, so that they never remain still or pure (but neither do they set in classic poses). If, as we are often told, music is the purest of the arts, then literature is the muddiest, up to its knees in the mud of life. But, though there may be magic words and sacred words, no words are 'dirty' words in themselves. A writer always wants to pick them up and make them fresh again, by the power of his love. (Sometimes, admittedly, he has to decide that certain of them are past redemption, in his generation at least.)

Whatever else it does, a training in English should bring an increased ability to appreciate the many ways in which the literary imagination explores human experience—ways that range from the directly literal and moralistic to the oblique or apparently irrelevant.

A work of literature may have formal qualities beyond and irrelevant to the needs of meaning and the ordering of experience. A sonnet is not only an exploration and pattern-

247

ing of significant experience; it is also a playful pattern, made for its own sake and enjoyed for its own sake. And some of the deepest meanings of literature may come in the most indirect ways—through the odd, the fantastic, the grotesque. Although in fact the technically fantastic and the apocalyptic vision run right through English literature, Jacobean drama being only the most immediately striking instance, we tend to be uneasy about such elements. When we discuss the novel, in particular, we tend to speak about narrative skill or close moral explorations—even though this may cause us to underread Richardson, to ignore Sterne, to put Emily Brontë in an aberrant corner, and to leave Lewis Carroll to children and psychologists. Today we talk chiefly about, for instance, Angus Wilson's skill as a social satirist whereas he is at bottom a novelist of horror, horror at cruelty and at final meaninglessness. More often than we recognize, English writers see the skull beneath the skin, and can only express their vision by moving outside the more literal conventions.

But I am chiefly concerned here with literature as it deals with what E. M. Forster calls 'the life by values'. It starts in absorbed attention to the detail of experience, in immersion in 'the destructive element', in 'the foul rag and bone shop of the heart'. It, first, 'blesses . . . what there is for being'. It works not by precept and abstraction but by dramatization, by 'showing forth', in a fullness of sense and feeling and thought, of time and place and persons. In ordering its dramas it is driven by a desire to find the revelatory instance, the tiny gesture that opens a whole field of meaning and consequence. It does not do this pointlessly, nor explicitly to reform; it aims first at the momentary peace of knowing that a little more of the shifting amorphousness of experience has been named and held, that we are now that bit less shaken by the anarchy of feeling and the assault of experience. To push for this kind of truth, no matter how much it may hurt, is a kind of moral activity. As Jung says, the poet "forces the reader to greater clarity and depth of human insight by bringing fully into his consciousness what he ordinarily evades or overlooks or senses only with a feeling of dull discomfort".

I do not believe that reading good books necessarily makes us behave better—that if we appreciate Jane Austen's *Emma* we will henceforth act with greater self-knowledge. Yet how well would we be able to apprehend, let alone express, the complexity of personal relations, if it were not for literature working as literature? I do not mean that we all need to have read the best books; but what has the fact that they have been read, and that their insights have to some extent passed into the general consciousness, contributed to our understanding of our own experience?

Though literature has to do with meanings it is not primarily analytic or discursive, or it would be something else, something valuable perhaps but not art. Only art re-creates life in all its dimensions—so that a particular choice is bound up with space, people and habits. Only here do we at one and the same time see ourselves existentially and vulnerably; and also as creatures who can move outside the time-bound texture of daily experience. The two make up, in Auden's phrase, 'the real world of theology and horses'.

So English studies are important at any time. But it is harder to live up to our own professions than we realize. Those of us who teach in Schools of English assert a case for the importance of great literature and tend to assume that we have thereby made the case for the importance of Schools of English. Which is to assume that our practice as teachers lives up to the challenge of the works we study, and this is not often so.

An increased respect for the life of language, and for the unpremeditated textures of experience—how are these qualities, which a training in English ought to encourage, valued in contemporary society? In what ways might a literary person concern himself with them today?

SPEAKING TO EACH OTHER

Years ago Ezra Pound wrote a striking rhetorical passage about this:

> Has literature a function in the state, in the aggregate of humans? It has . . . it has to do with the clarity of "any and every" thought and opinion. It has to do with maintaining the very cleanliness of the tools, the health of the very matter of thought itself. Save the rare and very limited instances of invention in the plastic arts, or in mathematics, the individual cannot think or communicate his thought, the governor or legislator cannot act effectively or frame his laws, without words, and the solidity and validity of these words is in the care of the damned and despised literati. When their work goes rotten . . . by that I do not mean when they express indecorous thoughts . . . but when their very medium, the very essence of their work, the application of word to thing, goes rotten i.e. becomes slushy and inexact, or excessive or bloated, the whole machinery of social and of individual thought and order goes to pot.*

Is language neglected and despised today? In one way, certainly not. A BBC current affairs producer, who had spent years in interviewing and reporting, once told me: "We've talked enough about the 'affluent society', 'the meritocratic society' and the rest. I propose 'the articulate society', the society in which everyone is ready to and feels they ought to speak on invitation about anything. They are often talking nonsense—*but they do it in whole sentences*, and with a vocabulary that would have surprised their grandfathers."

If language is decaying today, it is doing so not from neglect but from a surfeit of insensitive attentions. The 'Use of English' is one of today's proliferating trades, and any English School could within a year or two treble its size by setting up peripheral agencies—some sensible and useful, some dangerous—from courses in English for foreign students, through courses in English for science students or technical students, or for apprentices or for executives, to courses in 'the prose of persuasion' for advertising men or public relations men or politicians.

* *Literary Essays of Ezra Pound.* London: Faber; New York: New Directions.

We have no equivalent to 'commercial artist' for his counterpart in writing and speech. 'Commercial writer' on a visiting card would be a good deal less 'slushy, inexact, excessive and bloated' than 'creative copywriter'. I wonder whether in any previous period so many words were being used inorganically— not because the writers had something to say about their experience, but on behalf of the particular concerns of others. So much language is used not as exploration but as persuasion and manipulation; so much prose has its eye only slightly on the object and almost wholly on the audience; so many words proclaim, if you listen to them carefully, not 'I touch and illuminate the experience' but 'this will win them over'.

It would be easy to compile a list of words that are by now unusable, until they have been redefined by each writer within each particular context. Not the old words we are all used to laughing about—'tragedy' for the popular press, or 'magnificent' for Metro-Goldwyn-Mayer: the process goes on quickly and the newer men have quieter voices. So words like 'sincere', 'creative', 'vital', 'homely' and 'love' go out of use. Try writing an obituary notice for a respected old man, or a speech in honour of a quiet, decent life:

> *All words like peace and love,*
> *All sane affirmative speech,*
> *Had been soiled, profaned, debased*
> *To a horrid mechanical screech:*
> > *No civil style survived*
> > *That pandemonium*
> *But the wry, the sotto-voce,*
> *Ironic and monochrome.*

The process works at many levels, and at each level the language can seem alive—as in the high nervous pseudo-life of some magazine stories. But the snags and roughnesses of real response have been smoothed away.

Even more: much writing does not address itself to the experience of whole men. It addresses us as parts of men, since on those parts (for one reason or another) pressure has to be brought to bear. So we are addressed as bits, bits who belong to large lopsided blocks—as citizens, as consumers, as middle-aged middle-class parents of one and a half children, as voters or viewers, as religiously inclined car owners, as typical teenagers or redbrick professors.

It is too easy to blame the advertisers and the public relations men for all this. It is part of a larger problem, part of the price of self-consciousness (up to a certain point and of a certain kind), a consequence of the endlessly working, conveyor-belt productiveness of modern communications, and of the increasing centralization and concentration of societies. Governments are under this pressure as much as advertisers—to influence us through words, for limited but urgent purposes.

A way of using language toward people is a way of seeing people, of making assumptions about them. This goes further than seeing them as, say, limited in vocabulary or background; it indicates how much respect we have for them as human beings. In short, changes in contemporary English— Government prose, *Daily Mirror* prose, *Observer* prose, the changing prose of social occasions, of public occasions or of love-making—these are not narrowly linguistic matters but can only be understood socially, psychologically, morally.

Schools of English should obviously be aware of all this. So should any teachers within the humanities, and perhaps all teachers. As it is, too many of us stay most of the time within our well-defined academic areas—but succumb easily to occasional invitations from the world outside. We do not with sufficient confidence separate ourselves from that world nor sufficiently critically engage with it. By insisting on the difficult but responsible life of language, and on the over-riding importance of the human scale, we can try to do our part in resisting the unreal, unfelt and depersonalized society.

Yet there is a great deal to be hopeful about: that so many now have the chance to become articulate may mean that self-consciousness will lead to self-awareness—and both

are better than dull illiteracy; that so many people are subjected to various kinds of verbal persuasion indicates at least
that they have some freedom to choose.

Each year's groups of graduates, presumably with a sound
training in English language and literature, leave the universities anxious to communicate their heritage in the schools.
They soon find that the voices that most readily speak to
their schoolchildren are very different from the voices heard
in that high art they are now trained to teach. Jane Austen
does not speak with the accents of *Honey*, and *Honey* is much
read even in girls' grammar schools. 'Only connect'; how
many teachers make sense of this split, although many of
them listened to those popular voices before they came to
university and some might still do so with some part of
themselves? In my experience few resolve the contradictions.
They can rarely assert their truths with the assurance of the
communicators on the other side of the cultural fence. They
are often confused and baffled; they despise without understanding and feel like keepers in the museum of high but
irrelevant art, training a few in the next generation to be
keepers in their turn.

It would be better if more of us were more informed, if
we sought more relevance and connection, if we encouraged
a stronger sense that the life of the imagination has always
to be fought for. Today especially—when commercial media
consume whole areas of artistic possibilities as though
working-out an automated mine, when we subject language
to elaborate misuse—we need to make these connections.
Some secondary schools already attempt it; they do not get
much help from university English departments.

Listen to this voice, to this kind of voice:

We live in the realm of the *half* educated. The number of
readers grows daily, but the quality of readers does not improve rapidly. The middle class is scattered, headless; it is
well-meaning but aimless; wishing to be wise, but ignorant
how to be wise. The aristocracy of England never was a
literary aristocracy, never even in the days of its full power—

of its unquestioned predominance did it guide—did it even seriously try to guide—the taste of England. Without guidance young men, and tired men are thrown amongst a mass of books; they have to choose which they like; many of them would much like to improve their culture, to chasten their taste, if they knew how. But left to themselves they take, not pure art, but showy art; not that which permanently relieves the eye and makes it happy whenever it looks, and as long as it looks, but *glaring* art which catches and arrests the eye for a moment, but which in the end fatigues it. But before the wholesome remedy of nature—the fatigue arrives —the hasty reader has passed on to some new excitement, which in its turn stimulates for an instant, and then is passed by forever. These conditions are not favourable to the due appreciation of pure art—of that art which must be known before it is admired—which must have fastened irrevocably on the brain before you appreciate it—which you must love ere it will seem worthy of your love.

That paragraph occurs in, of all places, a critical essay on the poetry of Wordsworth, Tennyson and Browning. I do not agree with all its formulations but I admire its boldness in tackling interconnections between history, politics and the aesthetics of popular taste. That kind of voice should be heard more often in Schools of English. But if a teacher were to produce such a paragraph in the middle of an otherwise straightforward critical essay, some of his colleagues would advise him to delete it—on the grounds that it wasn't sufficiently specialist and scholarly, might well make people wonder whether he wasn't "becoming 'journalistic'," and might even affect his chances of promotion. Actually the passage is about a hundred years old and is by Bagehot*

The approach I have been outlining may be provisionally called Literature and Contemporary Cultural Studies. It has something in common with several existing approaches, but is not exactly any one of them. And it has many ancestors;

* From "Wordsworth, Tennyson and Browning; or, Pure, Ornate and Grotesque Art in English Poetry" (1864).

but Dr. Leavis in his culture and environment work and Mrs. Leavis in her studies in popular fiction are more important than most.

The field for possible work in Contemporary Cultural Studies can be divided into three parts: one is, roughly, historical and philosophical; another is, again roughly, sociological; the third—which will be the most important— is the literary critical.

We need to know more about the *history* of what is called 'the cultural debate'. In *Culture and Society* Raymond Williams did some interesting work in the line from Burke to Orwell, and got praise and punishment from people whose specialist fields he had been bound to encroach on. It would be useful if those others would now make their contributions.

Probably even harder: we need to define the terms of the debate more closely. At the moment they are muddled; more even than is usual, semantic shifts hide confused assumptions. The clash of undernourished generalizations and of submerged apologetics takes the place of what should be a dialogue.

Talk about 'highbrows, middlebrows and lowbrows' continues, although it is now almost entirely useless as critical terminology. The educational press (still following Ortega y Gasset talks about 'your common man' and 'the masses' as though these were well-defined terms rather than conditioned gestures. Most of the discussion of conformity, status, class, 'Americanization', mass art, pop art, folk art, urban art and the rest is simply too thin.

Or look at the language used in the debate about advertising: the most intelligent and seriously received of the apologists are so high-minded—high-minded but semantically cavalier—that it is painful to read them. And how easily the organs of opinion create new little cultural patterns; the 'Angry Young Man' movement or the 'U and non-U' controversy. The promotion of all such patterns is almost wholly lacking in precision or historical perspective. We have as yet hardly begun to get any of the terms in the debate straight, partly because to do so will require us to reconsider a lot of comforting notions. It would be better if more philosophers came into this field; but until they do literary people will have to try to clear the undergrowth for their own enquiries.

Some students of sociology have worked in the areas traditionally called the sociology of literature or of culture during the last few years and so have some students of literature.* But we need much more varied work in contemporary cultural sociology. We need enquiries into such questions as:

(a) *About writers and artists*: Where do they come from? How do they become what they are? What are their financial rewards? (One can, of course, make historical comparisons at any point.)

(b) *What are the audiences* for different forms and what the audiences for different levels of approach? What expectations do they have, and what background knowledge do they bring? Is there such a person as 'the common reader' or the 'intelligent layman' today? What are the ins-and-outs of a line running from Jude the Obscure through Kipps and Mr. Polly to Koestler's anxious corporals and the readers of egghead paperbacks?

(c) What of *the opinion formers and their channels of influence?* . . . the guardians, the élite, the clerisy (if there is such a body today)? Where do they come from? Who, if anyone, has succeeded the Stephens and the Garnetts? We realize how much could be done here when we remember how exceptional is such a book as Noël Annan's *Leslie Stephen, His Life and Times*.

(d) What about the *organizations for the production and distribution of the written and spoken word*? What are their natures, financial and otherwise? Is it true, and if so what does it mean practically (whatever it may mean in imaginative terms), to say that the written word (and perhaps all the arts) are progressively becoming commodities, to be used

* For instance, Professor Altick in the U.S.A., Professor Dalziel in New Zealand and Dr. Louis James here.

and quickly discarded? What, to take a small instance, are the commercial facts, what the pattern and what the significance of 'the paperback revolution'?

What of the rise of reputations? How far are they the creation of commercial forces, seeking concentration and rationalization here as in motor car production, and so tending to give excessive attention to a few and almost wholly to ignore other artists?

(e) Last, how little we know about *all sorts of interrelations*: about interrelations between writers and their audiences, and about their shared assumptions; about interrelations between writers and organs of opinion, between writers, politics, power, class and cash; about interrelations between the sophisticated and the popular arts, interrelations which are both functional and imaginative; and how few foreign comparisons we have made.

Most important of all: the directly literary critical approach in cultural studies is itself neglected. Yet it is essential to the whole field because, unless you know how these things work as art, even though sometimes as 'bad art', what you say about them will not cut deep. Here, we particularly need better links with sociologists. It is difficult, outside a seminar, to use a literary critical vocabulary—to talk about 'the quality of the imagination' shown; or to discuss the effect on a piece of writing of various pressures—for instance, to talk about corner-cutting techniques, or linguistic tricks, or even (perhaps especially) about what tone reveals. All this needs to be analysed more, to be illustrated and enforced—and at all levels, not just in relation to mass arts.

The mass or popular arts about which we know too little and in which there is room for developed critical practice include: film criticism; television and radio criticism; television drama (which tends to be ignored or overrated); popular fiction of many kinds—crime, westerns, romance, science fiction, the academic and academic's detective story;*

* Orwell did some good early work here and a few others have followed him.

the press and journals of all kinds; strip cartoons; the language of advertising and public relations; popular songs and popular music in all their forms.

Some people say they don't want or need to know more about any of this, that it is all beneath serious critical consideration. The same people will often make sweeping and uninformed generalizations about mass art. A few make handsome exceptions for the *News of the World* or 'Z Cars'.

If only for a start, a little more humility about what audiences actually take from unpromising material would be useful.* Perhaps no one should engage in the work who is not, in a certain sense, himself in love with popular art.† One kind of 'love' is a disguised nostalgia for mud. Assimilated lowbrowism is as bad as uninformed highbrowism. It is hard to listen to a programme of pop songs, or watch 'Candid Camera' or 'This Is Your Life' without feeling a complex mixture of attraction and repulsion, of admiration for skill and scorn for the phoney, of wry observations of similarities and correspondences, of sudden reminders of the raciness of speech, or of the capacity for courage or humour, or of shock at the way mass art can chew up anything, even our most intimate feelings. All this is related also to hopes, uncertainties, aspirations, the search for identity in a society on the move, innocence, meanness, the wish for community and the recognition of loneliness. It is a form of art (bastard art, often) but engaging, mythic and not easily explained away.

Of course, this art is being increasingly machine-tooled: there are thirteen-week sociological soap operas, with a crisis at every natural break; predigested tales for the women's magazines; the extraordinary sophistication of today's Westerns; the offbeat commercials. But even with these, there are sometimes spaces between the brittle voices in which a gesture sets you thinking in a new way about some aspect of human experience.

* I was glad to see just this point hinted at by—surprisingly, to me— C. S. Lewis in *An Experiment in Criticism*.

† Some American critics are very interesting here, such as Benjamin DeMott.

We cannot, then, speak of the effects of all these arts as confidently as some social scientists do unless we have a close sense of their imaginative working; we have to recognize the meaningfulness of much popular art. If we do, we shall not be left with that 'passion of awe' which we can find in the best works of art. Nor shall we be left only with contempt. We may more often be ironic than contemptuous; and we may well have moments of awe.

I have admitted the danger of too contemporary a slant in English studies, of too social a slant and even of too 'moral' a slant. If we forget the 'celebratory' or 'playful' element in literature we will sooner or later stop talking about literature and find ourselves talking about history or sociology or philosophy—and probably about bad history and bad sociology and bad philosophy. But that truth has been used by some Schools of English as a shelter. English, once again and finally, has to do with language exploring human experience, in all its flux and complexity. It is therefore always in an active relation with its age; and some students of literature—many more students of literature than at present—ought to try to understand these relationships better.

1963

THE LITERARY IMAGINATION AND THE SOCIOLOGICAL IMAGINATION

W E say that a good writer has imagination, intuition, insight. We expect to see these qualities in his work; perhaps—to come straight to the theme of this essay—in his eye for 'significant detail' about society (that some gestures or habits seem to tell more about a society than other gestures or habits); or in the way he discerns deep secular trends within his society—that it is moving in this general direction rather than that, or is expressing unconsciously some ambiguity in its own sense of itself.

But this is a claim about much more than literature and a bigger claim than literary critics always realize. It points to truths outside literature and cannot be contained in what are called 'purely literary values'. It points outside the literature to the life that literature examines, and claims to say something true about that life. It claims that the literary imagination can give insights into the nature of society itself, insights which cannot be contained within a self-enclosed aesthetic world; insights which, it is often assumed, can affect a reader's own sensibility thereafter. Or, it seems to follow, insights which may express themselves not only in a writer's formal works of literature but may be brought to bear by him as direct commentary on his society—as in the debate about culture and society which runs through the nineteenth century and to which many literary critics contributed.

Yet the claim is still larger, even when it is made solely about formal works of literature. It is a claim that these works are at their best much more than reflectors or mirrors of their society, more than symptomatic evidence. I am doubtful whether, since literature is produced by individual human beings, any work of literature can be explained wholly as a symptom. But certainly some are more 'symptomatic' than others, than what—to beg a big question for the moment—we call important works of literature. The run-of-the-mill romantic novel in the eighteenth century, or the popular novel of sex and violence today, will probably yield more if they are regarded as mirrors of movements within their society rather than as 'disinterested explorations' of aspects of that society. But if we regard even such works from outside simply as mirrors, to be easily understood, we may miss the most important elements through which they do reflect their society; moreover, it is much more difficult to read them properly even for what they 'reflect', and may require closer critical attention than literary critics or social scientists have commonly thought.

But, as I say, we usually make larger claims than that. We claim that somehow the literary imagination can, by exploring a society in its own way, tell us something new about aspects of that society, provide illuminating hypotheses about it, suggest orders within it that are exceptionally revealing. We claim that it can in itself and by its insights (not by being used as 'symptomatic evidence') assist the understanding of society.

What does this enormous claim mean? Does it mean more than that we seek to attribute to a writer's personal impressions the status of objective truth? If more, how are these insights arrived at? Is the process in any way related to procedures in the social sciences? Can these insights be 'checked'? How far and in what sense can they be said to be 'true'? I can't indisputably answer these questions. But I will lay out some of the considerations which seem relevant to beginning an answer.

I need to turn from literature for a while and look at the way in which one kind of social scientist works. He has, say, a mass of material about whatever field he is investigating, a great mass of material. How does he make any sense out of it, find any patterns? Because he has an initial frame; he starts with a hypothesis, or with several. But there are an endless number of possible hypotheses with which to 'make sense' of the material. Of course, some are ruled out by what he might call his general 'feeling for the material itself' (though that phrase also begs a lot of questions); perhaps some never occur to him—he just happens not to think of them. All of them he tests against the material, to see how well they stand up. From his sense of recurrent stresses, recurrent shapes, recurrent omissions, he moves towards testing and modifying his hypotheses. Perhaps some people would say that this way of putting it gives too much weight to the initial hypothesis-making; that if we have a sufficiently full body of material, of facts, and if we feed it through a suitably complex computer, that computer will itself find within the material, objectively, the recurrent stresses, shapes, omissions and so on. But that only puts the question one stage further back. What is a full picture? And what is a fact? We might say that there are some objective facts and some that are 'objective'. An objective fact would be of this kind: the library issued ten million hardbound books in the last year. So long as careful definitions are made at the start, this is testable and enforceable. It is therefore, if one wishes to use that term, scientific; it can become part of the social scientist's objective data. I am using this description because one social scientist has suggested to me that his aim must be to make his 'facts' so far as possible into 'data' of this kind; and naturally I see what he means. He agreed that he soon leaves that level and arrives at questions like these: why were that number of books taken out? or those proportions of different kinds of books? how were they read? what needs did they seem to fulfil? . . . and so on. Answers to questions of this kind can produce much the most important knowledge he seeks. They are more likely to do so if the social scientist does his best so to refine his methods that as many facts as possible become data in the sense described above. But the most important of them can never finally become objective data in that sense; at their best—a very good best—they become 'objective'. How many facts, then, would we need so as to arrive at 'the truth' about the library services in Birmingham? If we had, say, 200 thousand or 2 million or 20 million facts we would (a) only scratch the surface of possible facts and (b) more important, we would angle things. Each different angle from which we look at any given object will throw up a range of new facts and new relationships. Every enquiry contains within itself, must contain, a range of assumptions and concepts before it can begin to recognize 'facts' to collect. One can easily imagine all sorts of bad, that is to say patently and narrowly subjective, analyses of 'class' in English life. There can be no objective analysis of it, even by someone who is not English or even by a non-European. We can and should push more and more towards objectivity, but we can never reach it. I am not saying all this so as to criticize the social sciences, and don't suppose I have given that impression; after all, this particular debate is a long and live one within the social sciences themselves. Here is just one quotation, taking much the view I take. From Myrdal:

> The chaos of possible data for research does not organize itself into systematic knowledge by mere observation. Hypotheses are necessary. We must raise questions before we can expect answers from the facts, and the questions must be 'significant'. The questions, furthermore, have to be complicated before they reach down to the facts. Even apparently simple concepts presume elaborate theories. These theories —or systems of hypotheses—contain, of necessity, no matter how scrupulously the statements of them are presented, elements of *a priori* speculation.*

I am pointing to an inescapable fact of our lives. I say 'ours' since it is, phrased rather differently, a fact of the writer's life also. We none of us 'know' anything in the blue; we know things within the conceptual and imaginative frames available to us.

How does a creative writer's way of arriving at 'truths'

* G. Myrdal, *Value in Social Theory*. London: Routledge & Kegan Paul; New York: Harper & Row.

compare with that of social scientists of the kind I have
described? I spoke of a social scientist sitting, so to speak,
before a great mass of material and making raids into it with
his hypotheses so as to see what sense they make of it (though
the actual process is more subtly concurrent than that makes
it sound). Some of the less sophisticated objections to literature as evidence about society take the form of saying that
it really produces no evidence, that whatever the writer
happens to bring forward and work his rhetoric on is called
evidence. I think this is a misguided view and that the position of the writer may at this point be close to that of some
social scientists. I suspect that what literary critics usually
call a 'social insight'—the sense that such and such a gesture
is 'significant'—is the result of the writer holding in his
imagination an enormous amount of material, of 'facts' about
society. I believe he holds this material in a kind of suspension, and that it is at the moment of his finding a unifying
image—a single gesture or a large theme—that we say he
has had a 'significant' insight. Here is Conrad on a moment
of 'inspiration':

> There must have been, however, some sort of atmosphere
> in the whole incident because all of a sudden I felt myself
> stimulated. And then ensued in my mind what a student of
> chemistry would best understand from the analogy of the
> addition of the tiniest little drop of the right kind, precipi-
> tating the process of crystallization in a test tube containing
> some colourless solution.*

I believe this material in bulk, if we were able to count it,
would be as voluminous as that deployed in the most elaborate social scientific project we can imagine. I think that with
a great writer the weight of material being drawn upon in
the background would be (if we could lay it out discursively)
of a complexity that would daunt even the most energetic
team of social scientists, with the largest foundation grant
we have ever known, working for years and years. How else

* J. Conrad, author's note to *The Secret Agent* (1907).

can one begin to explain the range of material about society or about the individual brought to bear in Shakespeare's plays? I am talking at the moment about sheer material, not about the way it is ordered. I am pointing to the fantastic complexity of the observation itself, a complexity which Shakespeare himself did not and could not realize. At the moments when a gifted writer is working at great heat the capacities brought to bear are beyond the conscious control of any man, and yet are all co-ordinated. If one could write out a description of all the abilities being used instantaneously by a superb tennis player in action, and then multiplied it several times, one might just begin to have an idea of the complexity of the material being held in suspension by a great writer at the time of writing. One has to think not only of the mass of individual details and skills but of the capacity also to find within them an overall structure or movement. To do this is to act almost incredibly quickly and co-ordinatedly.

So I am suggesting that a writer may have at least as many 'facts' to work on as a social scientist. And that he orders them so as to make 'significant explorations' not by conscious, controlled aggregation but by imaginative power. His imaginative power is the social scientist's capacity to frame hypotheses; or the other way round, the social scientist's capacity to find hypotheses is decided by his imaginative power. Is there, in fact, a difference in kind between the literary imagination at work on a society and the social scientific mind 'making sense of' its material? Are not the imaginations of the two at their best close to each other? I have to say 'at their best' because it seems obvious that not all of us are as quick at ordering, at finding 'significant detail', as others.

Instead of 'significant detail' there I almost wrote 'ideal type'. In some ways it would be attractive to be able to claim that the artist's 'significant detail' is the social scientist's 'ideal type'; and they are probably related. But more importantly they differ; and their differences go to the heart of the differences between the two disciplines. Ideal type analysis abstracts from the detail of society so as to make a usable theoretic design; creative writing recognizes 'significant detail' whilst at the same time recognizing and recreating the flux of untypical life. Part of the experience of literature is this sense of pattern-and-lack-of-pattern at one and the same time.

But to come back: not all of us are equally good at finding order and 'significant detail'. Some people are so quick that they seem able to find illuminating instances from the tiniest amount of material, as though by a sudden 'gift'. I think it was Aristotle who said that the greatest gift of the writer was the power to make metaphors—and in my sense every metaphor is a significant hypothesis or making of relationships—and perhaps one either has that power or not. It is easy to find similar prescriptions for social scientists. Talking about the relation between material and hypothesis Adorno says: "I would put the greatest emphasis on audacity and originality in proposing a solution."* 'Originality' seems to mean there what Berelson meant when he said: "In the last analysis, there is no substitute for a good idea",† and both seem to be contained in what literary people call 'imagination'. Incidentally, Adorno goes on: ". . . [this solution] *will itself of course have to be criticized constantly*"; and Popper says: "For although we cannot justify our theories in a rational way, nor even prove them to be probable, we can nevertheless criticize them in a rational way".** There is a sense of intellectual discipline behind those two statements from which literary critics could learn.

But still I think it is wrong to talk as though 'a sudden gift' or insight can greatly explore society in itself, without reference to what it has to feed on. We all know of very young writers who can produce memorable work. But they

---

* T. W. Adorno, 'On the Logic of the Social Sciences', in *Kölner Zeitschrift für Soziologie und Sozialpsychologie*, No. 14, 1962.

† B. Berelson, 'Content Analysis', in *Handbook of Social Psychology*, ed. G. Lindzey (1954).

** K. R. Popper, 'The Logic of the Social Sciences', in *Kölner Zeitschrift, op. cit.*

are more likely to produce marvellous lyrics about individual experience or illuminating, successive, single insights into aspects of society than a sustained exploration into and ordering of a society's life. It is sometimes said that mathematicians can be at their best in their teens; I don't see how a writer can be at his best at that age in his insight into society. He simply has not experience enough, even unconsciously. He cannot get far without some material to work on; he has to have the material. It is true that Henry James was dry on this point:

> I remember an English novelist, a woman of genius, telling me that she was much commended for the impression she had managed to give in one of her tales of the nature and way of life of the French Protestant youth. She had been asked where she learned so much about this recondite being, she had been congratulated on her peculiar opportunities. These opportunities consisted in her having once, in Paris, as she ascended a staircase, passed an open door where, in the household of a *pasteur*, some of the young Protestants were seated at a table round a finished meal. The glimpse made a picture; it lasted only a moment, but that moment was experience. She had got her direct personal impression, and she turned out her type. She knew what youth was, and what Protestantism; she also had the advantage of having seen what it was to be French, so that she converted these ideas into a concrete image and produced a reality. Above all, however, she was blessed with the faculty which when you give it an inch takes an ell, and which for the artist is a much greater source of strength than any accident of residence or of place in the social scale. The power to guess the unseen from the seen, to trace the implication of things, to judge the whole piece by the pattern, the condition of feeling life in general so completely that you are well on your way to knowing any particular corner of it—this cluster of gifts may almost be said to constitute experience, and they occur in country and in town, and in the most differing stages of education.*

But that was partly Henry James's way of putting in their

* Henry James, 'The Art of Fiction', in *The Art of Fiction and Other Essays*, ed. M. Roberts (1948).

place the grosser forms of naturalism. His woman novelist and James himself were no doubt more 'gifted' than most of us; still, they could only know how to 'read' such a snapshot of a scene, could only recognize it as what James called a 'germ', because they had had years of slowly observing, not necessarily while knowing they were observing, other places and other times, perhaps other societies. Later in that passage from which I have just quoted James added: "I am far from intending by this to minimize the importance of exactness—of truth of detail"; and the same passage produced that famous injunction to novice writers: "Try to be one of the people on whom nothing is lost! "—which in its turn reminds one of the importance Lévi-Strauss gives to 'participation'. Sustained imaginative perception of any depth into a society only looks like a sudden gift; it takes off from saturation in experience.

So our insights have been selected and ordered. But this finding and ordering of insights is a process of evaluation of evidence, according to the penetration they seem to give into the life of a society. It implies that these insights and this order have more 'real' or long-term significance than others. But suppose someone else, who presumably would claim to have observed society, consciously or not, as much and as well as those who are called good imaginative writers or good social scientists, claims that his picture is at least as 'real' and 'true' as theirs? His picture might be quite different and, in our view, plainly wrong. We cannot simply accuse him of lack of evidence. Such people usually love their evidence and have masses of it. One often hears public speakers make large assertions about the extent of the corruption in British society today, based on a great deal of 'evidence' and observation. Why is their observation or that of a 'bad' novelist less significant, less meaningful, than that of a 'good' novelist or, for that matter, of a social scientist gifted with Adorno's 'originality'? So we have reached now a broader question than we have looked at so far. Not only: "What is an insight into society and how is it arrived at?", but how do we judge between the value of different insights, between different people's insights? Why should we not accept the extreme evangelist's or the 'bad' novelist's or the unoriginal social scientist's selection and ordering? I'm not sure that in the last resort we can give a final answer to this question. But we can go some way before we reach the last resort. At least, I will suggest some criteria which help me to begin to choose different insights and different interpretations. Though if you tell me that they are all at bottom circular or self-validating, because of the questions begged in the use of such words as 'adequate', 'relevant', 'conformity' and 'compatibility', I might have to agree.

First of the rough criteria, then: a range and a command of complexity in the writer adequate to this complex and wide-ranging subject, the study of men in society. A range and sense of complexity are not the same as a love of mass and complication. Second, a kind of economy or, in the mathematician's sense, elegance—a relevance or conformity between the treatment itself and the particular areas under examination, a lack of hysteria (which can often be recognized, in the writing itself, by the obsessive recurrence of certain themes or images), a lack of excess. Finally, a reasonable compatibility with findings from other disciplines; a compatibility with 'truth' found, with as much range, complexity and elegance, by different routes; the sense that each illuminates as well as mutually qualifies the others.

Rules such as these might be a rough way of separating sheep from goats. But they don't get us much of the way. What about fantastic art, surrealist art, art which is deliberately distorted, excessive, obsessional, which appears to turn 'reality' on its head or narrows its interest to one tiny and aberrant aspect of society? What about, say, William Burroughs's *The Naked Lunch*? Can that lead us to some 'truth' about contemporary American society (again, other than being in itself symptomatic of certain strains in that society)? Certainly, it has complexity and so passes my first test. Yet it is also excessive and distorted. But such penetration as it has, such illumination as it offers, probably comes from its submission to and belief in the need for excess and distortion in the face of the experience it is exploring. Yet I do not think this particular problem is one of the most difficult. These kinds of work can also be put to my third test. If we read them properly (that is, obliquely) we can check how far they sit with the findings of other disciplines. One might find a useful interaction between theories of alienation and anomie and much that is recreated, dramatized, explored in Kafka, William Burroughs and others. The point is that such evidence does not necessarily breach the major principle but helps define it better; we shall only see what art of this kind is 'saying' about society if we learn to read it 'as art'.

If we do not first 'submit' to it in this way we may go astray. A social psychologist may use works of art as symptomatic evidence and find in them, say, what seems like corroboration of his views about anomie. He may raid them with a preconceived set of theories.* But if he first 'submits' to them they may not simply reinforce but modify and qualify his understanding of anomie. At this stage the interaction has become fruitful; each side is helping the other in its own best way.

Literary evidence does not simply illustrate that 'X' is what a society believes, assumes, feels. It recreates what *it seems like* to be a human being or a society which believes, assumes or feels 'X'. So it helps itself to define 'X'. If it is true, as a social scientist has said, that sociology always risks missing what it is trying to discover because of its 'love of clarity and exactness' then we can say that literature may help to keep open our sense of the richness of human experience, the virtually inexhaustible meanings in each gesture and word spoken, if they are understood in their contexts. But even that way of putting it emphasizes too much the particular local detail. One needs a way of describing (and I haven't found one) the *whole* experience which we undergo in read-

---

* In this connection, see T. W. Adorno, 'On Popular Music', in *Zeitschrift für Socialforschung* (1941).

ing a great work of literature. With that, we might be nearer understanding how much and in what ways such a work may alter our sense of man in society, may inform our sense of human life.

All this underlines the importance to social science of learning to read art expressively as well as instrumentally; and of doing this with the arts at all levels, mass art as much as 'high art'. Literature is 'evidence', then, but evidence which has to be read in quite a subtle sense, evidence through fictions, or through myths and rituals which can body out tensions and confrontations well below the overt level. This is why content analysis is particularly interesting, as a frontier area between the two disciplines. One can learn a good deal about how to 'read' a text from the best social-scientific content-analysis. For its part, literary critical method can help towards a fuller reading of the expressive meanings within works. It can thus help to inform the social scientist's initial hypotheses when he gets to work, in his own way, on aspects of modern society; and it may help to show that many expressive phenomena are not only symptomatic of the consciousness of their age but themselves help to alter that consciousness.

I don't underestimate the effort and intelligence that go into the search for objectivity in social scientific work; nor do I undervalue the results. Still, I do not think that any of us, whether literary critics or social scientists, can claim that we are showing 'the truth'. The most we can say is that we have shown 'something true about' a society, when seen from this angle or that. This changed phrasing is more than a play on words. I cannot imagine an accurate use of the phrase 'the truth about so-and-so . . .'. There are, of course, many levels of error and misleading subjectivity which can be cut through and must be cut through in search of 'something true about' any aspect of a society. Much current talk about teenage behaviour or about changes in class consciousness shows that well enough. But at a more intellectually-trained level the difficulty remains. Suppose six contemporary historians sat down together to produce: "a brief objective account of what Mr. Chamberlain's visit to Munich in 1938 meant politically." There would be agreement on only a few small items. How could there be more? Such a question brings into play the most delicate and deep-rooted patterns of assumptions and judgments. We can drive hard to get clear of them, and sometimes for limited practical purposes we may just manage to do so. But at the end of this line we reach bedrock; all findings, whether in literature or the social sciences, must be based on a set of agreed hypotheses, all rest finally on assent rather than proof, on a common conceptual frame with which we begin to make sense of the world. What we call proof or 'truth' indicates our hope that we have pushed past all possible recognizable subjectivities; to go further really would be to lift ourselves up by our own mental bootstraps.

It is not unnecessary or tautologous to say this; the issue is important and neither simple nor closed. We may have to act 'as if' we can drive right through to 'objective truth', so as to get down to the conceptual bedrock at all. But if we think we can easily ignore or break through that bedrock we will have deluded ourselves at the crucial stage of our work; and we will then, ironically, not even reach true bedrock.

This is where I become particularly interested in the developing study of linguistics. I am thinking now not of the degree to which our modes of thinking, the casts of our minds, are decided by the history of our race and society; but of the way in which the language we use can respond to changes in sensibility. I do not mean, bluntly, that language is culturally conditioned; and in any case I think art not only draws on the language made available by its culture but probably feeds back into the culture new forms of language and so of experience. I mean that the same words seem to change with changing sensibilities. True emotional north must always look like true emotional north or we should feel too threatened. We must always be able to speak of 'love', 'tenderness', 'charity', 'cruelty', 'folly', 'right or wrong', even though the emotional and imaginative realities meant by all these words may have changed enormously over the decades. Of all social changes the most difficult to trace are those which take place within the sensibilities or consciousnesses of societies, in their emotional registers, over time. In a famous *New Yorker* cartoon a married couple are sitting in a suburban drawing-room watching television. One of them turns to the other and remarks cheerfully that critics of TV who say it is turning us all into morons must be mad. You look closer— and see that both the man and his wife have the heads of apes. Who ever admitted to being 'alienated', one feels like asking? Part of the answer is that under the impact of art we sometimes do. We can recognize what 'alienation' may mean on the pulses and may even see something of it in ourselves then.

My reference to a common bedrock was not meant to be dispiriting but quite the contrary. That there should be some common frame is, to begin with, inevitable and useful; or we could neither talk to each other nor make sense of our material. If the material were just there, outside, and if we were without even the beginnings of a possible frame of reference, that material would be totally inexhaustible, amorphous and bewildering. But then, having admitted that our consciousnesses suggest certain frames and not others, we are involved in a sort of battle with those consciousnesses, a battle we will in the end always lose but in which we can make gains. And this seems to me as true of the social sciences as of literature, even though their modes of procedure are so different. Literary artists are not objective, admitted; social scientists can only be 'objective' within inverted commas. But literature, we say, best illuminates its age when it 'stands outside it . . . sees beyond it'. And I think one can say much the same of the best social science, that in which 'originality', to use one of the words I borrowed earlier, is most in play.

So I do not see that a creative writer is inherently more likely to lead us astray in our understanding of society than a social scientist. The rules of his kind of work may not be as plain as those of the social scientist but they are at least as numerous and probably more tricky. So long as we learn to read and listen to him—read his fictions, understand their obliquity and so on—we may learn a good deal from them. Not that those of us who are literary critics always do this well. The world of literary criticism, like all professional worlds, has its own deceptions and self-justifications. We jump to too many cultural conclusions, taking off quickly from the works to large evaluative generalizations with very few historical or sociological checks and balances. Our cultural ideas are too comfortable, limited and enclosed. This is a pity when we are making cultural generalizations about works of literature. It is at least as great a pity when literary critics move out to observe and comment on society directly. I think they should do so, as their nineteenth-century predecessors did. But they usually move too easily into undisciplined impressionism. As Alan Shuttleworth says: "There is a way of writing here, biographical, particular, actual, vivid, responsive, on a human scale, which is aware of its limitations."* He is at that point regretting that the conservatism of the literary tradition has led to either a suspicion of cultural judgments or, where they are employed, has encouraged a generalized impressionism unaware of its own limitations.

The equivalent error in social science is that attitude which claims to be 'value-free' (and I have defined the sense in which I think this is a proper ideal), but is really a hard-nosed unimaginativeness. And this is finally as damaging to social science as it would be to literary criticism; we are acting most intelligently when we face valuations, not when we evade them.

1967

* A. Shuttleworth, *Two Working Papers in Cultural Studies*, Birmingham University, 1966.

INDEX

275

INDEX